Rhinegold Study Guides

A Student's Guide to A2 Religious Studies

for the **OCR** Specification

by

Michael Wilcockson

with Nicholas Heap, Rohan Preece and Robert Stewart

Rhinegold Publishing Ltd
241 Shaftesbury Avenue
London WC2H 8TF
Telephone: 01832 270333
Fax: 01832 275560
www.rhinegold.co.uk

Rhinegold Religious Studies Study Guides
A Student's Guide to AS Religious Studies for the AQA specification
A Student's Guide to AS Religious Studies for the Edexcel specification
A Student's Guide to AS Religious Studies for the OCR specification

A Student's Guide to A2 Religious Studies for the AQA specification
A Student's Guide to A2 Religious Studies for the Edexcel specification
A Student's Guide to A2 Religious Studies for the OCR specification

Other Rhinegold Study Guides
Student's Guides to GCSE, AS and A2 Music for the AQA, Edexcel and OCR specifications
Listening Tests for Students: AQA, Edexcel and OCR GCSE Music
A Student's Guide to Music Technology for the Edexcel AS and A2 specification
Student's Guides to AS and A2 Drama and Theatre Studies for the AQA and Edexcel specifications
A Student's Guide to AS and A2 Performance Studies for the OCR specification

Rhinegold Publishing also publishes *Classical Music, Classroom Music, Early Music Today, Music Teacher, Opera Now, Piano, The Singer, British and International Music Yearbook, British Performing Arts Yearbook, Rhinegold Guide to Music Education, Rhinegold Dictionary of Music in Sound, Teaching Drama*

First published 2005 in Great Britain by
Rhinegold Publishing Ltd
241 Shaftesbury Avenue
London WC2H 8TF
Telephone: 01832 270333
Fax: 01832 275560
www.rhinegold.co.uk

You should always check the current requirements of the examination, since these may change.
Copies of the OCR specification may be obtained from Oxford, Cambridge and RSA Examinations at
OCR Publications, PO Box 5050, Annesley, Nottingham NG15 0DL
Telephone 0870 770 6622, Fax 0870 770 6621.
See also the OCR website at www.ocr.org.uk

A Student's Guide to A2 Religious Studies for the OCR specification
British Library Cataloguing in Publication Data.
A catalogue record for this book is available from the British Library.

ISBN 1-904226-16-7

Printed in Great Britain by WPG Group Ltd

Contents

The author

Michael Wilcockson is head of divinity at Eton College. Prior to this he was head of divinity at Aldenham School and then The Leys School. He has recently written *St Mark's Gospel: A New Approach* (Hodder Murray 2005) as well as two books for Hodder and Stoughton's Access to Philosophy series: *Issues of Life and Death* (1999) and *Sex and Relationships* (2000), and articles in recent issues of the journal *Dialogue*. He is an ISI school inspector and principal examiner for A-level religious studies at a major examinations board.

The editors

Emma Whale (project manager), Charlotte Regan (senior assistant editor), Jonathan Wikeley (assistant editor), Joanna Hughes (designer), Lucien Jenkins (managing editor).

Acknowledgements

In the writing of a guide such as this many people have contributed. The author and publishers are grateful to the following people for their specific advice, support and expert contributions: Hallam Bannister, Emily Boswell, Julian Dobson, Manowar Hussain, Jonathan Paull, Dick Powell, Hugh Sadleir and Abigail Walmsley. Above all, Michael Wilcockson would like to thank his wife Alison, for her careful reading, commentary and corrections.

The authors and editors are also conscious of having drawn on a lifetime's reading. More recently the growth in use of the Internet has made an unparalleled amount of exciting information and challenging opinion widely available. Although every attempt has been made to acknowledge both the primary and secondary sources drawn on, it is impossible to do justice to the full range of material that has shaped the creation of this book. The author and editors would therefore like to apologise if anyone's work has not been properly acknowledged. They would be happy to hear from authors or publishers so that any such errors or omissions may be rectified in future editions.

Introduction

What's different?

This A2 course builds on all the work that you will have covered at AS level. The major differences are:

- that you will now write single continuous essays rather than stepped two-part answers
- the new material covered will expect a greater command of technical language and more sophisticated analysis.

Keep your AS notes to refer back to when examining the connections between your modules for the synoptic paper.

Throughout this guide you will find references to *A Student's Guide to AS Religious Studies for the OCR specifcation* by Michael Wilcockson (Rhinegold 2003). For simplicity's sake, this will be referred to as the *OCR AS Guide*.

'Synoptic assessment' is a technical expression used in many A-level subjects. It describes the element of the course that tests your ability to connect ideas from your two chosen A2 units, **as well as** the material you learnt at AS.

Choice of units

At A2, you must continue with your units from AS – you cannot choose different ones. As at AS, you will be examined on three units, but at A2 each examination is one-and-a-half hours long. For the papers on your two chosen units, you must answer two questions from a choice of four.

Timing

At A2 there is no Foundation unit; instead there is a compulsory paper called 'Connections in Religious Studies', which examines certain themes that link your other two units. This combination of your two choices is referred to as a route. For example, if you are studying Philosophy of Religion as well as Religious Ethics, this is Route A; Jewish Scriptures with New Testament would be Route P.

Connections

As at AS, there are certain combinations of units that cannot be taken. Check the latest edition of the specification to see which combination of units is permissible. Equally, in some units there is a choice: if you study the New Testament module you must choose between either Gospels or Early Church; if you look at Eastern Religions, you must choose between either Hinduism or Buddhism. See www.ocr.org.uk.

Skills

Examination skills

Whereas for AS you were asked to write one answer showing your knowledge and understanding of the question, and another evaluating a problem or issue, at A2 you are asked one question in which you have to show all the appropriate skills (knowledge, understanding and evaluation) throughout the essay. Examiners assess each essay according to two criteria:

AO1 (knowledge and understanding): the specification defines this as the ability to 'select and demonstrate clearly relevant knowledge and understanding through the use of evidence, examples, and correct language and terminology appropriate to the course of study'. This area is weighted at 64.6 per cent.

AO2 (evaluation): the specification defines this as the ability to 'sustain a critical line of argument and justify a point of view'. This area is weighted at 35.4 per cent.

At A2 your essays need to be much more sophisticated and to demonstrate many of the following qualities:

- The ability to quote **sources** and explain them
- The ability to quote **scholars** and discuss them
- Signs of **reading** outside the standard text books

✦ Your own **judgements** and assessment of ideas

✦ Your own ability to **organise** an argument, including a clear opening and concluding paragraph.

Further reading

Read *Shaping the Tools: Study Skills in Theology* by Ruth Ackroyd and David Major (DLT 1999).

Essay skills

The most important new element of A2 essay writing is the ability to evaluate and assess ideas as you develop your argument. Never leave evaluation to the end of an essay, as if you were writing the second part of an AS question.

What is evaluation?

Evaluation may cover any of the following within a single essay:

Strengths and weaknesses. This is one of the simplest and clearest ways of making an assessment. It can be done by contrasting two ideas and pointing out why one idea is more successful than another. For example, I could argue that the strength of pacifism is that it upholds the integrity of Christian principles, but on the other hand it could lead to greater suffering of innocent people.

Coherency. Often when pointing out strengths and weaknesses you are also drawing attention to the consistency or coherence of a point of view. In the example of pacifism you might propose that a strong pacifist position is incoherent because it contradicts the Christian principle of protecting the innocent or weak.

Further reading

See *Thinking A–Z* by Nigel Warburton (Routledge 1996).

Fallacy. A fallacy is an argument that makes a logical leap from premise to conclusion. There are a number of well-known fallacies that are worth learning. For example, in ethics the so-called 'naturalistic fallacy' is used to reject any statement that begins with a fact or observation and then moves on to a value judgement.

A premise is an assumption from which other arguments follow.

False premise. A useful form of evaluation is to argue that the premise is wrong or faulty. This might be due to false factual information, or that it is too general and you can think of exceptions, or that it can be contradicted by another more coherent premise. You can make a good argument simply by looking at the problems of defining a particular word and considering what premises are implied.

Counter-argument. At GCSE and AS, many candidates write evaluative essays using the simple formula 'on the one hand... on the other hand... so therefore...'. However, at A2 it is not always wise to write a whole essay divided in this way. It is far better to arrange your paragraphs so as to present argument/ counter-argument as you proceed. For a counter-argument to be effective, you must ensure that *your* personal judgement is clear, using phrases such as 'and therefore', 'consequently it can be seen that', 'for that reason', 'hence' and so on.

Essay plan

Make sure that your essay follows a coherent structure:

Opening paragraph. At A2, even more than at AS, the opening paragraph needs to isolate the issue and to suggest the direction in which your essay will be proceeding. Make sure you explicitly **refer to the question**, perhaps by isolating a key word or idea.

Main paragraphs. Each new paragraph should represent **one key idea**. Whenever you are moving on to a new idea or presenting a counter-argument, you must begin a new paragraph. This is fundamental to the structure and coherency of your essay. Paragraphs should introduce an idea, develop it (with examples, quotations, explanation) and if necessary give an evaluation.

Conclusion. You must allow yourself time to write a conclusion. A conclusion enables you to return to the essay title and **give an answer**. This should be a brief summary of the main ideas you have made in the central part of your essay.

Sample essay

Below are some extracts from a good student essay. Commentary is provided to help you see where this candidate has scored highly, and where they need to improve.

You can learn from these points even if you are not taking the unit discussed (New Testament: Early Church).

'Paul's teaching on justification encouraged lawless behaviour.' Discuss.

Paul defined justification as God's act of remitting the sins of guilty men, accounting them righteous, free of sin. But this is not achieved by their own works, but through the sacrifice of Christ and his resurrection. Theoretically, man should be able to justify himself before God by his own works. In reality, because of man's sinfulness, God is the only one who can justify people.

Paul was not a fan of the law, and he made this quite clear. However, 'lawless behaviour' in these terms applies only to the Mosaic Law, not moral law. Paul still says we need to live by God's eternal law.

Paul used a cumulative argument to set out his views of justification. Firstly, man sins and will be judged by God. Secondly, man will be judged by his actions. Thirdly, man will be judged according to God's natural law/Mosaic Law. Finally, all those who keep the Law will be made righteous.

However, in Romans, Paul clearly states that 'we have all sinned, no one is free from sin.' Elsewhere he states 'if the Law makes people righteous, then Christ died for nothing.' And finally, elsewhere in Romans, Paul states 'God makes the unrighteous righteous and the ungodly Godly.' This however presents us with a problem. Is God unfair?

Paul describes the Law like a prison sentence (Romans 7: 7) and it is by justification through faith in Jesus Christ that we are released from our 'sentence'. However, Paul is not saying that just because God releases us from the Law that gives us a reason for lawless behaviour, we as Christians, still abide by God's law. In Romans he clearly states that justification does not exempt us from death, we are just assured an after-life.

It can be seen that Paul doesn't encourage lawless behaviour, he sees the Mosaic Law as a cause of sin and death – yet the heart of God's law is to give life. This is a life of unconditional love. In conclusion, Paul's teaching of justification does not encourage lawless behaviour. It encourages correct lawful behaviour through God, Jesus and the Spirit.

Good attempt to define key terms from the essay title.

Reasonable point, but he needs to say why it is 'theoretically' possible.

The opening sets up the argument, although the second part of the title has been neglected. Sin is an important part of Paul's teaching. The candidate could indicate that they know this.

Try to avoid colloquialisms. A quotation with explanation would have made the point far better.

The point is well made and makes the contrasts clear, but ideally should have been made in the opening paragraph.

Good points, but need elaborating with direct reference to the set texts.

This is fine if you cannot remember the exact reference.

Well-chosen quotations but they need some comment and evaluation.

Try to avoid 'us' or 'we' as this assumes a faith commitment on the behalf of the reader/examiner. Be objective.

Explicit reference to the title shows that you are answering the question.

This may be true, but it doesn't quite follow on from the previous point.

The second use of 'law' here needs to be explained.

The point is made a bit late – a quotation would clarify and provide evidence.

The conclusion refers back to the essay title and answers the question.

This is from a very sound essay on the A/B border. Its argument is a little circular, and without more explicit references to the texts, the ideas are often a little too general. A really good candidate would have referred to Paul's differing views in Galatians and Romans, the

Examiners mark all essays on seven bands, where band 7 shows 'an excellent understanding of and engagement with the material' and 'knows exactly what the complexities of the question are'. Bands are then converted into marks. The total mark available for these units is 45 (29 for AO1 and 16 for AO2).

use of dualistic metaphors such as law/life, body/spirit, death/freedom, old man/new man and so on. However, generally it has a good structure and the conclusion certainly helps to gain a few extra marks. There was appropriate use of quotations, but a few more would have helped. This essay was awarded a top band 5 mark of 23 for AO1 (knowledge and understanding) and a low band 6 mark of 13 for AO2 (evaluation) giving the candidate 36 out of 45.

Connections unit

What is it, and why do I have to study it?

The Connections unit can only be examined in June and cannot be offered as an extended essay. 'Synoptic assessment' is a technical expression used in many A-level subjects. It describes the element of the course that tests your ability to connect ideas from your A2 **and** AS material.

The Connections unit is a very important part of your A level – it's worth 60% of your mark at A2. The exam board states that:

> Synoptic assessment assesses the candidates' knowledge and understanding of the connections between elements of the areas of study selected. It involves the explicit drawing together of knowledge, understanding and skills learned in different elements of the Advanced GCE course. It also contributes to the assessment of the skill of relating such connections to specified aspects of human experience.

The routes

The specification sets out a number of topics for each combination of the two areas of study. Questions are limited to these particular areas and they will not be set on the whole of each paper.

Route A:	Philosophy of Religion with Religious Ethics
Route B:	Philosophy of Religion with Jewish Scriptures
Route C:	Philosophy of Religion with New Testament
Route D:	Philosophy of Religion with Developments in Christian Thought
Route E:	Philosophy of Religion with Eastern Religions
Route F:	Philosophy of Religion with Islam
Route G:	Philosophy of Religion with Judaism
Route H:	Religious Ethics with Jewish Scriptures
Route J:	Religious Ethics with New Testament
Route K:	Religious Ethics with Developments in Christian Thought

Preparing for the Connections exam

The examination paper on Connections in Religious Studies sets three questions covering these selected areas and candidates must select **two** essays. The examination is 1½ hours long, which gives you about 45 minutes to plan and write each essay.

Look out for this jigsaw sign. These boxes contain the details of the route they refer to, as well as which areas are being connected. So, for example, a box entitled **Route M: Religious ethics and environment** will give you information on links between Islam and environmental ethics.

In the margins of this book, the connections between topics will be brought to your attention. At the end of each chapter you will also find more information on the areas that you will need to prepare for. There are also some example examination questions for each route. If you can't find material on the connections between your chosen modules in a particular chapter – don't panic! Simply turn to the end of the other relevant chapter and it will be there.

Preparing for the Connections unit will be part of your revision and you can use the time to go over old material and get to know it really well. The questions can be set *only* on the specified areas, so make sure you know exactly what to expect.

Make sure you have brief quotations for each topic to help reinforce your argument. Quotations also help to give some depth to your essay and to ensure that it doesn't become too subjective. Make sure you explain the quotation or lead up to it. A quotation by itself does not add anything to an essay and must be relevant.

As you have 45 minutes to write each question, you should spend five minutes on preparing and writing an **essay plan**. Make sure that each paragraph shows how you have connected the topics and what *your* evaluation or assessment of the ideas is going to be. Make it very clear in your opening paragraph where and how you are making the connections between the two topic areas. Remember, though, that the essay title is always open-ended, and this gives you plenty of scope to interpret it according to your particular interests. It may be, of course, that you think that there are no connections, or that they are very weak and not of major concern, in which case you should make this a feature of your essay.

Quotations
This guide provides many quotations for you to start your own quotations sheet. Have a place in your file where you add quotations, perhaps with a brief comment explaining why each one is important.

In the exam

Sample question

Let's look at another good student answer, this time to a Connections question on the links between philosophy of religion and religious ethics (Route A).

'God creates us and knows in advance all the choices we will make; therefore we cannot be held responsible when we do wrong.' Discuss.

Free will and determinism are issues that have been debated over for many years. Most people would like to believe that they have, in many ways, a sense of free will. However, many people would argue otherwise. Some see free will as an illusion and believe that really their actions have merely come about due to a series of events outside their control. This would be referred to as causality, or cause and effect. When discussing free will and determinism from a religious point of view there is a contradiction between having the gift of free will and believing in an omniscient and omnipotent God. In this essay these ideas will be analysed from both philosophical and psychological angles.

> This is a warm-up type of opening and is not a particularly inspiring start.

> A fair point that could be related explicitly to the idea of moral choices.

> An awkward sentence. The idea doesn't need to be introduced here and should have been left out.

> Succinctly summarises the problem and refers explicitly to the essay title.

From a traditional Christian point of view as God is omniscient he knows what is going to occur before it happens. If this is so, then how can a person be held responsible for her actions if God knew what she was going to do but did not intervene? This is problematic for Christians and presents a conflict between God's qualities and the gift of freewill that he has supposedly given humans.

> The point is a good one, but needs to be developed a little more. A reference to a scholar who has advocated this idea would ensure this.

An alternative point of view is that God knows exactly what is going to happen and humans have no freewill. If this is so, humans are like robots and they cannot be held responsible for their actions because they couldn't have done anything different. If God did not want something to happen and knew about it in advance then he could have stopped it.

> There is only a problem if omniscience entails omnipotence. The point was made in the opening but really needs to be made explicitly here.

> An example would be good, perhaps with a reference to God and suffering, such as the holocaust or a biblical story – there is a lost opportunity here to link philosophy and ethics clearly.

William James argued as a determinist that everything happens for a reason as the result of a chain of cause and effect. If this is so then everything that happens could not have happened any other way. This view suggests that we should not be held responsible for our actions, as they are all predetermined. However, in contrast to these views there are the compatibilists who argue that freewill and

Presumably intended as an example of the psychological views referred to in the opening paragraph, but it is too brief, unsubtle and lacks analysis. Psychological determinism is complex and requires more than a couple of sentences.

This example is fine. It is kept brief and the points drawn from it are good.

Good piece of evaluation, which a subtler candidate could have developed to include God as the ultimate agent. The question could then have developed an agnostic determinism.

Never use 'yes' or 'no' like this. It is far too chatty.

Some evaluation of Augustine is necessary here.

Not a startling conclusion but it does refer directly to the essay title and answers the question.

determinism can co-exist. Compatabilists such as Hobbes and Hume thought that there did not need to be a contrast between determinism and freewill. They argued that you are free to make your own choices, unless there is an external agent coercing you to do otherwise. For example, a person may wish to walk out of a bank but there may be man holding a gun to his head coercing him to do otherwise. If this view is taken then it is hard to say whether one should be held responsible for one's acts or not. The problem is deciding whether a person is affected by an external agency.

Another view may solve this uncertainty. Augustine believed that humans have free will and that although God knows that these choices will be, he does not will them – he is just knowledgeable of the future. If this view is taken, then yes you should be held accountable for your acts, as God has not predetermined that you will do that.

In conclusion, although there are many arguments suggesting otherwise, I feel that you should be held accountable for your actions, even though there will always be a degree of material effects that led you to doing that particular action.

This is a sound and competent essay on the A/B borderline. It was not good on James' ideas and missed the opportunity to develop an interesting argument – he could have been left out completely. This essay came very close to listing arguments, and this must be avoided if you are to gain high marks on evaluation. There needed to be much more on Augustine and this would have helped focus on the question. The example was good but the candidate missed a chance of developing the ideas so as to make God the agent and thereby relate it back to the question. Finally, although the candidate mentioned God's omnipotence at the start of the essay, they failed to consider this explicitly with reference to God's action in the world, a topic that was covered in the AS Foundation unit. There were no quotations. However, the structure was sound and this enabled the candidate to present a reasonably coherent answer. The essay was given a low band 6 for AO1 (knowledge and understanding) scoring 31, and a high band 5 for AO2 (evaluation) scoring 16, giving a total of 31 + 16= 47 out of 60.

Remember that you don't have to include everything you know and essays are sometimes improved by discussing a few things well.

Extended essay

Instead of sitting one of the A2 units as a timed examination paper in June, you may, as an alternative, write an extended essay. The exam board sets the questions and issues the examination paper in September. This gives you about three months to write a 2,000–2,500 word essay for the January examination session. The essay is submitted to the exam board in early January (usually around 10 January) and is marked by the board's examiners.

The extended essay titles (usually a choice of three per unit) are available on the OCR website (www.ocr.org.uk) and are sent to your school once you have

Key points to remember

Word limit

The essay must not exceed 2,500 words. Examiners are very strict about length and simply will not read beyond the word limit.

Bibliography and footnotes

It is very important that you show where you have found your ideas. If you quote from a book, you should put a numbered footnote at the bottom of the page or the end of the essay, giving the author's name, the name of the book and page reference. In some cases, it is worth including in brackets the date when the book was published and which edition you are using (later editions sometimes revise an author's ideas). Do not include books in the bibliography that you have not actually read – it is far better to list a few books that you have truthfully referred to, rather than an implausibly long list. Websites should also be cited in your footnotes and bibliography.

Footnotes do not count as part of the word count. Footnotes are used mostly for referring to the books you have used. You should not put comments of any kind into the footnotes, as these cannot be credited in the overall word count. You will have to ensure that any extra comments or information you want to include is contained in the main body of the essay.

Quotations

One way of showing off your own research is to quote passages from the writers you have been reading. Make sure you:

- keep these quotations brief – no more than two sentences
- choose quotations that make an unusual or controversial point
- quote passages that are not contained in the standard textbooks
- always comment on any passage you cite.

Structure

A chief problem with many extended essays is that they cover a lot of material, but lack careful organisation and structure. Examiners can only give high marks if they feel that the essay is coherent. It is better to write a slightly shorter essay that does not repeat material, and has instead sharp and focused argument, than a longer one that contains a lot of ideas that are not wholly relevant. One method you can use is to give a subheading to each paragraph when you are drafting your essay. In this way you ensure that the essay is relevant at every stage. Remove all the subheadings when you submit your final version to the board.

Editing

When you have drafted your essay, read it through and cut out any sentences and even paragraphs that, although interesting, are not absolutely relevant to the essay title. If you are using a computer you can move paragraphs around and cut and save some material into another document in case you decide later to reuse it.

Language

Spend time checking the quality of your English and clarity of expression. Because you are writing this in your own time and not under timed conditions, examiners will expect a much higher level of expression. This also includes being able to use the appropriate technical terms accurately and in the right context.

Remember that you do not need to explain technical language. It will be clear from the way in which you use it whether you understand what it means or not.

Plagiarism

You must be very careful not to copy out material from books or your teacher's notes. Examiners are usually able to detect when you are plagiarising material and may disqualify your essay.

Never copy and paste large sections of information from the Internet. Examiners can and do often look at websites and it will be very obvious if you have copied from them without acknowledging that you are quoting. If you do copy without acknowledgment it may be seen as plagiarism.

The right choice?

If you are allowed to choose whether or not to take the extended essay option, you might want to consider the following:

- Preparation for the essay will be much greater than ordinary research because the level of expertise expected by the examiner is far higher than for an essay written under timed conditions. Have you the interest and skills to succeed?
- You might be the kind of person who generally does better in timed examinations – and given the extra six months preparation and revision for the June examinations, you might perform much better in the summer than in December.

- You will still need to cover all the areas of the paper in order to know enough to write good answers in the Connections unit.
- On the other hand, research can be fun, and in polishing your style and developing a better understanding of the subject you will certainly improve your competency in the subject over all.
- You will only have to sit two religious studies papers in June, and can therefore concentrate your revision on just these areas.

Reading, note-taking and using resources

Further reading

The aim of this guide is to sketch out the main areas you need to cover for each unit, and to highlight key ideas, but you cannot get a high grade simply by reading this guide. Each topic within a unit requires you to do further reading and research. If you don't do this, you cannot expect to get a high grade. You will see in the margins of this guide some suggestions for **further reading** – sometimes from some of the standard textbooks and sometimes from more specialised books on certain topics. Where possible you should try to read at least a couple of the more specialised books for each of the units you are studying.

Notes

This is covered in more detail on page 6 of the *OCR AS Guide*.

The only way to concentrate on your reading is to make notes. If you keep your notes neat and tidy, they can then be used for essay writing and later for revision. Make a mixture of linear notes and diagrams. Linear notes (for example, making a summary of the chapters of a book in the order in which they appear) are good for getting a lot of information down but can sometimes be too detailed. Diagrams (such as mind-maps or spider diagrams) really help to indicate the key areas and can be very useful when planning an essay. When reading from other sources, write out key passages that you can then quote in your essays. Make sure you note down from what book and which page number they come.

Resources

The main resources for religious studies are books, journals and magazines. The advantage with all these sources is that they have been checked by publishers and are generally reliable. Newspapers can also be a useful means of acquiring up-to-date material, although they can present ideas in a very lopsided way – and sometimes simply get facts wrong.

There are some good television programmes and commercial videos available from which you can make notes. Visual material offers the advantage that you get a real sense of the personalities behind an argument or belief.

Philosophy of religion

Body and soul

Plato

Concepts similar to many modern associations with the term 'soul' can be found in Greek pre-Socratic thought during the 6th and 5th centuries BCE. The soul was seen as:

- Distinguishing a corpse from a living being
- The totality of the living person
- The animating force in all living beings
- The moral force in the human person
- The cognitive centre of the person
- The locus of extremes of passion
- That which was lost in battle
- That which survived into an afterlife.

A key philosophical issue at this time was the relationship between the body and the soul. Plato's teaching in this area may be extracted mainly from the *Phaedo* and the *Republic*. In the *Phaedo*, Socrates is shown discussing the question of the immortality of the soul before draining the cup of hemlock in his cell. In the *Republic*, Socrates discusses the tripartite division of society into those who rule, the military class and those who work. This corresponds to the tripartite division of the soul, whereby the **rational** part employs the **wilful** part – which in turn controls the **appetitive** part. In the governance of the state this division results in the quality of 'justice'. In the person, balance is only achieved when the appetitive aspect of the person is kept closely in check.

Overall, Plato conceives a clear body/soul split and in this sense is a **dualist**. The separation between the physical-yet-unreal from the spiritual-yet-real underpins his thought, as the analogy of the cave in the *Republic* reminds us. It is outside the cave in the sunlight that the spiritual and real world exists. Yet to turn from the shadows on the wall and to see the light from the sun is a painful and laborious process, which only the few who seek knowledge would be able to undertake. The few are those who could call themselves philosophers.

The soul of the philosopher strives to free itself from the 'prison' of the body. This can be done during a person's lifetime, when the soul is able to focus on the true reality of the realm of the 'forms'. After death, the philosopher's soul could then live on in the realm of forms. Those who did not control the demands of the body would be reborn in a lower form of existence in the physical world.

Plato's teaching as a whole presents the body as perishable because it is physical and subject to change and decay. The immortal, incorrupt and pure soul enters the body at birth and leaves the body at death. As part of the imperishable realm of forms, even

Further reading

See page 14 of the *OCR AS Guide*, as well as chapter 9 of *Philosophy of Religion* by Peter Cole (Hodder and Stoughton 1999).

Further study

Make sure you familiarise yourself with the dialogues of Plato given below. Plato's *Phaedo*, in particular, presents many of the topics covered here. Note the extensive use that is made of myth in *Phaedo* 107–115.

The cave

In the cave, prisoners who have been there all their life see shadows cast on a wall and hear echoes of voices. They mistake these shadows and the echoes they hear for reality. In truth, the prisoners are in the physical but unreal world. For more on this, see page 13 of the *OCR AS Guide*.

while it is in the body, the soul may be aware of the perfect world from which it comes and to which it returns. This awareness is due to the physical world having been made by the **demiurge** (a creator god) based on the pattern of the eternal realm of forms.

Simmias

Crito asks how Socrates wishes to be buried and is told, 'Any way you like if you can catch me and I don't get away from you... After I have drunk the poison, I shall no longer be with you, but departing, shall go away to the joys of the blest' (*Phaedo* 115).

In the *Phaedo*, Simmias proposes another way of looking at the relationship between the body and soul: that of a lyre and the harmony that is produced. Socrates refutes the argument, but the imagery Simmias uses remains powerful: 'Our body is strung up and held together by heat and cold and dry and wet and the like, and our soul is a mixture and a harmony of these same elements when they are well mixed in the correct relative proportions' (*Phaedo* 85–86). Simmias asks whether the harmony remains when the lyre is destroyed.

John Hick

Further reading

John Hick is one of the foremost British philosophers of religion whose plural view of religion has been very influential. Read pages 113–114 of the Development of Christian Thought chapter in this guide.

John Hick rejected Plato's dualism and developed his theory in *Philosophy of Religion* (1973) and *Death and Eternal Life* (1976).

Hick returns to Judaic-Christian beliefs concerning the body and the soul, and proposes a **psychophysical person**, in which the observable person *is* the whole person. The soul is therefore not 'temporarily attached to a mortal body'. The psychophysical person is made through the processes of nature and nurture, and is directed towards God. Hick's views about the body and soul are presented in the context of a discussion that focuses on life after death. Death marks the moment of complete extinction. What happens next is 'God's re-creation or reconstitution of the human psychophysical individual' as a spiritual body present in a spiritual world. Hick's **replica theory** asks us to imagine this:

Philosophy of Religion (Prentice Hall 1973), page 124.

- Firstly, John Smith of the USA disappears in front of his friends – and at that precise moment an exact replica appears in India. The similarity between both is complete in all aspects, from stomach contents to emotions. In addition, the John Smith in India believes himself to be the John Smith who disappeared from the USA. The friends who witnessed the vanishing would have to treat John Smith who appeared in India as none other than the one who disappeared from the USA.

Further discussion

Consider whether as a friend of John Smith you would accept the conclusion that the two Johns were the same.

- Secondly, if, rather than vanishing, John Smith had *died* in the USA and the exact replica had appeared in India, then the conclusion would still have to be the same: John Smith who appeared in India was none other than the John Smith who died in the USA.
- Thirdly, what if John Smith died in the USA and appeared in a world distinct from the one that we occupy? In this case he would appear 'as a resurrection replica in a... resurrection world inhabited only by resurrected persons.'

Philosophy of Religion page 126.

By emphasising the indissoluble psychophysical unity, Hick avoids many difficulties involved in maintaining a body/soul split. What, however, is the link between the 'resurrection replica' and the 'original person'? **Bernard Williams** (1929–2003) raised the problem of continuity. There is continuity as a baby grows through life until death, since spatio-temporal continuity can be observed.

With death, that continuity is broken and hence it could be argued that there is no life after death.

Richard Dawkins

Dawkins rejects such notions about the soul. In *The Selfish Gene* (1976), *River Out of Eden* (1986) and *The Blind Watchmaker* (1995) he builds a radically sceptical perspective on knowledge of DNA.

Richard Dawkins is a biologist and professor of the Public Understanding of Science at Oxford University. He opposes all theistic claims.

The replicator

Dawkins argues that in 'the primeval soup' could be found the **replicator** – the molecule able to create copies of itself. Over four thousand million years the replicator evolved from merely existing to constructing survival machines for continued existence. Replicators are now known as genes and the survival machines are human beings. Dawkins draws a parallel with the development of human beings.

> **Further discussion**
> Consider the extent to which Dawkins uses the language of myth in presenting his case. Has he simply replaced the 'myth of the soul' with the 'myth of DNA'?

- 'The primeval soup' has become 'the soup of human culture', and the unit of replication through which culture is passed on is the **meme**.
- The propagation of genes via sexual reproduction is matched by the propagation of memes through, for example, ideas, tunes and so on, 'leaping from brain to brain'.
- It is only through this process that individual consciousness and the sense of the self develops.

DNA survival

The process of evolution for the gene and the meme is concerned with only one purpose – DNA survival. Maximising this survival is the 'true utility function of life'. All of a person's actions – from aggression to altruism – can be explained by the furtherance of that end. Dawkins argues that the self or consciousness can be thought of as 'the culmination of an evolutionary trend towards the emancipation of survival machines as executive decision-takers from their ultimate masters, the genes'. Apart from maximising DNA survival, there is no other purpose in life. Indeed the very search for purpose is in some sense 'an exaggerated form of a nearly universal delusion'. The universe Dawkins constructs is 'one of blind physical forces and genetic replication… and you won't find any rhyme or reason in it, nor any justice. DNA neither knows nor cares. DNA just is. And we dance to its music'.

> **Further reading**
> *The Selfish Gene* (OUP 1976), page 63; *River Out of Eden* (Weidenfeld & Nicolson 1986), pages 96 and 133 respectively.

Death brings an end to the survival machine that is the human being. Our genes continue or disperse according to the life forms that they may have entered through reproduction. Our memes continue or disperse according to their propagation in the soup of human culture. Here, there is no place for a belief in the soul.

> **Further discussion**
> Consider whether, from a materialistic point of view, the human body can ever be fully destroyed so that none of its constituent parts remain.

Other concepts of the body/soul distinction

Dualism

Traditionally, dualism – the belief that body and soul have separate and different existences – dominated western philosophical and religious thought. **Aquinas** (c. 1225–1274), following Aristotle, wrote that soul or *anima* refers to that which first animates or 'makes alive' the living things with which we are familiar: 'the soul is what makes our bodies live; so the soul is the primary source of all those activities that differentiate levels of life: growth, sensation, movement, and understanding' (*Summa Theologica* II, 76, 1).

> **Further reading**
> *God and the Mind Machine: Artificial Intelligence* by John Puddefoot (SPCK 1996) discusses computer intelligence and traditional views of the soul.

Descartes

> **Further reading**
>
> See pages 15–16 of the *OCR AS Guide* on Aristotle's idea of the soul, plus *An Introduction to the Philosophy of Religion* by Brian Davies (OUP 1982), page 213.

For René Descartes (1596–1650) there was a clear distinction between the world of matter known to the senses and the world of thought known directly: 'My essence consists solely in the fact that I am a thinking thing.' As for his body, this was 'simply an extended, non-thinking thing'. The problem remained of how the non-spatial mind related to the spatial-temporal body. Descartes suggested that this interaction took place in the pineal gland. For Descartes, mental acts of the mind – where thoughts and feelings are known – were separate from, and controlled, physical acts, which were performed by the body.

Materialism

The response of materialists to this kind of thinking is to state that the 'self' is nothing more than a word describing a physical body and its actions. Among these actions are those that take place in the brain due to electrical, chemical or biological input. These actions in the brain might be described as thought or emotion but they are simply physical phenomena. Materialism is therefore **monistic** and **reductionist** – it reduces all mental activities down to material causes. **Gilbert Ryle** (1900–1976) argued in *The Concept of Mind* (1949) that those who followed in the footsteps of Descartes were mistaken. He coined the phrase **ghost in the machine**, which has been much used in discussions about the body/mind split.

> **Further discussion**
>
> Consider whether everything you think or feel is a result of input that affects the brain on a purely physical level.

> 'The dogma of the Ghost in the Machine… maintains that there exist both bodies and minds; that there occur physical processes and mental processes; that there are mechanical causes of corporeal movements and mental causes of corporeal movements. I shall argue that these and other conjunctions are absurd'.

The Concept of the Mind (Peregrine Books, 1970) page 23.

For Ryle, the mind simply describes the way in which we act as bodies.

Idealism

The idealist argument proposes that the world may not be the way it really is, but only the way we *think* it is. It questions whether physical reality is as knowable as reductionist materialists assume. Is the world real, independent of our observations of it? If not, the materialist case collapses.

> **Further study**
>
> Read chapter 10 of *Reason and Religious Belief* by Peterson, Hasker, Reichenbach and Basinger (OUP 2003). John Hick, unusually as a philosopher, places some weight on the evidence of near-death experiences (NDEs) and out-of-body experiences (OBEs). Spiritualism (communication with the dead) and hauntings (ghosts) might also be added. Read, for example, Celia Green's *Out of the Body Experiences* (Institute of Psychophysical Research 1995) and consider the amount of weight you would give to each of these as evidence for life after death.

Life after death

Disembodied survival

Disembodied survival after death initially seems plausible for dualists, since if, as Descartes argues, human beings can exist without their bodies, then the fact that the body dies does not mean that the person as a soul dies. Davies quotes from the writings of **H. D. Lewis**: 'My own conclusion is that no recent discussions of the mind-body problem have succeeded in showing that we can dispense with an absolute distinction between mind and body'. Mental processes, quite distinct from physical ones, suggest that a non-physical self can continue after death.

An Introduction to the Philosophy of Religion, page 215.

Light bulbs

Richard Swinburne (b. 1934) links the soul and the brain together. 'The soul is like a light bulb and the brain is like an electric light socket. If you plug the bulb into the socket and turn the current on, the light will shine. If the socket is damaged or the current turned off, the light will not shine.' Swinburne concludes that if the brain is destroyed or 'dead', the soul will cease to function – there will be no mental life. What if the socket is repaired or the current turned

The Evolution of the Soul (Clarendon Press 1986) page 310.

on again? Swinburne suggests that the soul could be reawakened if it was reconnected to a brain. This would be something that an omnipotent God could do without violating natural law.

An image world

H. H. Price (1899–1985) proposes another theory. He argues that the **survival hypothesis** – life after death – has a mass of evidence supporting it. The problem people have in believing this lies in accepting a 'disincarnate human personality'. But this could happen, he proposes, if the 'new world' after death were an 'image world' of mental images. The closest analogy to what Price proposes is the difference between the world of waking experience and that of dreaming. Death would simply mark the end of waking experience and the beginning of an imaging consciousness. The new world would be one where personality could continue and interaction take place, since: 'It would be the joint-product of a group of telepathically-interacting minds.'

> **Further reading**
>
> Read 'The Soul Survives and Functions after Death' in *Philosophy of Religion: Selected Readings* eds. Peterson, Hasker, Reichenbach, Basinger (OUP 1996).

Embodied survival

If we associate person and body, then the continuation of the body implies the continuation of the person. As we have seen, Hick proposes this view in his replica theory. **Brian Davies** challenges this, arguing that 'knowing that a replica of myself will be wining and dining somewhere is not at all the same as knowing that I shall be wining and dining somewhere.'

An Introduction to the Philosophy of Religion, page 223.

Davies adopts a conclusion similar to that of Swinburne, although their premise is entirely different. Davies argues that the dead body in the grave is clearly recognised by others as physically continuous with the live body to which they related before death. There is no logical reason why the dead body could not have the power of living again after death if there was 'a power' that could make this happen, so that people who lived again were physically continuous with people who had died. As with Swinburne, the argument proposed by Davies requires God to be that power. Consider the argument that if God did not exist he would have to be invented, in order to provide people with immortality. Is belief in immortality more fundamental than belief in God?

Resurrection

Resurrection is particularly associated with Christian thought. In the New Testament, the idea of the restoration of life can be found in miracle stories where Jesus brings the dead to life. Jesus teaches that belief in him guarantees eternal life: 'I am the resurrection and the life; whoever believes in me, even if he dies, will live, and everyone who lives and believes in me will never die' (John 11: 25–26). The Gospels all concentrate on two important aspects of Jesus' resurrection: the empty tomb and the appearance of the risen Jesus to his disciples.

For example, see the Raising of Lazarus (John 11: 1–44).

> **Further reading**
>
> Read pages 113–115 of the *OCR AS Guide* for a more detailed discussion of the resurrection narratives in John and Mark.

Nothing is said in the New Testament about the **process** of resurrection. The risen Jesus can suddenly appear so that he seems like a ghost (Luke 24: 36–37). He later asks for something to eat and eats fish in front of the disciples like any other person (Luke 24: 41–43).

> **Further study**
>
> Consider Paul's words to the Christians in Corinth: 'If Christ has not been raised, then empty is our preaching; empty too your faith. ...Of all people we are the most pitiable' (1 Corinthians 15: 14, 19). Is Paul right?

In 1 Corinthians 15, Paul discusses the resurrection body and the resurrection event to raise the following points:

✦ To express continuity between the person who dies and the

same person risen, he uses the analogy of the seed becoming the plant (1 Corinthians 15: 36–38).

- To express the qualitative difference between the body before death and the risen body he writes about the natural body becoming the spiritual body (1 Corinthians 15: 42–44).
- In an image of the Last Judgment, Paul describes how the dead will be raised incorruptible and immortal through the power of God (1 Corinthians 15: 51–54).
- Christians share the same belief 'in the resurrection of the body and the life everlasting' that is stated in the Apostles' Creed.

> **Further reading**
> An issue with the idea of a post-mortem state is posed by the **qualia** question, namely, what would it be like to be resurrected person? The question is famously explored by Thomas Nagel in his essay 'What is it like to be a bat?' in *Mortal Questions* (CUP 1991).

Rebirth

Rebirth is the belief that when the body dies the self is transferred to another body of some kind.

> **Further reading**
> See pages 134 and 147 of the *OCR AS Guide* and the chapter on Eastern Religions in this book.

Hinduism teaches **samsara**: a series of rebirths in which the atman, the eternal soul, moves from body to body dependent on the qualitative sum of actions performed in past lives – karma. By keeping to dharma or duty, good karma is accumulated. The aim of life is therefore to obtain moksha (freedom from rebirth), when the atman is reunited with Brahman, the Godhead. During samsara, the reborn atman carries no apparent memory of its past life.

Buddhism rejects the idea of atman; there is nothing that can be passed from life to life. Atman is replaced by the doctrine of **anatta** – there is no permanent, underlying self. Instead, the individual is compounded of five elements of consciousness that are constantly changing according to environment and conditions. Karmic law links each life together so that the individual is the union of all lives lived in the past. The aim of life is that through following the Noble Eightfold Path and the dharma, suffering can be overcome and nirvana – enlightenment – achieved.

Hans Kung

Hans Kung presents a useful evaluation of rebirth. On the positive side, a life before and after the present life is necessary for a truly moral world order. A person's actions in past lives determine that person's present quality of life. A person's actions in the present life determine their quality of life in the next. This would encourage morality to flourish. Furthermore, cumulative evidence of people living past lives is empirical evidence of rebirth.

However, Kung continues to point out that if past life is forgotten, how does that help in developing morality? There are also problems in replacing the concept of a loving God with a harsh law of karma. No allowance seems to be made for past or future actions that are determined by environment and nurture. Kung also doubts that the evidence of rebirth has any empirical value, no matter how bulky.

Kung appeals to nature: 'In nature what are not repeated are... the concrete details. Nature in particular, from the atomic nuclei to the stars... goes through a history.' *Eternal Life* (Collins 1984), page 89.

Heaven and hell

Heaven and hell as concepts are found in both Christianity and Islam. The Qur'an teaches that there will be a day of resurrection and of judgement. Descriptions of hell are similar to those of Christianity, while those of heaven are much less figurative (surahs 4 and 90 give a vivid picture of hell while a reference to the pleasures of Paradise can be found in Surah 36).

> **Further reading**
> Read chapter 10 of *Death and Eternal Life* by John Hick (Collins 1976) on the development of heaven, hell and purgatory in Christian thought.

Heaven in the New Testament is the abode of God and the angels. Some imagery is very focused, such as when Jesus explains that 'in my Father's house there are many dwellings' (John 14: 2). Other imagery is more complex, such as that found in the book of Revelation, where heaven is a temple, a bride and the New Jerusalem (Revelation 21: 1–4). Heaven is where 'good' people go. Hell in the New Testament is the abode of the devil, and a place of torment. Many of the parables of Jesus contain the warning of being sent to a place where there will be 'weeping and gnashing of teeth' (Matthew 25: 30). It is a place of 'eternal fire, prepared for the devil and his angels' (Matthew 25: 41). Jesus used the Hebrew word **Gehenna** to refer to hell. This referred to a valley outside of Jerusalem that was used as a rubbish dump and burned day and night. Jesus also taught that the devil could 'destroy both soul and body in Gehenna' (Matthew 10: 28). Hell is where 'the wicked' go.

New Testament

Further discussion
Consider the word 'eternal' when applied to life in heaven or hell. What concept of time is being used? Is Milton's Satan right in suggesting that, 'Our torments also may in length of time become our elements, these piercing fires as soft as now severe'?

Although a simplification, there is a sense in which heaven and hell are inevitable constructs in response to the realities of life. Many of the Psalms in the Old Testament raise this problem. If the wicked are not punished in this life, and the virtuous and those who suffer are not rewarded, then wherein lies the justice of God? If this argument is pushed too far, however, the problem remains of whether in the next life those who have not suffered receive a lesser reward than those who have. Another line of argument suggests that suffering is acceptable because all will be put right in heaven. But does that justify the suffering of the innocent?

Suffering

Route E: Philosophy of Religion with Eastern Religions. Read pages 134–135 and 148 of the *OCR AS Guide*. Consider how eastern religions offer an idea of 'hell' in terms of failing to achieve moksha or nirvana and therefore continuing to live in maya (Hinduism) or dukkha (Buddhism).

For many, the idea of hell as being a place where people are punished by fire forever is hard to accept. Hick agreed and argued that hell was scientifically fantastic, morally revolting and self-contradictory. Aquinas argued that finite sins against an infinite God could only justly be punished by infinite time in hell. However, the problem of justice remains when there is no allowance for the wicked to repent. The Roman Catholic doctrine of **purgatory** could be seen as a response to this, in that those not quite ready for heaven were punished for a duration until purified. Attempts have been made to ignore the figurative language describing hell and refer to it instead as being the absence of God. Yet, logically, it might be suggested that if that can be done for hell, what about the figurative language regarding heaven?

Purgatory means literally 'cleansing' from sin. This 'intermediate state' is rejected by Protestant theologians, often because between death and final resurrection the person is not conscious and not aware of time.

Revelation and religious experience

The concept of religious experience

Natural theology approaches an understanding of God through the use of reason and knowledge. Thus a rational focus on creation reveals God's presence. This approach is distinct from revelation, which refers to God's self-disclosure in a way outside of the Natural.

See pages 69–70 of the *OCR AS Guide*.

Religious experience was analysed by William James in *The Varieties of Religious Experience* (1901–1902). James argues that religious experience might differ according to the religion of the person and their particular temperament but, in essence, all religious experience is comprised of two parts:

- Uneasiness on the part of the person that there is something wrong about them
- Being saved from this wrongness is achieved by making proper connection with the higher powers.

Further discussion

Consider whether some individuals are more prone to religious experience as a result of their personality type, genetic make-up and upbringing.

Religious experiences can be mystical – with God being found through internal reflection or external observation. Many saints are described as having such experiences following long periods of prayer and meditation. Alternatively, a focus on beauty – particularly of nature – might result in a religious experience. James describes such experiences as being ineffable (defying description), noetic (containing knowledge), transient (of short duration) and passive (under the control of a 'higher power').

Types of religious experiences

Many examples of visions, voices, numinous experiences and conversions have been noted. Before the battle of the Milvian Bridge in 312 CE, Constantine declared he had seen the 'chi-ro' in the sky and heard a voice say 'in this sign conquer'. In 1537 Ignatius of Loyola claimed to have had a vision of God and Christ, and heard a voice say, 'My will is that you should serve us'. In 1858, Bernadette of Lourdes declared that she had seen a vision of the Virgin Mary in a grotto and heard the voice declare, 'I am the Immaculate Conception'.

Otto

Further study

Read Isaiah 6: 1–8. Identify those parts of the account that are natural and those that might be described as supernatural. In what non-religious ways can the vision be interpreted?

The prophet Isaiah, who lived in Jerusalem in the 8th century BCE, responded to his vision of God in the Temple with fear, declaring, 'Woe is me! I am doomed' (Isaiah 6: 5). This fear is based on being in the presence of the divine, the **numinous**. The term is a descriptive one used of religious experience and was coined by **Rudolph Otto** (1869–1937) from the Latin 'numen' (god).

In *The Idea of the Holy* (1923), Otto explored the non-rational apprehension of the divine as being a wholly other, separate reality. God was encountered as 'mysterium tremendum et fascinans' – provoking awe and fascination. He argued that the awe was in response to the transcendence of God and the fascination in response to the immanence of God, since God had disclosed himself to the person in establishing a relationship.

Otto's description of the numinous does not remove all problems. A non-religious person might have a sense of the numinous in terms of fear and awe while climbing a mountain, watching a frightening film in the cinema, and so on. Wayne Proudfoot makes a similar criticism when he notes that terms such as 'numinous', 'holy' and 'sacred' are used of religious experience precisely so that the experience *cannot* be fully described and analysed: 'Otto's use of numinous is an example of how one can employ the term to create a sense of mystery and present it as analysis.'

Wayne Proudfoot, 'Religious Experience as Interpretative Accounts' in *Philosophy of Religion: Selected Readings*, page 358.

Conversion

Conversion is often regarded as a result of religious experience. At the end of his vision, Isaiah hears God ask if there is anyone that he can send to do his work. Isaiah replies, 'Here am I. Send me!' (Isaiah 6: 8). Isaiah has had a conversion experience, as now he changes the direction of his life and becomes a prophet. James argues that in a conversion 'the habitual centre of personal energy' in a man or woman is taken over by religious aims. Precisely what this 'habitual centre' is, James does not make clear. Humans, he argues, possess a subconscious region that yields access to higher spiritual agencies. From the evidence he gathered, James concluded that in conversion the person who had such an experience was 'the undergoer of an astounding process performed upon him from above. There is too much evidence of this for any doubt of it to be possible.' James does not ignore other factors that might be at work. He points out the dramatic way in which some emotions manifest themselves – sudden anger or love – which might be similar to the conversion experience.

Quotes in this section are from *Variety of Religious Experiences*, pages 196, 126, 204 and 257 respectively.

One common feature of conversions is the struggle between the personal will and the imperfect sinful self. In this struggle the person is overcome either suddenly or gradually. Isaiah's conversion experience suggests this process as he declares 'I am a man of unclean lips', which admission of sinfulness leads one of the seraphs to declare: 'Your guilt is taken away' (Isaiah 6: 5, 7). James recognises that in some people the struggle between the will and sinful self never takes place. Their religious energy remains dormant: 'some persons… never are, and possibly never under any circumstances could be, converted.'

James recognises two types of conversion:

- ✦ **Volitional:** over a lifetime a person gradually places religious aims at the centre
- ✦ **Involuntary:** a person is suddenly forced by a religious experience into a position of self-surrender, which pushes religious aims to the centre.

Further discussion

Consider the fact that some people might have conversion experiences at moments of moral crisis or psychological vulnerability. How would that impact on one's understanding of their conversion?

Once the conversion has taken place, in general, a person remains identified with the new religious vision of life that they have experienced. Even if the conversion experience does not have a lasting effect, James argues that it has still served its purpose in showing 'a human being what the high-water mark of his spiritual capacity is'.

Corporate experience

Conversions are sometimes the result of what might be termed corporate religious experience – when a number of people are involved. A key text is the account of Pentecost in the New Testament (Acts 2: 1–11), which describes the events following the resurrection and ascension of Jesus, as the disciples gathered in Jerusalem and the Holy Spirit came down upon them. In response, the disciples start speaking in different languages as they are filled with the Holy Spirit. Some people's response was amazement but others believed that the disciples were drunk.

Further study

Read Acts 2: 1–11. Identify those parts of the account that are natural and those that might be described as supernatural. In what non-religious ways can the experience be interpreted?

A modern counterpart of the account of Pentecost is the **Toronto Blessing**, which involved the Toronto Airport Vineyard Church. A South African evangelist, Rodney Howard-Browne, had had a dramatic impact on those to whom he preached. Many declared themselves 'drunk in the Holy Spirit' which caused them to act in bizarre ways. One phenomenon was 'holy laughter' where people were subject to fits of uncontrollable laughter. Pastor Randy Clark was one of those influenced by Howard-Browne's preaching. Clark

Mel Thompson suggests that experiences such as these are very difficult for the philosophy of religion to deal with. 'This is because the experience itself is not rational; the person concerned is ecstatic...having let go of normal controls... The charismatic experience is one that, however powerful and transforming for the person having it, is not a source for reasoned evidence or propositions of any sort.' *Philosophy of Religion* (Teach Yourself, 1997).

was invited to preach at the Toronto church and when he had finished, the type of corporate religious experiences noted above began to happen in the congregation – but with more intensity. There was holy laughter; hysterical crying and shouting; people barking like dogs or roaring like lions; people dancing and leaping. This first took place on 20 January 1994 and became known as the 'Toronto Blessing'. Similar events have continued to take place in the Toronto church on most evenings, with visiting members of evangelical churches often returning to their own congregations to document similar behaviour upon spreading the 'blessing'.

Further discussion

Consider the evidence presented on the 'Toronto Blessing'. What is your evaluation of the reported experience?

Not all evangelical churches have responded positively to the concept of the Toronto Blessing and some have even gone so far as to question whether God and the Holy Spirit have anything at all to do with the manifestations that took place.

Miracles and the problem of evil

Further study

Make sure you look up these references to miracles in the Bible to inform your understanding of this section: Exodus 7: 8–13; Joshua 10: 7–14; Matthew 8: 23–27; Mark 8: 22–26; Luke 9: 37–43; John 2: 1–11. Consider the purpose of these miracles. For more on the problem of evil, see pages 70– 72 of the *OCR AS Guide*.

Aquinas

Thomas Aquinas defined miracles as 'Those events... which happen by divine power beyond the order commonly observed in nature' (*Summa Theologica* III, 101, 2–4). He categorised three ranks of miracles:

- Something done by God that nature can never do – such as the sun standing still.
- Something done by God that nature can do, but not in that order – such as a person living, seeing or walking *after* being dead, blind or lame, respectively.
- Something done by God that nature usually does, but in the case of the miracle is done without the operation of the principles of nature – such as being cured of a fever 'by divine favour'.

Hume

Read page 18 of the *OCR AS Guide*.

It was against this type of understanding of miracles that David Hume (1711–1776) reacted in his chapter 'On Miracles' in *The Inquiry concerning Human Understanding* (1748). Hume argues first of all that: 'A miracle is a violation of the laws of nature; and as a firm and unalterable experience has established these laws, the proof against a miracle, from the very nature of the fact, is as entire as any argument from experience can possibly be imagined.' To believe that a miracle has taken place would be irrational, since it would mean setting aside the evidence of natural laws established by human observation.

Quoted by Michael Palmer in *The Question of God: An Introduction and Sourcebook* (Routledge 2001), page 206.

Four principles

Secondly, Hume applies a principle of absolute scepticism to any accounts given of miracles on four grounds.

1. No account of a miracle is to be found 'in all history' that is supported by enough witnesses possessing 'unquestioned good sense, education, and learning'.
2. In human nature there is a 'passion for surprise and wonder' that leads people to believe in the unusual and incredible. When this passion is linked with religion, then 'there is an end of all common sense'. People *want* to believe in miracles and therefore conclude that accounts of miracles *must* be true.

3. Accounts of miracles are chiefly found among 'ignorant and barbarous nations' and these accounts decrease in number in accordance with the advance made by nations to 'the enlightened ages'. On these grounds such accounts can be dismissed as lies.

4. Accounts of miracles can be found in the testimony of different religions, and in refusing to believe the credibility of such testimony for one religion and trying to accept the credibility for another, it has to be concluded that all such accounts are to be regarded as contrary and opposite to each other – and can therefore be discounted.

Hume establishes as a maxim: 'No human testimony can have such force as to prove a miracle.' Reason can therefore never be sufficient grounds to believe in miracles – such belief would depend on *faith* which gives a believer 'a determination to believe what is most contrary to custom and experience'.

Consider whether Hume's absolute scepticism mitigates his argument in terms of its neutrality. Could there be any grounds on which he might accept a miracle?

Wiles

Another critique of miracles is provided by Maurice Wiles (b. 1923). Following the line of argument adopted by Hume regarding the laws of nature, Wiles posits that: 'Miracles must be, by definition, relatively infrequent or else the whole idea of the laws of nature would be undermined, and ordered life as we know it would be an impossibility.' If miracles are accepted as rare events of God's direct action then they 'have been sparingly and strangely used'. Wiles points out the problem of believing in relatively minor miracles when God was seen as intervening, when on those major occasions – such as Hiroshima – when intervention would seem utterly necessary, God did not intervene.

God's Action in the World (SCM Press 1986), page 66.

To reconcile such difficulties, Wiles proposes a rethinking of God:

- ✦ He rejects the idea that God intervenes directly but occasionally in the world.
- ✦ He proposes a single act of God in which the whole world is encompassed.
- ✦ He argues that if God does not intervene in the world in particular actions, then it follows that he has never done so.
- ✦ This being the case, the miracles recorded in the Bible and the life of Christ – including the Resurrection – never happened.

Further study

Consider 2 Kings 2: 19–25. Here there are two miracles involving the prophet Elisha. In what ways do these miracles benefit Elisha, other people? What is their religious significance? How would they support the argument proposed by Wiles?

Vardy

Peter Vardy highlights the same type of **moral problem** regarding miracles: 'A God who intervenes at Lourdes to cure an old man from terminal cancer but does not act to save starving millions in Ethiopia… such a God needs, at the least, to face some hard moral questioning. Some may hold that this God is not worthy of worship.' He argues that the moral problem with miracles may have much to do with human incapacity to fully understand the mind of God. He also notes the 70 carefully attested miracles at the Roman Catholic shrine of Lourdes. He states that the evidence – given by doctors – is incontrovertible.

The Puzzle of God (HarperCollins 1990), page 191.

Revelation through holy scripture

Scripture as divinely inspired

Route E: Philosophy of Religion with Eastern Religions. See pages 49–51 of the of *OCR AS Guide*. Note the distinction between texts that are *sruti* (revealed) and *smriti* (remembered). See also pages 88–89 of the *OCR AS Guide*. Note that this is a fundamental debate between Orthodox and Progressive Jews about the divine status of Torah and especially Oral Torah.

Most religions rely on a **propositional** concept of revelation. This provides a record of events, teachings and people – often from a distant past or place – through which a revelation has taken place. The propositional form of revelation is then written down and becomes a holy scripture for that religion. Examples of such scripture can be found in the *Pali Tipitaka* of Theravada Buddhism, the sutras of Mahayana Buddhism, the Vedas and Upanishads of Hinduism, the Qur'an of Islam, the Torah of Judaism, the Avesta of Zoroastrianism, the Old and New Testaments of Christianity, and the Book of Mormon of the Church of the Latter Day Saints.

Different approaches to sacred writings

With all such works, a key question is one of **hermeneutics**: how is the scripture to be interpreted? In a literalist approach, the text as it stands must be understood in the most literal sense, given its divine inspiration. This is the case in Islam:

The Qur'an

- Muslims accept the 'chain' whereby the Qur'an came from Allah himself, then to the angel Jibril and then to the Prophet Muhammad.
- The wording of the Qur'an lies with Allah – not with the Prophet – and it is fixed word-for-word in Arabic by Allah.
- A translation of the Qur'an from Arabic immediately ceases to be the literal word of Allah.

The Bible

The Bible is very different from the Qur'an in terms of content and methods of interpretation.

'Canon' literally means 'rule' and refers to the rules that early Christian scholars used to decide which texts were authoritative and could be included in the Bible. For example: accept books that have a connection with an apostle, or that have a connection with a person closely associated with an apostle; reject books that are too bizarre, magical or extreme, and books that are known to be late.

- The biblical canon represents books that, in terms of composition, range over at least one millennium with a wide variety of authors.
- The biblical canon for the Protestant churches includes some later books rejected by the Catholic Church.
- Biblical scholarship suggests that a number of books show the presence of separate accounts from sources that have been edited and woven together.
- Scholars point to passages in the Gospel attributable not to the direct words or memory of Jesus but to the debates and responses to events at the time they were composed.

Most people approach holy scripture within the parameters of beliefs and rules on how to read and interpret what is set before them. In Christianity, there is a strong tendency within Protestantism to believe that the Bible speaks directly to the heart and mind of the reader, providing that there is openness to the words being read. The Catholic approach to the Bible teaches that for an authentic understanding, passages need to be read in the context of the whole of the Bible, within the tradition of the Church, and with an awareness of the 'truths' of faith already revealed.

In terms of divine inspiration and the Bible, three perspectives can be noted.

Three perspectives

Further reading

See pages 37–42 of the *OCR AS Guide* for a more detailed survey of biblical interpretation in relation to some modern ethical problems.

A literalist perspective: the Bible is the inspired word of God as the Holy Spirit was at work in its authors, ensuring that the message was written down free from error. As Billy Graham once said: 'The Bible is a book written by God through 30 secretaries.'

A conservative perspective: the Roman Catholic Church states that the books of the Bible 'have been written down under the inspiration of the Holy Spirit, they have God as their author'. The catechism attempts to combine two approaches: in paragraph 107 it puts forward the literalist view that 'the books of Scripture firmly, faithfully, and without error teach that truth which God wished to see confided to the Sacred Scriptures', whereas in paragraph 110 it takes a more liberal approach: 'The reader must take into account the conditions of their time and culture, the literary genres in use at that time, and the modes of feeling, speaking and narrating then current.'

Catechism of the Catholic Church (Bantam 1995), paragraph 10.

A liberal perspective: God inspired the writings of the authors of the Bible, and so they are generally sound in theological terms. Specific texts have limitations that reflect the limitations of their authors – their limited awareness or understanding of science, cosmology, morality, psychology, geography and so on. In this way, the books of the Bible contain errors and inaccuracies. A radically liberal approach might suggest that the Bible is no more and no less inspired than a great work of poetry or literature.

Further discussion

Consider this saying of St Augustine: 'If you believe what you like in the Gospel, and reject what you do not like, it is not the Gospel you believe but yourself.' What arguments could be produced to support or oppose what he says?

The Bible can be approached from a **propositional** perspective – 'words of God' are given in the texts for believers to accept – and also from a **nonpropositional** perspective. From the latter point of view, the Bible represents a two-way process of communication:

- Human beings, in searching for fulfilment, receive an awareness of God.
- God reveals himself in the events of human history.

It is this process of divine address *and* human response which is recorded in the Bible. The nonpropositional approach removes some of the problems of trying to maintain the divine inspiration behind inerrant texts. Instead, divine inspiration has more to do with the faith of the authors of the Bible, who, because of that faith, are part of the process of revelation.

Religious language

In religious language it is assumed that God can be spoken of in the affirmative. The **cataphatic way** (*via affirmativa*) looks at the positive qualities of human experience and applies them by analogy to God. Words such as 'good', 'just', 'truth', 'love' and 'light' seem obvious terms to use. It makes sense to speak of God as good, or God as just and so on. These qualities are ones that people understand in their own lives and experiences, and can apply to God.

Via affirmativa

Further reading

Religious Language by Ian T Ramsey (SCM Press 1967) is still an important classic; chapter 5 of Hick's *Philosophy of Religion*; chapter 11 of *Groundwork of Philosophy of Religion* by David Pailin (Epworth 1986).

However, there are limitations to this approach. Each person's experience of the good or the just in their lives could vary considerably. In that case, what is being said of God? When God is described as good, it is assumed that he is good in the best kind of way that good could possibly be understood or imagined. Yet God as good would have to be beyond the limits of human understanding, since God transcends all the positive qualities that might be ascribed to him. In that case, what is being said of God?

Via negativa

The opposite way of approaching God is to speak in negative terms, following the **apophatic way** (*via negativa*). This rejects the possibility of describing God in terms of what he *is*, since God's being cannot be encompassed by use of analogy with human life and experience. It accepts that the way to really know God is to remove language itself, since this serves to place God within the limits and constructs of the grammar of human language.

The apophatic way was developed by Pseudo-Dionysius the Areopagite (c. 500 CE), author of a number of Greek treatises in which he tried to reconcile neo-platonic philosophy with Christian theology. In *Divine Names* and *Mystical Union* he developed the view that through prayer an individual could become united with God by abandoning senses, images and language. 'We pray that we may come unto this Darkness which is beyond light, and, without seeing and without knowing, to see and to know that which is above vision and knowledge through the realisation that by not-seeing and by unknowing we attain to true vision and knowledge.'

Further study

See www.ccel.org/ccel/rolt/dionysius.html

Verification and falsification principles

Verification

The verification principle developed out of questions concerning the way in which language is used to convey knowledge. Its origins can be found in the Vienna Circle – the name given to a group of philosophers with a mathematical and scientific background who met in Vienna in the 1920s and 1930s.

The verification principle lay at the heart of the **logical positivism** movement. The basic idea of logical positivism was that the true task of philosophy was to clarify the *meaning* of *meaning*. The question at issue was whether propositions were meaningful or meaningless. It was argued that only two forms of propositions can have meaning: analytic *a priori* and synthetic *a posteriori*.

Further reading

Read pages 63–64 of the *OCR AS Guide* to refresh yourself on these basic terms.

Analytic propositions are true or false in terms of the words used and do not require external verification. Such statements are ones we can make that are certain because they are concerned with the rules of logic. They are necessarily true independently of external empirical evidence. Typically such statements might be used in mathematical statements and definitions. Statements such as these are *a priori* in that the knowledge contained in them comes before (prior to) sense experience.

Synthetic propositions are true or false depending on empirical examination, which is required before verification can take place. Such statements are ones we can make that may or may not be logically true. Their being true or false is necessarily dependent on external empirical evidence. Statements such as these are *a posteriori* in that the knowledge contained in them comes after (post) sense experience.

It is in this context that we can understand the verification principle as follows. Propositions are meaningful on two grounds:

- They can be verified by the meaning of the words themselves, the grammatical structure of the proposition and the inherent logical reasoning behind them.
- They can be verified by external empirical evidence.

In the first case such propositions are analytically true or false, and in the second case such propositions are synthetically true or false. A. J. Ayer's *Language, Truth and Logic* (1936) brought the verification principle to a wider audience. Ayer distinguished two forms of verification:

- **Hard verification** referred to propositions where there was no doubt as to the truth of the statement, because it fulfilled either of the two grounds given above.
- **Weak verification** referred to propositions such as those that dealt with past or future events, which could be verified by observation and external empirical evidence obtained at that time, and which had then to be relied on by others.

The implications of this linguistic analysis in terms of religious language are clear: all talk about God is meaningless. The proposition 'There is a God' is not analytic – it cannot be verified by the internal logic of the statement. Equally, it is not synthetic – it cannot be verified by external empirical evidence. Being neither of these two, religious propositions and statements such as this are meaningless and nonsense. Simply because the word 'God' exists, does not mean that there has to be a corresponding reality.

Further discussion

Consider John Hick's **eschatological verification** principle, which argues that religious statements will only be verified in the hereafter. Would such verification only be possible for a believer?

Falsification

Further reading

Anthony Flew, 'Theology and Falsification' in *The Philosophy of Religion* ed. Basil Mitchell (OUP 1971).

Arguably, the falsification principle is a variation on the verification principle. **Anthony Flew** developed the scientific approach of Karl Popper, which posited the view that for a statement to be meaningful, it must be falsifiable, namely one must be able to prove it to be false. This may sound confusing, but Flew illustrated his point by using John Wisdom's Parable of the Gardener. Two explorers come across a clearing in the jungle that appears to have been cultivated. One explorer says that the evidence shows a gardener tends the plot. The other, on the basis of the same evidence, replies there is no gardener. To test it, they set a watch, put up an electric barbed-wire fence and patrol with bloodhounds. At no point is there any external empirical evidence that there is a gardener. However, the believer will not change his initial assertion. He declares: 'There is a gardener, invisible, intangible, insensible to electric shocks, a gardener who has no scent and makes no sound, a gardener who comes secretly to look after the garden which he loves.' The sceptic replies: 'What remains of your original assertion? Just how does what you call an invisible, intangible, eternally elusive gardener differ from an imaginary gardener or even from no gardener at all'.

Further reading

See page 355 of 'The Falsification Challenge' in *Philosophy of Religion: Selected Writings*.

The believer qualifies his assertion until nothing meaningful remains. His original assertion cannot be proved false, because he is constantly adjusting his original hypothesis – this is a 'death by a thousand qualifications'. Flew argued that religious believers often use the claim 'God is mysterious' to deal with any evidence that appears to confront their original belief in his existence. This means that it can never be proved false.

Further discussion

Consider *bliks*, formulated by R. M. Hare in answer to Flew's conclusion. A *blik* is an unverifiable and unfalsifiable interpretation of one's experience. Religious beliefs are *bliks*. Is this a successful answer?

Flew gives examples of religious assertions that are made in this way. A believer might state to a loving father, 'God loves us as a father loves his children'. This reassurance is then undermined when the father's child is dying of inoperable throat cancer. The reassurance is repeated but this time with a qualification: 'but his love is not merely human love'. The death of the child is then met with the reassurance being repeated, with a further qualification: 'and God's loving ways are inscrutable'. No matter what further tragedies befall this father, the believer will always have qualifications at hand to confirm belief. Flew concludes: 'What would have to occur or to have occurred to constitute for you a disproof of the love of, or the existence of, God?'

Philosophy of Religion: Selected Writings, page 355.

Symbol, analogy and myth

Symbol

One response to the relationship between language and our experience of the world is to argue that there are levels of reality that can be known outside of the merely empirical. Such levels of reality can be understood through the use of the language of symbols. A useful approach to the area is provided by Paul Tillich.

A brief definition of a symbol is that it is like a sign, in that it points beyond itself to something else. However, a symbol moves one step further than a sign. 'Symbols, although they are not the same as that which they symbolize, participate in its meaning and power.'

'Religious Language as Symbolic' in *Philosophy of Religion: Selected Readings* eds. Peterson et al (OUP 1996), page 358.

Tillich uses the classic example of a national flag, which on the one hand can be a coloured piece of cloth, and on the other a coloured piece of cloth that happens to enshrine a nation's beliefs and values. He criticises the approach of those such as Ayer, because in their work, symbol has been reduced to sign.

Tillich develops the distinction between the two by proposing that symbols open up otherwise hidden levels of reality, which cannot be grasped in any way other than through symbols. However, this requires a two-way process – the symbol opens up the soul of the person involved *and* the most fundamental level of reality: 'the ultimate power of being', namely that which is Holy. All religious symbols are therefore symbols of the Holy.

Tillich argues that on the transcendent level God is both symbolic and non-symbolic. Thus God is 'Being in itself' *and* the highest being in which everything that people have exists in the most perfect way. In communication with God, these two points have to be considered, and so the human person must symbolise in order for there to be a relationship. Everything that is said about God in terms of his attributes is said in a symbolic sense. Likewise, expressions about God, which refer to God's actions in a temporal, spatial or causal sense, are symbolic and not literal expressions.

Tillich avoids a number of criticisms of his use of symbolic language by arguing that symbols themselves are independent of empirical criticism: 'You cannot kill a symbol by criticism in terms of natural sciences or in terms of historical research.' He recognises

Philosophy of Religion: Selected Writings, page 364.

that symbols can die, in the sense that the situation in which they were created can pass. Thus symbolic language can adequately convey the truth of the situation in which it is created – but in another situation, it might be inadequate in doing so.

Further discussion

Consider whether symbols really convey any factual knowledge. Could they give the wrong insights about the ultimate reality?

Analogy

Analogy in religious language was the construct of Thomas Aquinas, based on Aristotle. While acknowledging the contribution of the apophatic way, Aquinas upheld the possibility of following the cataphatic way. The question at issue was that of taking concepts from ordinary meaningful discourse (loving, good, wise and so on) and applying them to the transcendent God so that meaningful discourse could be had about God.

Aquinas argues against two forms of language that might be used in discourse about God:

- **Univocal language**, whereby the same word when applied to God and human beings means exactly the same thing.
- **Equivocal language**, whereby the same word when applied to God and human beings means something totally different.

In the first case, univocal language does not allow for the fact that God is infinite and his virtues cannot be limited or separated out. Thus to say that 'God is loving' and 'the mother is loving' cannot mean exactly the same thing, given that the mother is finite and her virtue of love can be separated out from other virtues she might have, such as strength, courage, wisdom and so on.

In the second case, equivocal language does not allow for the fact that the human being can, through the use of reason, come to knowledge of God. If the word 'loving' when applied to God meant something totally different to 'loving' as applied to the mother, then human beings would remain completely in ignorance about God.

Aquinas recommends therefore **analogical language**. God is not 'loving' in exactly the same way as the mother in the example above, nor is God 'loving' in a completely unrelated way. There is a relationship between the language used to describe God and the language used about human beings. By using analogical language, God can be spoken of correctly if not comprehensively.

Aquinas distinguished two types of analogical language:

- **Analogy of proper proportionality** means that a quality can be ascribed to one thing, which then points to another thing with the same quality. For example: A mother loves her daughter. Her daughter knows what love means. God loves all people. The daughter thus has some understanding of what it means to say that God is loving.
- **Analogy of intrinsic attribution** means that a quality can be ascribed to one thing because it is caused by another thing. For example: God is the source of all love. God loves all people. The mother loves her daughter. The mother's love is caused by and is a reflection of God's love.

Further discussion

Consider whether analogies really allow for meaningful discourse about God and his characteristics.

Myth

Myth, in the context of religious language, refers to a symbolic narrative relating stories of God, gods, goddesses, heroes and heroines. They can be understood as religious stories that give an insight into the values and self-awareness of the people from whom they come. However, when religious stories are called myths, it is implied that the stories are false. No matter how much a believer might be told that the myth has to be taken as revealing insights about God, the believer might feel that the meaningful question is being avoided: did it happen?

Further study

Read and consider the passage in Acts 1: 9–11, the Ascension of Jesus. What arguments can you propose for and against describing this event as myth?

In 1941, a radical approach to myth was presented when Rudolf Bultmann published *The New Testament and Mythology*. Bultmann argued that:

- The worldview of the New Testament was a mythological one, too out-of-date for the modern age.
- In order for the true message of the New Testament to be understood, it had to be demythologised.
- This process meant a radical existentialist approach to the New Testament and the elimination of unnecessary imagery or myth.

Further reading

Bultmann's work was popularised by John Robinson's *Honest to God* (1962). Robinson approved of Bultmann's efforts in questioning 'the mythological language of pre-existence, incarnation, ascent and descent, miraculous intervention, cosmic catastrophe, and so on… which make sense only on a now completely antiquated world-view'. *Honest to God* (SCM Press 1962) page 24.

In contrast to Bultmann's approach, Maurice Wiles argued that a myth cannot be true or false in the way that empirical statements can be judged. However, that does not rule out applying categories of truth and falsity to myths: 'Insofar as they express certain fundamental aspects of the human condition, they may do so in a way which… turns out to be false.' The key question is 'whether a myth can continue to function as a potent myth, once it is acknowledged that it is not literally true'.

'Myth in Theology' in *The Myth of God Incarnate* ed. John Hick (SCM Press 1977), pages 159 and 165 respectively.

Route D: Philosophy of Religion with Developments in Christian Thought. See page 113 of the Developments in Christian Thought chapter and consider how myth and metaphor have affected John Hick's liberal Christian views of Jesus and Christianity's relationship with other religions.

Test yourself

1. 'God can only be understood in terms of analogy.' Discuss.
2. 'Rebirth after death makes less sense than resurrection.' Discuss.
3. Consider the view that holy scriptures are sources of revelation.
4. 'Religious experience is distinctive and offers the best evidence for God's existence.' Discuss.

For material on making connections between Philosophy of Religion and your other chosen module, including some sample questions, see the relevant pages of the chapter on that module. For example, for material on the connections between Islam and Philosophy, see pages 158–159, as well as the margins of that chapter.

Free will and determinism

What are the nature and limits of our freedom? For someone to hold moral responsibility for the choices that they make, there must be some element of free choice in their decision-making. If everything they do is determined by genetics, psychology or the will of God, then we cannot talk of moral culpability or sin in the way that many religious believers are accustomed to.

> **Further reading**
> See chapter 1 of *Free Will* by Thomas Pink (OUP 2004).

Determinism

Environmental determinism

Environmental determinism is the view that what we do is determined by where we find ourselves in the world. We hold certain roles, such as student, worker or teacher, and these roles are shaped by influences such as class, wealth or power. These factors create attitudes towards our situation, society and the structures of power that affect us. Free choices made by a peasant farmer in Africa, for example, are different from those of a middle-class worker in Britain.

Genetic determinism

Research into the human genome has highlighted patterns arising from particular genetic make-ups.

Genetic determinism highlights the role that genes have played in determining personality and behaviour. Those who hold an idea of **genetic fixity** claim that the genes that parents pass on to their children determine the characteristics of those children.

Social conditioning or psychological determinism

This position is based on the belief that our relationship with society – and with particular individuals within society – determines our personality and sense of identity. In particular, psychologists have identified the importance of attitudes towards sexuality and authority, and how these are formed by those closest to us.

> **Further reading**
> See pages 18–21 of *Ethical Theory* by Mel Thompson (Hodder and Stoughton 2005).

Hard determinism

> **Further reading**
> See chapter 5 of *Moral Problems* by Michael Palmer (Lutterworth Press 2001).

Hard determinists take the view that everything in the universe has a preceding cause, and that events of type A always lead on to events of type B.

This can be expressed in various ways, but the most basic argument is that environment, genetics and psychology act as the causes of certain feelings and behaviour. Hard determinists will argue that the amount you can find out about an individual's social context and psychological and physical make-up determines the degree to which you can predict that individual's response to a moral situation. If you know everything about a person in relation to these causal elements, then you can accurately predict all their actions.

Hard determinism has huge implications. Some philosophers, such as John Locke (1632–1704), would argue that free moral choice is simply an illusion. They claim that while we have an impression of freedom, in reality we find that we are not actually free and that, as we cannot control our choices, we cannot be held responsible if we make bad moral choices. This view has obvious repercussions for legal courts in assessing the actions of criminals, but also for priests in assessing the sins of their flock.

Libertarianism

Libertarians acknowledge that physiology and psychology affect our choices, but argue that these do not actually determine them entirely. According to libertarianism, we do possess moral freedom and are therefore responsible for the choices we make.

Libertarians talk about individuals possessing a moral self, which they say exists so that people can make causally undetermined choices out of moral duty rather than self-interest. According to Michael Palmer, there is a distinction between our nature and our character. The nature of an individual illustrates an aspect of their character. For example, the nature of a greedy person may predispose them towards gluttony, but they can nevertheless choose to refuse a second helping at lunch. In other words, character cannot be reduced purely to nature.

As a result of this, libertarians state that criminals are still culpable for their actions, even though courts may recognise psychological or physiological factors. Priests may sympathise with a sinner but still insist on their acknowledgement of sin.

Further study

Freedom is especially important for existentialism because, as Sartre argues, humans develop their being (or 'essence') by the totality of their free acts. Not to do so is to suffer from 'bad faith' and to live a false existence. But can it be achieved? Read Jean-Paul Sartre's novel *The Age of Reason* (Penguin 2001) to consider this question.

Soft determinism

Soft determinists, as might be expected, hold a view somewhere between the two positions outlined above. They disagree that actions are uncaused and the product of completely free moral choice, but they do insist that individuals must have sufficient freedom to act if we are to talk about moral responsibility. If actions are not caused, then they are chaotic and random – a view that itself poses questions about moral responsibility. Instead, they believe that actions are caused, but that individuals still possess some freedom in relation to the cause. There are two related points here:

- **Internal and external causation**. For example, in the case of Mohandes K. Gandhi's decision to fast, his act was contingent on a particular historical situation in British India, but his choice was free. In the case of a man lost in the desert without food, on the other hand, the external cause of his situation denies him a choice of whether or not to eat.
- **Determinism and choice**. Without desires, beliefs and character, our actions would be completely random; these elements in our make-up are caused by the factors outlined in the hard determinist position. In order for moral choice to be real, conscious decision-making, action and choice need to precede the actual decision of an individual.

Route A: ethics and philosophy of religion. Consider the implications of hard determinism for arguments about the problem of evil. Consider the view that without human freedom, God has to take responsibility for both moral and natural evil. Read page 41 of *Free Will* by Thomas Pink.

Further reading

See pages 18–21 of *Ethical Theory* by Mel Thompson (Hodder Murray 2003).

Historical antecedents to the debate

The arguments of the reformer John Calvin (1509–1564) have shaped some attitudes towards this issue. His idea of 'double predestination' promoted the idea that human choice is shaped entirely by the will of God: he argued in his doctrine of election that God not only decides whether an individual will join the elect and find salvation, but also whether someone will choose to reject that salvation. As a result, there is nothing an individual can do that will affect their final destiny, although Calvin would

Further discussion

Consider what Calvin's response would be to this statement: 'We do not possess any genuine freedom to act ethically.'

encourage moral living on the basis that it is a sign that an individual who pursues it is among the elect.

An earlier debate in the history of Christian belief was that between Augustine (354–430) and Pelagius, a British theologian who was declared a heretic by Pope Innocent I in 417. Pelagius claimed that all human beings came into the world in the condition of Adam. Sinlessness is therefore a real possibility for an individual if they choose to use their God-given freedom of choice appropriately. Augustine, on the other hand, suggested that freedom had become limited after the Fall and that the sin of Adam was passed down to his descendents. Baptism was necessary if humans were to be able to turn away from sin. Human freedom had been severely limited and there was a consequent need for God's grace.

Route A: ethics and philosophy of religion. Consider the question of God's omniscience in relation to human freedom. If God has knowledge of all things, can humans be truly free? If humans are externally free, does this mean that God cannot fully know or control the future? Explore ways in which theologians might balance God's omniscience with human freewill.

Further reading

Read page 71 of the *OCR AS Guide*.

Conscience

Many religious thinkers have described conscience as a vehicle for divine revelation, while many secular thinkers have seen it merely as a reflection of the values of society: a set of values and principles that affect cultural and aesthetic awareness.

Despite disagreements as to its definition, many thinkers have acknowledged the primacy of conscience in moral decision-making. St Paul suggested that every human possessed an innate sense of right and wrong as a result of their possessing a conscience (Romans 2: 14–15). The New Testament coins the term **syneidesis** to describe the pain a person feels when they act in a way that goes against their moral principles. Natural law thinkers have suggested that conscience is correlative to natural law itself; it is built into our nature and allows us to flourish by making moral decisions that enable us to fulfil our natures as designed by God.

Conscience has also been described as the reaction of a person to objective moral law. The church has always placed an emphasis on informing conscience so that its judgements are in line with the teaching of the church or the Bible. Theologians have disagreed over its place in the process of reaching a moral decision. Some have argued that conscience should play a secondary role, while others have argued that its role should be central. Many acknowledge the personal nature of conscience and demand respect for its dictates, even when they go against the teaching of the church or scripture.

Route A: ethics and philosophy of religion. Consider whether conscience necessarily supports the view that God exists. Is it possible to believe that humans have a conscience and yet deny that God exists?

Thomas Aquinas

Thomas Aquinas (c. 1225–1274) belongs to the group of theologians who claim that conscience is primary in moral decision-making. He described it as an **intuition** of right and wrong. Bad action consists of ignoring what is known to be wrong and acting in a way that contradicted conscience. Aquinas claimed that humans should follow their conscience because it relates to the end or purpose of that person. To act against conscience is to be guided by something that lies outside our God-given nature.

Further reading

Aquinas by Brian Davies (Continuum 2003).

Aquinas also claimed that Christians needed to inform their conscience, clarifying what is right and wrong, with the aid of revelation. As long as conscience is informed, it is right to follow it even when it contradicts a public law. If church teaching contradicts conscience, then conscience should be a person's guide; Aquinas argued that it was better to be excommunicated or even martyred than violate one's conscience. This definition had problems for the church because it was not entirely clear as to its authority in relation to individual conscience.

'There is a principle of reflection in men, by which they distinguish between, approve and disapprove their own actions. We are plainly constituted such sort of creatures as to reflect upon our own nature... this principle in man... is conscience.' Joseph Butler, *Fifteen Sermons 1* part 3.

Joseph Butler

Joseph Butler (1692–1752), who served as Bishop of Durham, claimed that conscience has an enduring role in morality, superior to both reason and emotion. He claimed it was the starting-point for moral discussion; without conscience, moral issues and arguments would never have arisen. He described it as a principle that distinguished between the internal principles of the heart, as well as external actions.

Butler argued that our actions should be governed in conformity with a hierarchy of principles that define human nature. He claimed that duty and self-interest combine in conscience: that which brings us happiness is both what we should do and the thing that allows us to be good and virtuous.

Alistair Macintyre has highlighted the circularity of Butler's argument about the nature of conscience. According to Butler, we ought to perform actions that satisfy our natures as rational and moral beings, but our natures as rational and moral beings are defined by our adherence to certain principles. Butler's argument is also problematic when duty and self-interest do not coincide, and the bad person prospers and is happy without obeying moral principles.

Further reading

See chapter 9 of John Henry Newman's *An Essay in Aid of a Grammar of Assent* (University of Notre Dame Press 1979), although be warned, this is not for beginners!

The ultramontanes were Catholics who looked straight to the Pope for authority and guidance.

'Conscience is the aboriginal vicar of Christ, a prophet in its informations, a monarch in its peremptoriness, a priest in its blessings and anathemas, and, even though the eternal priesthood throughout the Church could cease to be, in it the sacerdotal principle would remain and would have a sway.' Newman quoted in *Cardinal John Henry Newman* by Ian Ker (Oxford University Press 1988), page 688.

'I add one remark. Certainly, if I am obliged to bring religion into after-dinner toasts (which indeed does not seem the thing) I shall drink – to the Pope, if you please – still, to conscience first, and the Pope afterwards.' Newman in *A Letter to the Duke of Norfolk concerning certain difficulties Anglicans have with Catholic Teaching.*

Cardinal Newman

In 1864, Newman (1801–1890) wrote a letter to the Duke of Norfolk outlining and responding to difficulties that certain Anglicans had with Catholic teaching. In this letter, he outlined his view of conscience in the Christian life. He faced the problem of reconciling his own Catholic ideas with those of the powerful **ultramontanes** who were dominant in the Roman Catholic Church in Europe at this time. He wanted to find room for freedom of conscience, while still defending the authority of the papal office.

He argued that conscience is the law of God that is available to and apprehended by individuals. Although it may suffer 'refraction' as it passes through the mind of each person, it never loses its character as divine law, and should always be obeyed because of its continuing role as an authority on matters of morality.

Newman distinguished between the authority of conscience and the authority of the Pope as defined by the doctrine of **papal infallibility**: the claim that the Pope cannot be declared wrong on matters of faith and morals when he speaks as leader of the church. He said that the authority of conscience 'bears immediately on something to be done or not done' while the Pope's infallibility is 'engaged on general propositions, and in the condemnation of particular and given errors'.

Newman acknowledged that the dictate of conscience can only prevail over the teachings of the Pope after 'serious thought, prayer, and all available means of arriving at a right judgement on the matter in question' had been explored. Newman remained very critical of a secular view of conscience that omitted any thought of God at all. He believed that self-will replaces conscience in the thinking of many liberals.

Route A: ethics and philosophy of religion. Consider Newman's moral argument for God's existence. Can we have a concept of a moral law without belief in a lawgiver? Read pages 37–41 of *Philosophy of Religion* by Peter Cole (Hodder and Stoughton 1999).

Sigmund Freud

Freud (1856–1939) adopted a secular approach to morality, claiming that conscience has nothing whatsoever to do with the existence of a God and revelation. He suggested that a person's early upbringing provides them with certain ideas that influence their moral awareness. According to Freud, the human mind can be separated into three functions:

- **ego** – the rational self
- **id** – the self at the level of its physical and emotional needs
- **super-ego** – the controlling self.

Further discussion

Consider how you would tackle the question of whether conscience is the voice of God. Read Anthony Storr *Freud. A Very Short Introduction* (OUP 2001) chapter 5.

Freud claimed that the super-ego performs the role of conscience. Like a parent, it imposes rules on what the ego, prompted by the needs of the id, can do. The id might drive a person towards a life of sensual pleasure, and the ego might allow this drive to affect the person's action, but the super-ego will warn the person against actions that society or family might frown upon.

Of course, a super-ego that has been shaped by the teachings of the church and the Bible might be too dominating, and Freud believed this could result in all sorts of neuroses and strange responses in an individual. Believing in a God who reveals truths about behaviour may, in Freud's view, result in a damaged personality.

Jean Piaget

Jean Piaget (1896–1980) was a biologist who moved into the study of the **cognitive development** of children. He shared Freud's view that every child goes through a series of distinct mental (cognitive) stages that allow innate **schemas** or organisational capacities to develop according to external experiences. These are:

- **Sensori-motor** (birth to two years): child differentiates itself from objects and is able to recognise itself as agent of action.
- **Pre-operational** (two to seven years): child learns to use language and to represent objects by images and words, but its thinking is still egocentric and it has difficulty taking the viewpoint of others.
- **Concrete operational** (seven to 11 years): child can think logically about objects and events. Can classify objects according to several features and order them in series along a single dimension such as size.
- **Formal operational** (11 years and up): child can think logically about abstract propositions and test hypotheses systematically. Becomes concerned with the hypothetical, the future, and ideological problems, and is able therefore to reason about moral problems.

Route A: ethics and philosophy of religion. Consider the links between Freudian psychology, Piaget's developmental cognitive views and moral relativism. Do their psychological profiles of the human mind necessarily raise problems for traditional religious views of morality?

See www.psy.pdx.edu/PsiCafe/KeyTheorists/Kohlberg.htm

Further reading

Stanley Milgram's famous electric shock treatment tested Kohlberg's hypothesis. Read pages 117–120 of *Psychology. A Very Short Introduction* by Gillian Butler and Freda McManus (OUP 1998).

As a reductionist, Piaget did not believe that there is a separate conscience, but thought that the brain develops like any other organ to fulfil its capacity – in this case for eventual abstract thinking – at the right stage in its development. The implications of Piaget's moral development theory were explored by **Lawrence Kohlberg** (1969). He argued that moral development of an individual is determined by the sophistication of their reasoning, not their age or necessarily the conclusions they come to. Some people never reach the higher levels of complexity. The third level in Kohlberg's analysis suggests that some individuals are able to posit universal ethical principles such as justice and respect for others.

Religious ethics: Christian ethics

The specification allows for the ethics of any religious tradition to be studied. For a good overview of the other main religions read *Ethics in the World Religions*, eds. Joseph Runzo and Nancy Martin (Oneworld 2001).

The main precepts and purpose of Christian ethical behaviour

The Bible is generally the most common source of Christian ethical teaching, but this teaching has also been shaped and developed through the church tradition. Christians continue to assert the centrality of the Ten Commandments (Exodus 20: 1–17).

Further reading

See pages 125–127 of the *OCR AS Guide* on the importance of justice and peace in liberation theology today.

Further discussion

Consider St Paul's teaching on the tension between law and love in his letters. Read the chapter on the New Testament in this guide.

Principles such as peace and justice guide moral behaviour. Ethical behaviour is directed at securing physical health and avoiding secularism. It aims at 'structures of grace': a set of administrative and practical arrangements designed to introduce graciousness and compassion into the lives of every faithful individual.

In the New Testament, there are two primary laws: unconditional love of God, and love of one's neighbour. These principles are rooted in the Jewish tradition, but also draw on the Greek concept of **agape** (unconditional or unselfish love). Christians seek to follow the example of Jesus Christ, emphasising humility and mercy alongside contrition and restitution and renouncing sin.

Christians work to secure the Kingdom of God, work that is explored and illustrated in the parables of Jesus. Christians act in opposition to the world (John 13: 35), and act as witnesses to God's love. They aim to perform good deeds and actions so that others can see the truth of the Gospels. Righteousness can come through faith (a Protestant idea) and through developing a strong and loving relationship with God through Christ. The importance of prayer is vital in relation to this aim, but also the process of sanctification (a Catholic idea), whereby a person grows in holiness towards salvation.

Further reading

This is most clearly set out by Paul in 1 Corinthians 15. Read the chapter on the New Testament in this guide.

Christians believe in a future resurrection of the body and eternal life, usually understood as a future transcendent state, but also a present reality made possible by God's grace as the result of a *metanoia* (the Greek term for a change of heart or conversion) and baptism.

Further reading

Rowan Williams 'Making Moral decisions' in Robin Gill (ed.) *Cambridge Companion to Christian Ethics* (CUP 2001). Dr Williams became Archbishop of Canterbury in 2002.

Rowan Williams developed his idea of Christian ethics around certain central aims: knowledge of oneself, fidelity to the one true God, recreation of self through the community of Christ and the work of the Holy Spirit. In addition he talks about obedience to the will of God, following Christ and bearing witness to his selfless holiness, and the building up of the Christian community.

Deontological Christian ethics

Christians talk about a set of moral laws or norms, and emphasise the importance of obedience to these. These laws are either explicit or grounded in the teaching of Jesus. Agape is the supreme moral principle, and the teaching of the Bible is built around this, especially in the New Testament. Conservative Christians will assert the objective and absolute nature of many biblical laws.

The natural law approach is based on the idea that Christians can use reason to construct moral laws based on first order observations of human nature. If human nature is fixed, then these laws are clear and absolute. If Christians are unsure of the veracity of our laws, we can confirm them by reference to revelation.

Many Christians regard the Gospels as a sublime moral code. The important principle is to act in imitation of Christ. Many relate this to **eschatology**. If Christians take a realised eschatological approach, and assert the fact that the Kingdom of God is an earthly state, then ethics is about acting in such a way as to achieve this state. Many others suggest that Christians are judged in the future on how they have acted in the world. Their 'corporate works of mercy' (Matthew 25) have been seen as central in relation to this.

The complex issue of eschatology or the coming of the state of perfection is discussed in the chapter on the New Testament, pages 82–94.

Teleological Christian ethics

Christians work towards certain principles or ends. Joseph Fletcher claimed that only the outcome (agape) justified the action. His liberal interpretation suggested that moral laws are guidelines and not straightjackets. Others argue that Christians live in such a way that they hope they will be redeemed and that life will ultimately be fulfilled in the realisation of Christian community. Christians aim to establish justice in the world.

Further discussion

Consider the view that religious ethics need not be deontological. Read page 21 of the *OCR AS Guide*.

If Christ's significance is seen in relation to the redemption of people, then it makes sense to talk about a moral disposition from which moral actions flow. Christ is seen as a source of revelation about a gracious God who is working for the sanctification of humans. This redeeming work becomes the focus rather than a set of moral laws.

Some Christian natural law thinkers suggest that there is a multitude of human natures, and that our observation of first-order principles is far from fixed. Some calculate morality not in relation to a set of fixed absolutes applied universally, but rather in relation to whatever allows individual fulfilment.

Environmental ethics

We are currently facing a huge number of ethical issues with regard to climate change, pollution and the use of the earth's resources. It is important to identify them before considering the various moral responses and the value of these responses.

The following topics all need to be considered in relation to the ethical approaches studied for AS; virtue ethics, natural law, Kant and the categorical imperative, utilitarianism and religious ethics. See pages 75–87 of *OCR AS Guide*.

Physical environmental issues

The burning of fossil fuels, the destruction of the rain forest and the use of CFCs have caused a 'greenhouse effect'. The resulting trapping of heat by 'greenhouse gases' has led to weather change,

Climate change

Further reading

Chapter 2 of *Environmental Ethics* by Joe Walker (Hodder and Stoughton 2000) on factual problems of the environment. Read also part three of *Replenish the Earth* by Lewis G. Regenstein (SCM 1991) for a good overview of Hindu, Jain, Buddhist, Muslim and Baha'i responses.

rises in sea-level, threats to the infrastructure of coasts and changes in the quality of fresh-water supplies.

In addition, the release of CFCs, nitrous oxide and methane into the atmosphere has depleted the ozone layer. This has allowed more UV light to penetrate the earth's atmosphere, causing damage to the DNA of living things, resulting in mutations. One example of this is an increase in the rate of skin cancer.

Pollution

Pollution has increased as a result of rises in the earth's population, the use of man-made fertilisers and more widespread industrialisation. Among the consequences is acid rain. Air pollution, by for example carbon monoxide, sulphur dioxide and nitrogen dioxide, has led to an increase in asthma and lung problems in humans. This is accompanied by pollution of rivers and seas, as artificial fertilisers drain into them, landfill sites produce toxic run-offs, and industrial and urban waste are dumped. This has affected the creatures that live in the water and thus our own food chain. In addition, there has been nuclear pollution through the disposal of radioactive material in the ground or the sea.

There has also been an increase in land and water-cycle pollution through industrial waste, and pollution of rivers and seas has occurred alongside this. The sea has been used increasingly as a dumping ground for waste, and rubbish in landfill sites has produced a toxic run-off. Mercury from batteries has got into the soil and has also affected the food chain. In addition, there has been an increase in nuclear pollution through the disposal of radioactive material in the ground or the sea.

Earth's resources

This projection was made by the ecologist David Bellamy and appears in Joe Walker's book *Environmental Ethics* (Hodder and Stoughton 2000), page 41.

There has been a depletion in the earth's resources. It is projected that all coal, oil and gas reserves will have been used up by 2636 – or even earlier if consumption increases along the lines of the current rate. Countries around the world have become dependent on the use of fossil fuels, and there is a vested interest in powerful countries maintaining their current levels of consumption. In addition, there are also arguments about the best possible alternative fuel supply.

Further discussion

Consider the arguments for and against the following energy sources: wind and solar power; hydroelectric power; nuclear power.

Ethical environmental responses

Deep ecology

Further discussion

Consider the ethical differences between preservation, conservation and protection of the environment.

Followers of the deep ecology approach hold the view that all objects in the universe have absolute intrinsic value. This means that the value of all created things is measured in relation to themselves and not other objects or life forms. Holders of this view oppose hierarchical views of power in relation to the environment. The deep ecological view opposes the exploitation of the earth's resources by humans. The use of animals, plants and other things to satisfy human needs alone is considered intrinsically wrong or evil. One version of this view was developed by **James Lovelock** in 1979, in a hypothesis he called **Gaia** (the ancient Greek term for the earth). The earth is a dynamic entity whose sum is always larger than its parts. The warning of Gaia is that the world can continue with or without humans – the choice is ours. Lovelock's hypothesis does not belong to one particular religious tradition and has been adapted by many to their own belief systems.

Further reading

Gaia: A New Look at Life on Earth by James Lovelock (OUP 2000). Andrew Linzey's work is also important here. His principal criterion is that Christian ethics state that humans have a primary duty to protect the weak: see his *Animal Theology* (SCM 1994).

People who follow instrumentalism take the view that objects in the universe are valued in relation to something else. Usually this something else is humans. Instrumentalists have problems assessing which objects are of the greatest use to themselves, and which objects will have the best instrumental value. Results such as human happiness dictate the value of things in nature. Naturally this can produce a hierarchy of value, implying that some things hold little or no value and are therefore superfluous.

Instrumentalism

Based on ideas in the book of Genesis, this approach considers that the world was created by God in the beginning. God then established a covenant with man, who had been created in his own image. The covenant relationship was based around the idea that man's continued worship of God would result in his sustained existence. In return, humans were given dominion over nature, based on the **imago dei** principle, which implied that humans adopted a role over nature comparable to the role God had taken in creation.

Biblical view

Further reading

Celia Deane-Drummond *A Handbook in Theology and Ecology* (SCM 1996) chapter 2.

The dominion of humans has been understood in two ways. The first is to see it as one of **domination**, whereby humans use the earth to satisfy their own needs. The second is **stewardship**, where humans see themselves as caretakers of God's property. In addition to these beliefs, many monotheists believe the doctrine of the Fall, which states that suffering and disorder entered the world through human disobedience. The natural world has shared the effects of the Fall through its own suffering.

Further reading

The Fall is described in Genesis 3 and commented on in Romans 5: 12. Read the chapter on the New Testament, pages 70–73.

As well as being an **androcentric** approach, this view is deeply hierarchical and again suggests that all things measure their value in relation to humans. Some argue that this approach has contributed towards today's environmental problems.

Process theology has challenged the hierarchical view. Process theologians claim that all reality is in the process of change. They challenge the traditional view that substance is unchanging and forms the core of existing things. God does not stand outside time and space, but rather is seen as developing in and through the world. God's nature emerges through interaction with the world. The divine uses persuasion upon all occasions and events in time, thereby shaping the future direction of the world and at the same time the being of God himself.

Process theology

Process theology is also referred to as panentheism. It is popular in North America (Ian Barbour is a good example) but has its followers in Europe, notably in Arthur Peacocke's influential book *Creation and the World of Science* (OUP 2004).

This approach offers a vision of 'creative transformation' of the world through the work of the **Logos**. It challenges the idea of God handing over stewardship of the world to humans, and thereby raises the value of other existing things alongside man. God's being is tied to the world, so how we treat that world and the environment affects God himself.

Further reading

See chapter 4 of *The Environment and Christian Ethics* by M. S. Northcott (Cambridge University Press 1996).

Feminists have argued that there is a correlation between men's treatment of women and their treatment of nature:

- Women and nature have bee oppressed and mistreated by a patriarchal society.
- By contrast with detached male reasoning, women are said to resemble relationships in nature by being empathetic and emotionally literate.

Feminist responses

Further reading

Read *OCR AS Guide* pages 121–122 for a quick overview of different types of feminism.

- Menstruation and childbirth link women to the natural cycles of the earth, incorporating seasons and periods of fertility, life and death.

Eco-feminists have called for direct political action to liberate women and the environment. In changing the attitudes and actions of men in relation to nature and the environment, feminists believe that women can reclaim some power over their own lives. This response does have its problems, as, in associating women with nature, it leaves the structures of oppression intact, while still alienating men by leaving them out of the dialogue. Some feminists therefore call for a rejection of all dualisms that divide men and women, humans and nature, and mind and body.

> **Further reading**
> Mary Daly's *Gyn/Ecology* (Women's Press 1979) is a classic radical feminist view. See also chapter 4 of *A Handbook in Theology and Ecology* by Celia Deane-Drummond.

These feminist responses emphasise the importance of partnership between humans and nature, aiming for a sustainable global environment. This deep ecological approach challenges the superficiality of an environmentalism that seeks to reform current structures rather than to reform underlying attitudes towards the environment.

Utilitarian responses

> **Further reading**
> Robert Elliot in *Companion to Ethics*, ed. Peter Singer (Blackwell 1993).

One utilitarian response concerns itself with a **human-centred ethic** that seeks to maximise the surplus of human happiness over unhappiness. This approach treats only humans as morally considerable, and is in line with the instrumentalist approach outlined above. However, it points to the way in which the natural world can contribute to human happiness by offering an ecologically richer environment, a focus for aesthetic pleasure, or even an outlet for recreational activity.

The **animal-centred ethic** highlights the way in which human activities such as clear-cutting forests, damning rivers, quarrying mountains and constructing pipelines can all increase the threat to non-humans. Peter Singer has encouraged humans to understand the principle of utility not simply in human terms. This approach seeks to avoid arbitrariness both in relation to the choice of one species (humans) but also non-human species in general. Singer argues that we can work out the value of a being/environment by determining the relationship between its own experiences and interests and our human experiences (namely our enjoyment) and interests (usefulness) of it. A **hierarchy of value** of all things is established by applying these two criteria. This view is contrary to the deep ecologists who value all things equally.

> **Further reading**
> See *Animal Liberation* (Pimlico 1995), Peter Singer's classic and influential book on animal rights.

A **life-centred ethic** counts all living things as morally considerable. It particularly values complexity (for example, valuing a pig-nosed turtle over a shrub), but also the goal of filling a particular ecological niche (for example, a rare plant above a pig-nosed turtle when other turtles exist). If we extend the value of all living things and suggest that they all have equal value, then human intervention in the natural world becomes harder to justify. This attitude may be harder to maintain, however, in relation to the principle of utility.

> **Further discussion**
> Consider to what extent you would agree that environmental issues are more of a concern to a religious believer than a utilitarian.

Ecological holism

This approach claims that there are two things that are morally considerable. The first is the biosphere as a whole, the second the large ecosystems that constitute it. The extinction of species may not be bad in itself, but rather in relation to the larger goal of maintaining the biosphere or ecosystem.

An **everything ethic** suggests also that non-living things, which lack consciousness and even basic biological organisation, can still be thought of as morally considerable. An action such as mining by smashing up rocks and disturbing geological structures should not be valued in relation to the task of mining effectively or satisfying a human need, but must rather be considered in relation to the thing in itself. This approach is open to accusations of irrationalism, but it can lead to a wider understanding of moral significance and a greater degree of biological egalitarianism.

Route A: ethics and philosophy of religion. Some might claim that a belief in life after death diminishes human concern for the environment. Consider the implications for environmental ethics of a transcendent vision of salvation. Explore also ways in which life after death is linked to concepts of stewardship. To what extent does a process-theological view rule out the possibility of life after death? Read pages 211–226 of *The Environment and Christian Ethics* by Michael Northcott (CUP 1996).

Sex and relationships

Marriage

Marriage is defined by law as the 'voluntary union for life of a man and woman'. Christians understand it as a form of companionship based on mutual relationship, rather than a legal contract for the production of children. The Christian church has sought to promote marriage as the ideal environment for happiness and for the raising of children. It has at the same time presented celibacy as a spiritual gift and as highly desirable for the spiritual life.

Further reading

See *God, Sex and Love* by Jack Dominian and Hugh Montefiore (SCM 1989). Dominion is a psychiatrist and Montefiore a theologian. See also chapter 5 of *Sex and Relationships* by Michael Wilcockson (Hodder and Stoughton 2001).

St Paul promoted celibacy as an ideal, but agreed nonetheless that if a couple got married it was important that they accepted their duties towards one another (1 Corinthians 7). They should avoid lust and a lack of control over their sexual natures, as this would lead them to neglect their spiritual duties. Augustine (354–430) saw marriage as a sacrament ordained to allow humans to overcome sin and control the sexual urge. He also took seriously the command in Genesis to man: that he be fruitful, multiply and fill the earth.

Taking their lead from St Paul and other New Testament texts (Matt 19: 27–29, for example), and specifically the celibacy of Jesus, the Roman Catholic and Orthodox churches have celibate monks and nuns – and in the case of Catholicism, a celibate priesthood.

Natural law

Natural law teaching states that man is 'naturally disposed to pairing'. Marriage allows the proper ordering of sexual life, and is the right environment in which to raise children. Thomas Aquinas (c. 1225–1274) believed that the primary purpose of sex is reproduction, and so, by extension, the purpose of marriage is to provide a stable environment for raising children. It is also the basis for a relationship based on trust, mutual obligation and stability. More controversially, Aquinas believed that marriage completes woman because 'the male is both more perfect in reasoning and stronger in his powers'.

Christianity today

Today's churches all owe a debt to Paul, Aquinas and Augustine. Marriage is the basis of a healthy life and family, and the building block of human relationships and a strong society. It provides the moral basis for the development of children by providing fellowship, love and grace. Roman Catholics highlight the fact that sex within marriage fulfils both a unitive and procreative function. The act itself is a sacrament, whereby the couple undergoes an ontological change (a change in their state of being) to become one flesh.

For example, the Roman Catholic catechism states that 'the vocation to marriage is written in the very nature of man and woman as they come from the hand of the creator'.

Some churches today have distanced themselves from the early church idea of marriage as a way of containing sexual sin. Rather it

Route A: ethics and philosophy of religion. Discuss how the arguments of psychologists and sociologists have changed our awareness of human sexual behaviour. Explore how moral norms established in religious and other ethical systems have been challenged by the theories of sociology and psychology. Read pages 26–27 of *Sociology: A Very Short Introduction* by Steve Bruce (OUP 2000); chapter 1 of *Sex and Relationships* by Michael Wilcockson.

Further reading

An influential book on many feminists is Frederich Engels' *The Origin of the Family, Private Property and the State* (Penguin 1986), which was first published in 1884 and develops the Marxist suspicion of all institutions and all forms of ownership.

Further reading

Chapter 5 of *Sex and Relationships*; chapter 17 of Peter Vardy's *The Puzzle of Sex* (Fount 1997).

is seen as promoting a deeper loving union. Sex is seen as an expression of, and a means of enhancing, the unity between the couple. Protestants do not regard marriage as a sacrament and downplay natural law teaching and church tradition in deference to the word of God in scripture.

Utilitarians have supported a libertarian idea of marriage whereby responsibility is given to the couple to decide on the scope and commitment of their new relationship. While some have emphasised the importance of the utility principle, others such as Peter Singer have pointed to the way in which each couple has a different set of interests or preferences that need to be fulfilled.

Reconstruction feminists have sought to avoid marriage because of its links with patriarchy and the way in which it has traditionally been conceived in male terms, furthering in turn the exploitation of women and conservative notions of ownership on the part of men.

Divorce and remarriage

Traditionally the grounds for divorce in the Christian tradition have been adultery or 'unchastity' (Deuteronomy 24: 1–2). This is known as the **Matthean exception**, as it appears that Jesus opposed divorce on the grounds that it is against God's will (Matthew 5: 32). Some argue that Jesus' teaching on divorce is positive rather than negative: the married state is an expression of unity and love rather than divorce itself being a grave sin.

Christians have traditionally sought to steer a careful path between legalism and liberalism. The former runs the danger of descending into a list of technical reasons for divorce rather than teaching about the nature of fidelity, while the latter threatens the sanctity of the marriage relationship.

Christians find it difficult to adopt an absolutist approach to issues of divorce and remarriage. Trends in society have meant that there are a large number of divorced Christians, and the number of those choosing to cohabit has increased. In addition, there is the consideration that those who have experienced marital breakdown are often those most in need of the blessing and support of the church.

Catholicism

The Catholic Church does not recognise the possibility of divorce. If a marriage has taken place, then both the church and the law are incapable of dissolving it by decree. The implication of this is that remarriage after separation constitutes adultery.

The Roman Catholic Church allows separation to take place if the couple have reached a stage where marital reconciliation appears impossible. Some Catholics choose to remarry outside the church, and the Catholic Church allows couples to return to receive the sacraments if that relationship becomes celibate.

However, the most common response in a range of situations is to say that the marriage which took place was not a true marriage. An **annulment** can be granted by the church in cases of non-consummation, underage unions, forced marriage, consanguinity (blood relationship) or affinity (related to one another through law). It can also be granted on the basis that one of the partners failed to consent to the marriage vows through a lack of reason, judgement or psychological ability. The Church emphasises that this is different from divorce.

Many Christians argue that the Roman Catholic teaching about annulment encourages the legalist mentality that Jesus condemned. Some would argue that there are clear parallels between general Christian teaching about divorce and the Catholic teaching on annulment. Other Christians have therefore encouraged a more liberal attitude towards divorce and remarriage. The 1969 **Divorce Reform Act** was based on the principle outlined in the Church of England's teaching in 'putting asunder', whereby divorce was allowed after there was 'irretrievable breakdown' in the marriage.

> **Further study**
> Look at the way the remarriage in 2005 of the Prince of Wales to a divorcee was treated in the media.

Cohabitation

Cohabitation is defined legally as 'the co-residence of man and woman, living together within full sexual union, without that union being formalised by a legal marriage'. Most liberals and utilitarians would allow this as long as there was no abuse or intimidation. There are three types of cohabitation:

> **Further reading**
> Chapters 6 and 8 of *Sex and Relationships*; chapter 6 of *Something to Celebrate* by Rosemary Dawson (Church House Publishing 1997), the Church of England's report on family and changing attitudes to relationships.

- **Casual cohabitation.** A couple, usually in a short-term relationship, live together for convenience's sake.
- **Trial marriage cohabitation.** So called because a couple live together to verify their suitability for marriage.
- **Substitute marriage cohabitation.** A couple consciously rejects the institution of marriage on ideological grounds.

Most Christians would argue positively rather than negatively in relation to marriage and cohabitation. They say that those who reject marriage reject the trust and commitment that allows a relationship to stay strong. Also, marriage provides support or blessing from the church. Catholics believe that it provides grace.

Conservatism

Conservative Christians argue that cohabitation is 'living in sin' and as such is forbidden by scripture. The Bible teaches that virginity is a prerequisite of marriage (Exodus 22: 16, Leviticus 21: 13–15, Deuteronomy 22: 13–30). Cohabiting couples are regarded as less responsible, and it is highlighted that sex is often misused in these relationships, being understood simply as a recreational activity rather than for its traditional unitive and procreative functions.

Liberalism

Liberal Christians are much more likely to reduce the emphasis on the marriage ceremony as the moment in which a couple truly commit to one another. Many highlight the way in which marriage is rather a series of moments through which a couple grow in love and commitment towards each other. Many who undertake marriage do so without understanding the nature of a true relationship, while others who approach marriage more cautiously or avoid it altogether may actually hold a better understanding of commitment.

Homosexuality

> **Further reading**
> *Sex and Relationships* chapter 4; *Puzzle of Sex* chapter 18.

There is disagreement as to whether homosexuality is the product of nature or nurture, choice or biology, a complex web of genetic

Foucault's influential views have given rise to what is called 'queer theory', which argues that the 'normality' of heterosexual relationships is the result of external power structures. Read part 2 of Michel Foucault's *The History of Sexuality: The Use of Power* (Penguin, 1984).

factors or even a single gene. **Michel Foucault** (1926–1984), for example, has highlighted the cultural changes that have developed in relation to the question of sexuality. Under current law, sexual intercourse between two people of the same sex is not allowed under the age of 18, rather than the age of 16 for heterosexual intercourse.

Despite this uncertainty, Christian thinkers have generally opposed homosexuality, and taught that homosexual relationships are both different from and morally inferior to heterosexual ones.

Church of England

The Church of England renewed its condemnation of homosexuality in 1991, denying that it constituted a parallel form of human sexuality. At the same time, Anglican authorities recognised the value of homosexual people in the eyes of God. The church called for abstinence or, if that was not possible, a faithful relationship. Practising homosexual relationships are not allowed for ordained clergy. The church added the caveat that human conscience should be guided by present knowledge of biology and psychology.

Further reading

Issues in Human Sexuality: A Statement by the House of Bishops (Church House Publishing 1991).

Catholicism

The Roman Catholic Church regards homosexuality as contrary to both scripture and natural law. Homosexual sex is regarded as an improper and misdirected use of the sexual organs, given the impossibility of conception. Homosexuals are called to chastity, disinterested friendship and self-mastery. The church has declared homosexuality 'intrinsically disordered'.

The Bible

Both Genesis 19: 1–8 and Judges 19: 16–30 seem to confirm the immorality of homosexual acts, but these verses are as much to do with a condemnation of inhospitable behaviour, or even violence and depravity, as homosexuality. Likewise Leviticus 18: 22 regards lying with another male as with a woman to be an abominable sin, but two chapters later this sin is equated with a confusion of sexuality within the natural order, and associates the sin with Canaanite religious cult. Liberals would be keen to point out the contextual nature of its condemnation.

Utilitarianism

John Stuart Mill suggested that humans have sovereignty and inviolable rights over their own bodies. Utilitarians thus require both partners to consent to the relationship, and allow it as long as it does not harm public decency – usually defined as something that does not harm society. Preference Utilitarians would regard each relationship as different and might refuse to prescribe norms in relation to sexuality.

Contraception

Further reading

See pages 134–140 of *Sex and Relationships*.

Liberals often point to the dramatic changes in practice within both the Roman Catholic and Protestant churches in relation to contraception. They also point to significant advances in the range and effectiveness of contraception, and the new needs that its use meets. The Roman Catholic Church has maintained a conservative line, but all the leading teachers within that tradition have been under pressure to modernise their views.

Many Christian arguments against the use of contraception can be traced back to the natural law arguments about the function of sex for procreation. Fertility and reproduction were both blessed by God and those who advocated the use of contraception opposed the divine will. Forms of artificial contraception oppose this ordering, although natural forms of contraception do not contradict natural law. Catholics also regard many forms of contraception as abortifacients (an agent that causes abortion) as they destroy the potential for life after conception has taken place. Others see the use of contraception as propping up a promiscuous lifestyle opposed to all notions of either safe sex or chastity.

Natural law

The view is stated most clearly in the encyclical *Humanae Vitae* (1968): 'God has wisely disposed natural laws and rhythms of fecundity which, of themselves, cause a separation in the succession of births. Nonetheless the Church, calling men back to the observance of the norms of the natural law, ... teaches that each and every marriage act must remain open to the transmission of life.'

In 1968, many Catholics thought that Pope Paul VI would take up the spirit of the Second Vatican Council and liberalise the Catholic teaching on contraception. There had been at the council an increased emphasis on sexuality as a means to loving communion. However, *Humanae Vitae* condemned contraception and repeated that 'each and every marriage act must be open to the transmission of life'.

Church of England

The Church of England has moderated its condemnation of contraception in line with modern trends and pressures. These pressures have been increased by the threat of overpopulation and the spread of HIV, especially in Africa. In 1930, the Lambeth Conference ruled that contraception could be used when there was 'a clearly felt moral obligation to limit or avoid parenthood and where there is a morally sound reason for avoiding complete abstinence'. In 1958 the same conference emphasised the importance of responsible parenting. A year later it was decreed at the **World Council of Churches** that there was no moral difference between 'the use of the infertile period, artificial barriers to the meeting of the sperm and ovum, and drugs regulating ovulation'.

Reproductive technologies

Reproductive technologies range from IVF treatment to sperm or egg donation, freezing of eggs for later use or cloning using existing cells.

Christian perspectives

Conservative and Roman Catholic Christians have opposed their use because of the threats they pose to the integrity of marriage, and the one-sided view of sexual reproduction that their use encourages. Natural law teaching encourages Christians to examine reproduction in its proper context within a loving union between two partners. IVF treatment, for instance, can bypass the sexual act to allow conception to take place outside the womb. Given the potential destruction of human embryos in the process, many Christians would invoke the sanctity of life principle as a criticism for its use.

Further reading

See pages 85–87 of the *OCR AS Guide*; chapter 7 of *Sex and Relationships*; *Bioethics and the Future of Medicine: A Christian Agenda* by John Kilner (Eerdmans 1996).

Although there is no act of infidelity when a sperm or egg donor helps a couple conceive, the introduction of a third party into the relationship means that an analogy with adultery can be drawn. The birth of a child by this method can be source for uncertainty or alienation within the marriage. Nevertheless, it is important to remember that there are examples of a similar practice in the Bible itself: see the Old Testament story of Hagar and Sarah (Genesis 16).

Further discussion

Christians have argued that marriage reflects Christ's relationship with the church. What do you think this means and implies?

Feminists, including Christians, have raised objections about the use of reproductive technologies as a means of exploiting or

> **Further reading**
> Margaret Atwood's story *The Handmaid's Tale* (Vintage 1996) provides an excellent illustration of what might happen if reproduction became the means of power.

abusing women. Their use can be seen as the exertion of power over women's fertility. They can also be a source of trauma or suffering for women as the extraction of eggs, surgical operations and hormone treatment might all lead to greater frustration if conception does not occur.

Liberal Christians might argue that infertility treatments and reproductive technologies actually empower women and allow them to fulfil their potential in new ways. As well as providing renewed hope to infertile couples, they help women conceive and therefore fulfil the desire of women to become mothers, a goal that can also help save a marriage or prevent guilt over barrenness.

Utilitarianism

Utilitarians may welcome the use of reproductive technologies, but would potentially oppose its use in cases where a failure to conceive would result in greater suffering on the part of the woman or family. They may also question whether it is used appropriately in the context of single parenthood or a homosexual relationship. The good of the child needs to be addressed.

> **Further reading**
> Michael Wilcockson *Sex and Relationships* pages 147–151.

Cloning is also an issue in relation to reproductive technologies. Although the law prevents its use in most cases, some have called for advances in reproductive cloning, whereby a human being is cloned to provide certain matches with another human being for the purpose of blood transfusion, cancer treatment or other medical complications such as kidney failure. Many Christians oppose its use on the basis that it breaks natural law teaching about sexual reproduction, and also damages the embryo and exploits the child that is cloned. Utilitarians have highlighted the importance of therapeutic cloning and support the development of reproductive cloning if it provides medical treatment for those suffering at the moment.

> **Further reading**
> See pages 127–133 of *Sex and Relationships*.

Surrogacy is also a method that is opposed by many Christians on the grounds that it distorts natural law teaching about sex, reproduction and the raising of children. As it often involves a contract between three or four parties, it carries huge risks not only for the parents wanting that child, but also the surrogate mother and the child. Many Christians regard it as a form of commercialisation, even exploitation, if money changes hands.

War, peace and justice

> **Further reading**
> Chapter 6 of *Issues of Life and Death* by Michael Wilcockson. Chapter 19 of *Causing Death and Saving Lives* by Jonathan Glover (Penguin 1990). See also pages 81–85 of the *OCR AS Guide* (on the sanctity of life).

Christians have pointed to war as symptomatic of a fallen world. The justice of warfare has been examined and analysed by Christians over the centuries and there has been a huge variety of responses based around the need to limit the methods used in fighting, calculate the justice of any particular conflict, and seek ways of preventing unnecessary or innocent suffering in war. In addition, Christians have attempted to work out the relative values of pacifism, resistance to evil through force and militarism itself.

The just war

The just war tradition evolved over the course of centuries. Augustine (354–430) taught that war could be conducted by a public authority for the purposes of securing the common good. It could not be justified if its aims were unjust, such as a means of gaining power over others or as part of a private enterprise carried out for personal advantage or gain.

Thomas Aquinas (c. 1225–1274) criticised the fashion of many rich knights who fought for personal gain. He taught that authority for war must be given by a sovereign ruler; that it should seek to correct a real injustice, and that it should aim to promote good and avoid evil.

In the 16th century, the Church criticised the Spanish after their conquest of the native peoples of Central America, saying that they had killed too indiscriminately and many innocents had been slaughtered. The Church required innocents be spared as far as possible from attack during a conflict. Woman and children not holding weapons were not deemed hostile and should be spared from death.

The Lieber Code in 1863, the Hague Convention in 1907, and the Geneva Convention in 1925 all sought to place limits on what could and could not be justified within any given conflict. Building on the principles developed in previous centuries, these documents or agreements attempted to clarify how war could be fought justly.

Just war teaching can be divided into three sections: **jus ad bellum** (just conditions for going to war), **jus in bello** (just conditions for conducting a war) and **jus post bellum** (creating a just peace).

Jus ad bellum

- **Just cause:** protection from attack; the right to self-defence; humanitarian intervention; protecting innocents from aggressors.
- **Right intention:** war pursued for a just cause and not revenge, political expansion or land acquisition.
- **Proper authority:** traditionally a national sovereign or national political leader, but now also the UN.
- **Last resort:** all other means of achieving the same objectives (talks, sanctions etc) should be pursued exhaustively first.
- **Probability of success:** it is morally wrong to allow killing, suffering and destruction in a futile (even if just) gesture.
- **Proportionality:** the death, suffering and destruction caused by war should be proportional to the possible benefits.

Jus in bello

- **Discrimination:** there must be a differentiation between those who engage in harm (combatants) and those who do not (non-combatants).
- **Proportionality:** using only the amount of force that is proportional to the just ends being sought.
- **No evil means:** it is not allowed to use methods that are regarded as unlawful or morally evil, or to use weapons whose effects cannot be controlled.

This rules out mass rape, genocide, ethnic cleansing, and chemical and biological weapons.

Jus post bellum

This might mean that gains made from an act of aggression have been eliminated, victims' rights reinstated, formal apologies received and reasonable punishment given to the aggressor.

- **Just cause for termination:** a vindication of the rights whose violation led to the war in the first place.
- **Right intention:** there should be no motives such as revenge, and both victor and vanquished should be prosecuted.
- **Public declaration and legitimate authority:** all parties must declare peace and not just the victors.

- **Discrimination:** those responsible for the war should be punished and not innocent civilians. There needs to be clear differentiation between political and military populations.
- **Proportionality:** the vanquished retain their rights, and punishment should be proportional to the rights that are vindicated.

Further discussion

Consider how a Christian might apply the teaching of conscience to issues of war and peace.

Christian responses to the use of force

There is a sliding scale of potential Christian responses to situations of injustice. There are those who take an absolutist approach to issues of killing, and refuse to differentiate between killing in war and killing in peacetime. Both contravene biblical injunctions, and both fail to recognise the sanctity of human life. These Christians tend to adopt a position of non-resistance in relation to an act of aggression. This is a powerful response but it is often criticised by those who feel that it is part of the duty of a Christian to stand up for justice, especially where the lives of others are threatened. There may be an argument over the net effects of using force to repel an evil aggressor.

Others, such as Martin Luther King, also adopt a pacifist response to issues of conflict. Rather than promoting non-resistance they demand that Christians adopt a position of non-violent resistance. King used marches and peaceful protests to promote justice, and stated that Christians have a duty to oppose unjust laws. Non-violence is equated with biblical principles such as agape, which was defined by King as 'a creative redemptive love towards all men'. Many liberal Christians adopt this approach on the basis that it appeals to man's natural goodness and implies that such actions will appeal to a sense of justice within every human heart.

Further reading

Chapter 6 of *Issues of Life and Death* by Michael Wilcockson (Hodder and Stoughton 2001).

More conservative Christians regard the use of force as a necessary component in maintaining peace and in working for the victory of good over evil, justice over injustice. Many justify the use of violent resistance limited by the principle of discrimination along lines outlined in the just war tradition. Theologians such as Reinhold Niebuhr (1892–1971) measure goodness in relation to its outcome and the factors that require it. He distinguishes between times when non-violence works, and times when force is necessary.

Others adopt a more pessimistic approach and suggest that violent resistance is often required, limited by the principle of proportionality. With this approach, violent action could be used against the innocent, but only if the resulting good outweighs the level of force or violence used. Followers of **situation ethics** allow the use of violence as it adopts a consequentialist approach to Christian morality.

In the history of the Church there have been examples of all of the approaches listed above, but the official teaching of the Roman Catholic Church has certainly changed towards a more absolutist position over the use of violence and force. In the Middle Ages the church legitimised the crusades but recently has distanced itself from such a response.

Was Jesus a pacifist?

While this question cannot be clearly determined with the available evidence, it is clear that the Gospels present an ambiguous picture.

Jesus preached a message of non-violence, asking Christians to love their enemies and meet violence with acceptance or even forgiveness. At his arrest Jesus told his disciples to put down their swords when they were about to fight his captors. Jesus also respected authority, possibly in a situation of injustice, when he asked his followers to 'render unto Caesar that which is Caesar's'.

On the other hand, it has been argued that Jesus held many things in common with the Zealots who led an uprising against the Romans in 66–70. Jesus came from Galilee and drew support from the ranks of many of those opposed to the occupation of Israel by the Romans, along with their tax system. Jesus himself came up to temple at Passover and used force to drive those buying and selling from it. His action of overturning the tables of the money-changers was charged with righteous anger.

Jesus was arrested, tried, sentenced and executed in a manner fitting someone who was regarded as a dissenter and revolutionary. The punishment of execution was given mostly to those who threatened the peace and stability of Roman rule.

Nuclear war

There is a distinction between the tactical use of nuclear weapons and the use of nuclear weapons that carries a global threat and a much larger loss of human life. Many Christians regard the dropping of the atomic bombs on Nagasaki and Hiroshima at the end of the second world war as a grave moral evil. The destruction of life and property that such attacks wrought led many Christians to deny that nuclear weapons could be used as part of a just war.

Further reading

Chapter 7 of *Issues of Life and Death*; Richard Harries' *Christian and War in a Nuclear Age* (Continuum 1986).

It is possible to justify the use of nuclear weapons if the consequences of such an action outweigh the loss of life that accompanies their use. Christians may claim that the drastic consequences of using these weapons to attack another country have helped create a much more lasting peace than if they had not been available.

Deterrence

Deterrence is defined as the 'strategic deployment of nuclear weapons against targets of value belonging to a potential enemy to deter an attack'. The threat existing between Americans and Soviets in the Cold War was one of 'massive retaliation' on the part of the other if nuclear weapons were used.

Further discussion

Consider deterrence from a utilitarian and a Kantian point of view. Is it right to threaten violence even if you do not intend to act violently?

Christians are divided on this policy of **mutually assured destruction** (MAD). Firstly, nuclear weapons threaten life on earth and are contrary to the divine plan for creation. While deterrence has been effective, propaganda that is used both to justify the build-up of weapons and to convince an enemy that they will be used is highly dangerous and ultimately threatens to extend the likeliness of their use over time. There is also the problem of deception or lying on the part of the political leaders of a nation.

Many Christians have distinguished between threatening to use nuclear weapons with no intent, and threatening to use nuclear weapons with the intent in place. The problem with the former is that it is either a means of deception or an ineffective barrier to the aggression of an evil leader. The problem with the second is that it creates fear and threatens loss of human life on an unprecedented scale. Anyone approaching the topic from the perspective of **virtue ethics** would reject the morality of both approaches.

> **Further reading**
> See articles on deterrence, just war, nuclear war and pacifism in *A New Dictionary of Christian Ethics* edited by John Macquarrie and James Childress (SCM 1986).

Test yourself

1. 'In most matters about the environment utilitarianism offers the best solutions.' Discuss.
2. 'Whether to cohabit or marry is simply a question of conscience.' Discuss.
3. From the perspective of the religion you have studied, discuss the view that religious ethics must be deontological.
4. 'Without free will we cannot be held responsible for our actions.' Discuss.

Connections

These connections also apply to Routes AX and AY.

Philosophy of Religion and Religious Ethics (Route A)

The conscience or sense of moral responsibility as possible evidence for the existence of God. Consider how conscience is to be defined. Consider the Kantian argument that although the moral sense (conscience) of universal duty exists *a priori* (it is part of being human), it appears to be exercised separately from the will of God – but without God there would be no good reason to act reasonably. Consider the relationship between conscience and religious experience, especially experiences that are noetic (knowledge-giving) and regenerative (life-changing), and the moral effects that these have had on the recipients. Consider the psychological counter-arguments (Freud, Jung and so on).

> **Further reading**
> See pages 67–70 of the *OCR AS Guide* on the moral argument, and the chapter on philosophy of religion.

Make sure you give some examples of religious experiences and their moral/ spiritual effects, for example, Jeremiah, Ezekiel, Jesus, St Paul, Muhammad, the Buddha and the Toronto Blessing. Consider to what extent these moments 'prove' God or ultimate reality.

The concept of free will and determinism in relation to the nature of an omniscient God. Consider to what extent God can be held to know the future, and the implications of this for human responsibility. Firstly consider Augustine's weak predestination view that although God foresaw, he did not forewill Adam's act of rebellion, as part of the so-called free-will defence. Compare and contrast Augustine with Calvin's double predestination and view of election. Does Calvin's view represent a more coherent view than Augustine – while God foresees and forewills the Fall, he subsequently knows who also will be saved (but as humans do not know this they work on the assumption of acting freely)?

Read page 71 of the *OCR AS Guide*.

> **Further reading**
> See pages 150–151 on the Divine Decree (Al Qadr) for a similar debate amongst Muslim philosophers. Consider the relationship between samsara and karma in terms of free will and responsibility.

The relation between free will and the problem of evil. Consider the relationship between Epicurus' challenge to the omnipotence and goodness of God, and Plato's Euthyphro dilemma. Consider the idea that God respects the autonomy of humans to act according to their own sense of goodness but thereby reduces his involvement in the world (the position adopted by Kant), or the idea that if he commands acts such as the sacrifice of Isaac (Genesis 21) which appear to be evil, then there is no rational reason why we should obey. Consider these problems in terms of hard determinism: that as free will is an illusion, obeying an evil command of God is necessarily for the good, or soft determinism: that some form of suffering is part of the process of achieving good.

> **Further reading**
> Read pages 70 and 17 of *OCR AS Guide*. See the chapter on Judaism, pages 167–170 on the various theological responses to the holocaust.

The relation between ethical language and religious language. Consider the various ways (univocal, equivocal, analogical, metaphorical and analytical) in which religious and non-religious thinkers have attempted to define the following terms: justice, peace, love, good and evil. Consider whether 'good' in meta-ethics can mean anything in the same way that the apophatic way rejects any ability to talk of God. Especially note A. J. Ayer's use of the verification principle as the reason for rejecting all moral and theological language as meaningless, and contrast with the falsification principle applied to moral love/'God is love'. Consider the power of symbol in terms of moral/cultural relativism to express values held in a particular community and Tillich's argument for symbols as 'participating', yet nevertheless cultural and changing expressions of God. Consider the problem of defining justice in moral terms and analogically whether it can applied to God univocally or equivocally.

> **Further reading**
> See pages 40–44 of *The Puzzle of God* by Peter Vardy (Fount 1995). Also chapter 4 of *Ethical Theory* by Mel Thompson (Hodder and Stoughton 1999).

Read pages 19–21 of the *OCR AS Guide*.

See page 26–28.

Read pages 20–21 of the *OCR AS Guide*.

The implications for ethics of the theories of psychology and sociology. Consider the impact of the psychologies of Freud, Jung and Piaget on religious belief and ethics. To what extent are they reductionist – do they diminish the place of God and conscience merely to the level of neuroscience? Consider Jung's emphasis on the collective unconscious and to universal symbols found in all religions that reinforce the sense of community and collective spiritual values. Consider whether religions necessarily separate conscience from ordinary reasoning. Consider the impact of sociologists such as Marx, Durkheim, Weber and Berger, especially when wanting to separate irrational moral religious taboos from genuine contribution to religious ethics (Berger's argument). Consider, for example, debates about sexuality, and the place and effectiveness of organised religion in the present discussions. Consider Marx's critique of religion and ethics, and his suspicion of all systems that impose economic power over the weak.

> **Further reading**
> See pages 69–70 and 72 of the *OCR AS Guide* on William James, Freud and Jung.

Read pages 70, 73–74 of the *OCR AS Guide*.

The relation between moral behaviour and life after death. Consider the link between religious views about life after death and attitudes to war and peace, and whether a belief in a transcendent salvation diminishes moral concern for situations of injustice in the world. Consider to what extent religious teachings regard the conservation or transformation of the current political and social order to be morally important. Consider Kant's teaching on the kingdom of ends and to what extent it fits logically with the rest of his teaching.

See pages 16–19 on life after death.

Read pages 75–77 on Kant in the *OCR AS Guide*.

Test yourself

1. 'Religious and moral language are both meaningless.' Discuss.
2. 'Sociology has helped to show religious morality where it has gone wrong.' Discuss.
3. How fair is the claim that, as humans have free will, God cannot be responsible for evil in the world?

> For material on making connections between Religious Ethics and your other module, see the relevant pages of the chapter on that module.

For example, for material on the connections between Religious Ethics and Jewish Scriptures, see pages 65–67, as well as the margins of that chapter.

Jewish scriptures

The concept of reward and punishment

Bible quotations are from *Tanakh* (Jewish Publication Society 1985). You might also wish to use the Revised Standard Version where the translation follows more traditional wording. It is important that you can compare and contrast all the set texts in this unit with one another. Make sure you look up all the references given here. These notes attempt to place the passage in the context of the writer's overall theology. You must show this knowledge in the examination.

Route H: Religious Ethics and duty. When reading the set texts consider whether the idea of reward is consequential or deontological.

'Be not like slaves that minister to the master for the sake of receiving a bounty, but be like slaves that minister to the master not for the sake of receiving a bounty; and let the fear of Heaven be upon you.' *The Mishnah*, trans. H. Danby (OUP 1933).

The 'fear of God' is better thought of as reverence or awe of God.

Route R: Judaism. Consider the next three points in relation to contemporary Jewish debates about Zionism and post-holocaust theology.

Make sure you read through the rebukes or *Tochacha* in Leviticus 26.

Further reading

Read part 3 chapter 19 of Maimonides' *The Guide of the Perplexed*, trans Cahim Rabin (Hackett 1995).

In simple terms, reward and punishment are fundamental to the Jewish concept of God and his providential activity in the world. Fundamentally God is just and loving because he rewards the good and punishes the wicked. This idea is repeated again and again in the Tenakh, and reinforced by the rabbis and later Jewish writers. Maimonides makes it an article of Jewish faith in the 11th of his 13 Principles. Even so, there are many fundamental problems with such a view of God, which are discussed by the biblical writers and throughout Jewish history. These questions should be born in mind when discussing the prescribed texts below.

Should a good Jew worship God regardless of reward? This is classically expressed in the Mishnah tract *Pirke Avot* by Antigonus Soko. The question is left open ended: should the worship of God be sufficient in itself or should it imply God's love and protection?

Why be good? One might also ask, why should the *mitzvoth* be followed? Maimonides argued that initially the Torah should be followed because of its benefits to the individual, just as children want material rewards or praise from their parents. Only as adults is the reward seen in the development of social justice and a better world for all – not just for one's self. Therefore there is no entirely selfless act, and even the love and fear of God (*ahavat ha-Shem* and *yirat ha-Shem*), as expressed by the Talmudic writers, imply that God will reward the just and punish the wicked.

This world or the world to come? Earlier biblical writers see reward and punishment in this-worldly terms. As far as Leviticus is concerned, if Israel is obedient to the Covenant, God will protect her and she will thrive, but if she 'does not observe all these commandments', God in turn will 'wreak misery upon you.' (Lev 26: 14–17). However, as simple as the formula sounds, later writers conjectured that there must be some kind of after-life to reward the righteous who had not received their just rewards in this life. The rabbis interpreted Deuteronomy 22: 7 – '...in order that you may fare well and have a long life' – to refer to the life in the world to come (*olam ha ba*); likewise the passage in Numbers 15: 31 – 'But the person, be he a citizen or stranger, who acts defiantly reviles the Lord; that person shall be cut off from among his people' – was interpreted by the rabbis to mean that the soul would be extinguished or 'cut off' for ever at death.

Why do the wicked prosper? Despite the basic premise established above that God rewards the good and punishes the wicked, the biblical writers observed the obvious fact that this does not always appear to be the case (see, for example, Jer 12: 1). The atheistic response is, according to the psalmist, 'How could God know? Is there knowledge with the Most High? Such are the wicked; ever tranquil, they amass wealth.' (Ps 73: 11–12). But for the believing Jew there has to be a faith that God's justice will prevail; as Jeremiah states, 'You will win O Lord...' (12: 1). Maimonides accounts for the apparent success of the wicked in worldly terms as a risk that God takes when giving humans free will, but argues that all good actions will be rewarded. It is also the conclusion of the Book of Job – but many find this kind of conclusion far from satisfactory. The alternatives are that God may not have absolute power in the world or that he is not absolutely good.

Read pages 70–71 of the *OCR AS Guide* on the problem of suffering and God's goodness.

Are the many punished for the sake of the few? Another open-ended biblical debate is whether the individual is punished only for his or her own sins, or whether a nation or community can be collectively sinful and punished – including the innocent. The story of the flood (Genesis 6: 5–14) suggests that sin is collective and can be punished up to 'third or fourth generations' (Num 14: 18). On the other hand, Jeremiah and Ezekiel explicitly develop the notion of individual responsibility for sin and reject the older tradition.

'In those days, they shall no longer say, "Parents have eaten sour grapes and the children's teeth are blunted." But everyone shall die for his own sins: whosoever eats sours grapes, his teeth shall be blunted.' (Jer 31: 29–30).

Isaiah 53

Date and authorship

Traditionally, Isaiah is ascribed to one author writing during the time of the fall of the Northern Kingdom to the Assyrians in 701 BCE. Isaiah's call (6: 1) was 'In the year that King Uzziah died', namely, in 742 BCE. However, for many scholars there are distinct changes in mood and circumstances between the oracles of chapters 40–55 and 56–66, which suggest that 40–55 were composed by a pupil of Isaiah's writing during the time of the exile in Babylon (587–520 BCE), and 56–66 after the exile (520 BCE onwards). The anonymous author of 40–55 is often referred to by scholars as Second Isaiah or **Deutero-Isaiah**.

Abraham Ibn Ezra (1089–1164) first suggested different authors of Isaiah but the main arguments were developed in the 18th century by J. C. Döderlein and J. G. Eichhorn.

Purpose

Even if there are different authors writing during significant changes in Israel's history, there are several important themes that remain constant. The first is the holiness of God. In his call, Isaiah hears the seraphs proclaim: 'Holy, holy, holy! The Lord of Hosts! His presence fills all the earth!' (6: 3). Isaiah develops the notion that God is not just the god of Israel but of all the nations of the world (5: 26–29) and that as the controller of destiny it would be foolish of Israel to combat the might of the Assyrians. Israel should trust in God's protection (31: 1–3), and in reverence to God's holiness she must carry out social justice by helping the weaker members of society (5: 1–10). The punishment for not doing so is death. Punishment is there to teach Israel and Judah to become true followers of God and make the people a 'holy nation'.

'Assuredly, as straw is consumed by a tongue of fire and hay shrivels as it burns, their stock shall become like rot, and their buds shall blow away like dust. For they have rejected the instruction of the Lord of Hosts.' (Is 5: 24).

The circumstances in which Deutero-Isaiah found himself prompted a number of new themes. The **new exodus** is the most prominent – Israel exiled in Babylon will return in an exodus after she has received due punishment for her misdemeanours foretold in Isaiah 1–39. She can expect to be rewarded and begin a new life in a restored land. Now God's majesty is extended to such an extent that not only does he rule the whole world, but the gods of the other nations have no existence at all. Judaism is the only true religion (44: 6–20). Deutero-Isaiah dwells on the creative power of the **word of God** and God's providential action in the world (55: 11). But for many, the most intriguing aspect of Isaiah 40–55 is the relationship of the four **servant songs**. The identity of the servant poses considerable problems. The servant might be:

Isaiah 40 begins, 'Comfort, oh comfort My people, says your God, speak tenderly to Jerusalem, and declare to her that her term of service is over, that her iniquity is expiated; for she has received at the hand of the Lord double for all her sins.' (40: 1–2).

The four songs are usually thought to be: 42: 1–7; 49: 1–7; 50: 4–9; 52: 13–53: 12.

- ✦ **Redeemed Israel** (49: 3), or the wise 'remnant' (those who had remained faithful to God in exile) of the community (based on Daniel 12: 3). Or the prophet himself and his disciples – or a combination of individual and community.
- ✦ The **ignorant people of Israel** who are blind and deaf (42: 19) to God, and sinful (43: 23), but who have been forgiven by God and therefore become a light to the world (42: 6).
- ✦ **All Israelites** (41: 8–9; 44: 2 and Ps 113: 1) – in Is 56–66 the servants are the few faithful Israelites (63: 17) or even foreigners who carry out God's will (56: 6).

It is possible that at first the author thought the servant was the Persian king Cyrus (44: 26–45: 2) and only later, when he realised that Cyrus (549–530 BCE) would not bring about a spiritual renewal, did he adapt his ideas.

- ✦ An **actual historical character** whose life has embodied the values of the new community (53: 4–6).
- ✦ The **messiah**. This is especially true in the fourth servant song which Jesus or his followers equated with his role as the suffering messiah (1 Peter 2: 22–25). There are some Jewish texts that considered this servant to be the messiah, though most have resisted this interpretation because the messiah, the son of David, would not suffer.

The songs' function is to develop Isaiah's theology in a personal and immediate way. This is particularly the case in the fourth song, Is 52: 13 to 53: 12.

Commentary on Isaiah 53

In **52: 13–15** God speaks and praises his servant, who has 'prospered' because of his obedience to God's providential plan. His obedience has stunned his critics into silence – just as he himself has been silent against those who abused him (53: 7). If the servant represents Israel's faithful, it may be their loyalty to God in exile that has antagonised and astonished the Babylonian kings perhaps referred to in 52: 15. The second part of this verse emphasises that the life and death of the servant is quite unique.

Further study

Compare this to Job's friends who assumed that Job's disfigurement was due to his punishment by God.

53: 1–end The 'we' here is no longer God but the prophet or his disciples. The uniqueness of the message is reinforced – who could have believed that God was revealing his purpose through such an unexpected source as the rejected servant? The servant was not beautiful, so he seemed to be a man who had not been blessed by God (according to traditional teaching).

Vicarious means suffering on behalf of others.

Further discussion

53: 8–9 is difficult to interpret. Some suggest the servant was imprisoned, then was judged, died and was buried with the wicked. But it is not clear how and why he died. How important is this for the interpretation of the servant's vicarious suffering and atonement for sin?

Vicarious suffering. The unique element of the report is that the servant's suffering is the means of establishing God's relationship with Israel. It is described using Temple sacrificial language normally reserved for the sacrifice of animals, 'like a sheep being led to the slaughter' (53: 7 and see Leviticus 4–5) to be an 'offering for guilt' (53: 10). This has the psychological effect of causing the speaker to realise the nature of his sin: 'He bore our chastisement that made us whole' (53: 5). Just as the sacrificial animals in the Temple were muzzled, the servant is unable or unwilling to 'open his mouth' (53: 7). This aspect of his character stuns his audience – why should he atone for their sins without reward in this world?

Reward. Reward is given in two ways. Firstly, the remorse felt by the writer and his community enables them to repent and find a new level of moral and spiritual relationship with God based on the selfless example of the servant. Thus reward is not directly in terms of Leviticus' promise of earthly success. Secondly, the servant's own reward opens and closes the song. He will 'prosper' (52: 13) and share a place with the righteous (53: 11–12).

Punishment. The servant bears the punishment of those who mock him (53: 11). In traditional teaching, punishment is experienced as sickness and affliction sent by God. However, as is characteristic of Isaiah, he reverses this. Whereas the servant is the one who physically suffers, the significant suffering is of those who have unknowingly spiritually and mentally caused his anguish. Therefore, it is they who are punished by their own realisation of guilt – even though it is they 'who deserved the punishment' (53: 8). The novelty of this servant song is the shock of this discovery – 'Who can believe what we have heard?' (53: 1).

Further discussion

There is much debate about the nature of the servant's restoration by God – is he revived, healed or resurrected? Or has he died in the knowledge that his death will revive faith in God (53: 11)?

'Yet it was our sickness that he was bearing, our suffering that he endured' (Isaiah 53: 4).

Further study

Consider what the fourth servant song teaches about reward and punishment by comparing it with the ideas set out in the first paragraph of this chapter.

Jeremiah 7

There is considerable debate about the authorship and sources of the book of Jeremiah. Among scholars today there is a general recognition of Mowinckel's theory (published in 1914) that Jeremiah is composed from four sources, although there is disagreement as to authorship and date.

Date and authorship

Mowinckel's four sources are 1) poetic oracles; 2) biographical narratives; 3) deuteronomic discourses; 4) oracles of salvation and oracles against the nations. Number 3 causes the most discussion because its message of hope is sometimes considered to be a later redaction (or editing) of Jeremiah's original prophecy when the exile was over and many had returned home from Babylon. You will have to consider this when looking at Jeremiah's teaching on promise and reward.

Jeremiah preached for almost 40 years (1: 1–3) during the Babylonian conquest of the Assyrian empire which fell in 609 BCE. Nebuchadnezzar (626–605 BCE) extended Babylon's power by defeating the Egyptians at Carchemish. During this time, the succession of the kings of Judah alternated from those who absorbed the religion of their overlords to those, notably Josiah (640–609 BCE), who attempted to remain loyal to the covenant through reform (621 BCE). Jeremiah's message responds to all these new and complex situations. For him, politics and religion go hand in hand. The final events of his ministry witnessed the disastrous reign of **Jehoiakim** (609–598 BCE) who not only abandoned the reforms of Josiah but also tried to resist the Babylonians. Jehoiakim's son, Johoiakin was replaced by **Zedekiah**. But he was a weak king and, although at first he kept his oath of allegiance, he was finally persuaded by his anti-Babylonian advisors to rebel (Jeremiah 38: 5). The deportation after the fall of Jerusalem in 587 BCE indicated to Jeremiah the complete failure of Judah to maintain God's covenant.

Route R: Judaism and authority of scripture. Consider whether a good knowledge of the political events at the time of Jeremiah and Ezekiel undermines the authority of scripture. Read pages 469–480 of *Israelite and Judaean History*, by Hayes and Miller (SCM Press 1977).

Purpose

Jeremiah's mission was to define the proper worship of God and proclaim the punishments that would follow if this did not happen. Chapters 1–6 reflect the times of Josiah's reform and Jeremiah's hope for the full restoration of Judah. By contrast, chapters 7–20 reflect the time of Jehoiakim and the Babylonian defeat in 605 of the Egyptians; here Jeremiah's message is a strong warning and denunciation of the king and people. Chapters 27–29 and 32–45 reflect the years round 597–587 BCE and record (probably through his scribe Baruch) Jeremiah's ministry. At the heart of Jeremiah's message is the idea that the covenant between God and the people forms the basis of all moral and political life.

Commentary on Jeremiah 7

Read pages 93–94 of the *OCR AS Guide*.

Covenant. The vehemence of Jeremiah's words here reflects his disappointment with the early reign of Jehoiakim. He attacks those who think that simply by their presence in the Temple, God will protect them. They have broken the commandments of the

'The Temple of the Lord, the Temple of the Lord, the Temple of the Lord are these buildings' (7: 4). The phrase is repeated by Jeremiah to mock the people's false commitment to God. Compare this with Hosea 6: 6.

Decalogue (7: 9) with the **apostasy** of worshipping the prophets of Baal. Temple sacrifices are not considered to be part of their religious duties (7: 21–23) – their covenantal duty is summarised simply as 'I will be your God and you will be my people' (7: 23).

'The elements of promise for the future in these chapters may be in large measure due to later elaboration of the material, perhaps by the prophet himself, perhaps by his immediate followers in the years after 587; yet they attach intelligibility to words of exhortation, and the recognition of the closeness of the relationship which exists between God and his people'. Peter Ackroyd, *Exile and Restoration* (SCM Press 1976) page 52.

Punishment. Because of Judah's faithlessness, the time is coming when the people will be slaughtered and their bodies given to the birds (7: 32–34). Literally and symbolically the land – the promise of the covenant – will be in ruins (7: 34). The ultimate desecration is that the bodies and bones of the dead will be dug up and left to rot without proper burial (8: 1–3).

Reward. Despite the severity of the punishments there are glimmers of hope. Throughout the book Jeremiah notes that those who repent will be forgiven by God.

Ezekiel 18

Re-read the historical background to Jeremiah above. Also read pages 533–537 and 546–547 of *The Oxford Bible Commentary* by J. Barton and J. Muddiman (OUP 2001).

Ezekiel was writing at approximately the same time as Jeremiah. They share much in common but, whereas Jeremiah was preaching in Israel, Ezekiel, a priest, was exiled with other high-ranking members of society to Babylon (1: 1–2). Like Jeremiah, Ezekiel resisted Zedekiah's intentions to break his promise of allegiance to the Babylonians because the king had made it under oath to God (17: 13). Central to many of his ideas is **responsibility** and allegiance to the covenant. As a priest Ezekiel is conscious of the priestly ideal to maintain holiness, but without the proximity of the Temple and the land of Israel, Ezekiel's theology develops a new sense of religious and moral individual inner integrity.

Many have commented on the close relationship of Lev 17–26 (the Holiness Code) to Ezekiel's concern for purity.

Date and authorship

Ezekiel's ministry began in the fifth year of the exile (1: 2), namely in 593 BCE in Babylon, probably until 571 (29: 17). Some have suggested that as some chapters are repeated (3 and 33 for example), the book must have been edited. However, there is a very distinct and consistent style that suggests a single authorship of the book. As a prophet, his calling was to be a watchman for the house of Israel (33: 7) and to speak of his profound sense of the majesty of God whose holiness is beyond description.

Further study

Read 1: 4–28 and note the frequent use of 'likeness' throughout the vision to indicate the ineffable nature of God.

Purpose

Ezekiel never mentions Jeremiah by name, but his theology has so much in common with Jeremiah that many feel that he must have read or least heard Jeremiah's prophecy. Both claim that those who break the covenant through political disaster will be punished (Jer 4–6 and Ezek 17). Both hold that obedience to the covenant is possible even in exile (Jer 29, and Ezek 4 and 21). This leads to Ezekiel's reflections on the sinfulness of a people as a whole whose failure to maintain the statutes of the Torah has led to religious and political punishment. In one chapter Ezekiel argues that the nation has failed even from the time of the exodus, but that because of God's mercy and justness he has not punished them until now.

'However, I swore to them in the wilderness that I would scatter them among the nations and disperse them through the lands because they did not obey My rules, but rejected My laws, profaned My sabbaths and looked with longing to the fetishes of their fathers' (20: 23–24). Read Ezekiel 20 in preparation for chapter 18.

Commentary on Ezekiel 18

'As I live – declares the Lord God – this proverb shall no longer be current among you in Israel' (18: 3).

The chapter is made up of a number of questions posed by the exiles. They argue that, as their punishment for sin was due to the failure of their forefathers, either (cynically) there is no point in attempting to keep to the Torah, or (out of self-pity) they have to accept the punishment for someone else's wrongdoing. God rejects such notions (Ezek 18: 3). In simple terms, each person is responsible for his own moral conduct:

Reward. In 18: 5–9 the 'man who shall live' and who is blessed by God is the one who carries and upholds basic social justice. The phrase 'followed My laws' echoes Leviticus 18: 4 and suggests that such a person has achieved holiness. Reward is also available for the wicked person who repents (18: 21–23).

Punishment. The emphasis in this chapter is a response to the community's two hypothetical questions. Firstly, if the righteous man's son is a murdererand adulterer, idolater, and has cheated the poor (18: 10–12) he 'shall die' – receive God's punishment. Secondly, if his son is righteous (18: 14–17) 'he shall live'. So, even the righteous person who then sins is not protected by his past actions but will be punished (18: 24). Ezekiel concludes this chapter by calling for the people to be replenished by the Spirit of God (in chapter 36 he considers that they are spiritually dead), to 'Repent, therefore, and live!' (18: 32).

Route R: Judaism and covenant. Ezekiel still considers Israel's collective sin as a result of years of sinfulness; the righteous have been punished. Consider how Ezekiel's view of sin might be considered at, for example, Yom Kippur.

Further study

Compare Ezekiel's list of social virtues with Amos' prophecy and note the similarities.

Ezekiel's argument considers the relationship between distributive and retributive justice; popular and actual justice. Consider how he does this in his parable of the grandfather, father and grandson.

Job 19

Date and authorship

Further reading

For the authorship and dating of Job, see pages 95–96 of the *OCR AS Guide*.

In many ways, dating Job is far less significant than dating the prophetic books, which deal with historical events. Job's questioning of why the innocent suffer and the wicked prosper is timeless and does not need a historical setting. On the other hand, if, as many scholars argue, Job was written in the post-exilic period then his particular interest in the suffering of the innocent individual might be seen as a development of Deutero-Isaiah's servant theology, for both Isaiah and Job question the traditional view of sin and punishment.

Robert Gordis writes: 'For the first time the nexus between suffering and sin is severed. This insight of Deutero-Isaiah was destined to be developed by the author of Job.' *The Book of God and Man* (University Chicago 1965), page 145.

Commentary

Job 19 is a reply to Bildad's stinging criticisms in his second speech (Job 18). The thesis is clearly set out in 18: 5–6, where Bildad argues that as a wicked man's lamp does not shine, so his deeds will result in a life without joy – even death. Bildad's argument defends the traditional view that as God is creator and judge of the universe (Deuteronomy 11: 13–17) he will reward the righteous and punish the wicked.

Route R: Judaism and post-holocaust theology. Is Job's argument satisfactory in discussing suffering and the holocaust?

Job 19 questions the fundamental aspect of Bildad's defence: that God is righteous. Bildad has asked, 'Will earth's order be disrupted for your sake? Will rocks be dislodged from their place?' (18: 4) but Job responds that God has not protected him but has trapped him with his net (19: 6), and although he has called out for justice nothing has happened. God has become his adversary, his friends and not his enemies are fighting him, his children reject him (19: 18), his wife finds him repellent (19: 17) and his servants disobey him and treat him as a foreigner (19: 15). In this odd world even his bones stick to his flesh, not the other way round (19: 20).

This final insult is made worse by the fact that most servants were themselves foreigners.

Job negates Bildad's argument, word for word, from experience, 'How seldom does the lamp of the wicked fail, does the calamity they deserve befall them, does He apportion their lot in anger!' (21: 18). He does not accept that the righteous are rewarded in the afterlife and the wicked punished: 'So man lies down never to rise' (14: 12).

The idea of the afterlife is the solution offered in Daniel 12 and 2 Maccabees 7, both of which were written slightly later than Job.

The new idea of Job 19 is Job's hope of a **Go'el**, a redeemer or vindicator (19: 25). There is considerable dispute as to what exactly this term means and how it is being used here. It is not the

The Hebrew word Go'el is used in a general legal way meaning to avenge (Numbers 35: 19) or redeem (Ruth 4: 4–6).

first time Job has called on some kind of intermediary to plead his case. Previously has asked for an **arbitrator** (9: 33) and **witness** (16: 19). Job now hopes that this redeemer will read the permanent record of his life and sufferings cut into stone with lead letters (19: 23–24) and act in one of the following ways as:

- A heavenly redeemer who would champion his cause after his death and seek recognition of the wrongs done against him by God (19: 25)
- A heavenly redeemer who would raise him up after death to 'behold God' (19: 27). There is much dispute whether this is so. It is probably unlikely given Job's ambivalence about the after-life
- An act of vindication by God himself after his death (19: 25) justifying Job's innocence.

Further study

Consider which of these roles makes most sense. Compare different translations of 19: 25–27 to see the difficulties of this passage.

Does Job completely reject the traditionalist argument for reward and punishment, or is he applying it in a more personal and spiritual sense? The *Mishnah* (Sotah 5:5) concludes that Job realised that he has to serve God out of love: to what extent do you agree? From now on, Job's request is not for an intermediary but to behold or 'see God', which finally occurs in chapter 38.

Daniel 12

Further reading

Read *Daniel* by Norman Porteous (SCM Press 1979), or P. Davies in *The Oxford Bible Commentary* pages 563–571.

From very early times, there has been considerable dispute as to what kind of literature the book of Daniel is. In the Palestinian canon Daniel is placed in the third section of the Hebrew Bible – the Ketuvim or 'writings' – while the Greek version of the Hebrew Bible (the Septuagint) placed it in the second section – the Nevi'im or 'prophets'. The debate about the literary form of Daniel makes quite a difference to how he is to be interpreted. If, for example, it is a genuinely prophetic book predicting the future during the time of the exile under Nebuchadnezzar, Belshazzar, Darius and Cyrus, then the purpose of the book is to reassure the exiles that God will act decisively in the future. Indeed, the Jewish historian Josephus praised Daniel for predicting the future with such accuracy (*Antiquities* X.11.7).

Jewish and Christian Bibles today therefore differ as to where they place Daniel. For Christians, it is particularly important that Daniel is seen as a prophetic book because the figure of the Son of Man (Dan 7: 13) is equated with Jesus in the New Testament (e.g. Mk 14: 62). It was probably placed in the Ketuvim section of the Hebrew Bible because of the late date of its composition.

A general scholarly opinion today is that the latter part of the book (chapters 10–12) reflects the times from Alexander the Great until Antiochus IV. The author has a detailed knowledge of this period of history, which suggests that he is living during the time of the Maccabees (169–164 BCE).

Further reading

You should read the whole of Daniel 10–12. Daniel 11 gives a detailed account of Antiochus' atrocities.

Date and authorship

For the reasons given above Daniel was either written during the exiles or during the period of restoration and the Maccabean revolt. Ezekiel refers to a Daniel (Ezekiel 14: 4 and 20) along with Job and Noah, while the Book of Jubilees 4: 20 states that Daniel is the father-in-law of Enoch (which would make him the great-great-grandfather of Noah). In other words, there is no external evidence for the authorship of Daniel. Internal evidence suggests that he might have belonged to a special class of wise men or *maskilim*, whose job it was to teach the people to maintain righteousness during times when many Jews were adopting Greek customs and thought (see 1 Macc 1: 11–15). Some scholars have

Daniel 1: 4 refers to a group who were 'proficient in all wisdom, knowledgeable and intelligent and capable of serving in the royal palace'.

suggested that men like Daniel belonged to a new class of prophet – wise men whose ability to understand Greek ideas and adapt them within orthodox Judaism made them especially significant in this period. Therefore, it is not surprising that the role of Daniel is very similar to that of the patriarch Joseph, who also served in the court of the king and interpreted the king's dreams, while depending on God to sustain and reward him for his faith (Gen 39–45).

Purpose

'Apocalyptic' comes from the Greek meaning to 'reveal' or 'revelation'. It is often associated with elaborate visions and symbolism. See Daniel 7.

In many ways, Daniel marks a new form of literature, bridging the older forms of prophecy with an apocalyptic form of writing that was to become increasingly more significant in the first century BCE.

- ✦ **Apocalyptic**. Daniel is revealing God's plans for the future. His summary of the historical events that are yet to happen is a means of illustrating that the atrocities will come to an end and God will act decisively in history to redeem his righteous elect.
- ✦ **Prophetic**. Daniel follows the view of many of the prophets that history will come to an end when God judges the world.
- ✦ **Wisdom**. Daniel uses of stories and parables in a way that is intended to show how Jewish wisdom is superior to the wisdom of the foreign magicians (Dan 2), while stories of the fiery furnace (Dan 3) encourage the faithful of God's providence.
- ✦ **Pesher**. Daniel combines many of the above forms of writing to show how scripture, rightly interpreted, reveals that what God intended to happen is now coming true. Especially important here is Daniel's realisation (9: 1–2) that Jeremiah's prophecy of the land laid to waste and the 70 years serving the Babylonian king (25: 11) was happening now, and was a sign that they were entering the end time. The frequent references to the 'sealed book' (for example 12: 4) symbolise the power of God's word in scripture to reveal the truth at the right time.

Pesher means 'commentary'. At Qumran, for example, the pesher on Habakkuk states that Habakkuk wrote down words that had secret meaning until properly interpreted at the right time. 'And God told Habbukuk to write that which was to happen to the final generation, but he did not reveal to him when time would come to an end.' (1QpHab 7: 1–5).

Commentary on Daniel 12

The bulk of this chapter is about the reward promised to the righteous at the end time. 12: 1–4 completes the long outline of the recent history of Israel begun in chapter 10. **Michael** (12: 1) is Israel's guardian angel who will ensure that Israel will be protected at judgement when God intervenes in history. '**The book**' (12: 2) is the book of life (Psalm 69: 28), which contains the names of the righteous. It is not clear whether Daniel imagined that all would be resurrected, or only those who had responded to his message. The reference to those who **awake** (12: 2) is a reminder of Isaiah's picture of the resurrection (Is 26: 19). Daniel appears to have a special place for the *maskilim* or wise leaders (12: 3) who, like the servant of Isaiah 53, have inspired others to righteousness. The **sealing** of the book (12: 4) suggests either that the end is yet to come, or it is a way of saying that in the vision the book was sealed, but now, at the time of writing, the secrets of the end have been revealed and they are now on the threshold of the final moment.

In Deuteronomy 29: 26, God gives the nations their own patron angel. By Daniel's time, Michael was Israel's guardian angel (in the New Testament see Revelation 12:

Further study

Does Daniel think in terms of a general resurrection of the community as a whole or individual resurrection?

In the epilogue (12: 5–12), the two people (12: 5) are angelic witnesses to the angel – the **man clothed in linen** (12: 6) – who reveals the final secrets of the end first mentioned in 7: 25. The request to make the end time clearer has been much discussed, but seems to have been a correction of the time first given in 8: 14 (12:

Further study

Compare Daniel's idea of reward and punishment with Job. Who offers the more sophisticated view?

Further reading

Read pages 734–742 in *The Oxford Bible Commentary* by R. Doran (OUP 2001).

11). The punishment of the **wicked** (12: 10) is not explicit – and in that sense Daniel's apocalyptic lacks the detail of later apocalyptic writings. The reward to the **purified** (12: 10) is equally vague – but it is clear that, although God will act decisively after the death of Antiochus IV (referred to as the **appalling abomination** in 12: 11), the end time is only possible because God acts through the response of the righteous.

2 Maccabees 7

Date and authorship

The authorship and purpose of 2 Maccabees is set out in the Prologue (2: 19–32). The author's purpose is to summarise Jason of Cyrene's five-volume history (2: 23) of the Hasmoneans of 180–160 BCE, an **epitome** to please and edify those who wish to learn (2: 25). The unknown author probably also used eyewitness accounts and documents about the high priests from the Temple treasury. Some think it was written shortly after the first letter was added to the epitome (2: 19–15: 39) which was completed in 124 BCE (1: 9); others are less sure. Most agree that it was probably written before 1 Maccabees.

An epitome is a summary; the author makes it clear that if the reader wants more detail then he should read Jason's work (2: 28).

Purpose

Revise the history of this period and read page 27 of the *OCR AS Guide*.

Although the aim of 2 Maccabees is to outline the events that led to Judas Maccabeus overthrowing the emperor Antiochus IV, the epitomist's primary purpose is theological not historical. He shows that God is creator of the universe. This is absolute monotheism – God alone is just, merciful, kind, almighty, eternal and providential (1: 24). The aim is to contrast the place of the earthly rulers with God's ultimate rule. The theme of reward and punishment is developed in a way that contrasts considerably with earlier writers. The writer cleverly shows how the Jews maintain the Greek virtues of moral excellence by remaining true to the Law and to the Temple. It is not they who are the barbarians, but – through their brutality (and 2 Maccabees 7 is a good example) – the Greeks. God will defend them (7: 6) and offer them resurrection (7: 9, 23), but the barbarians will be punished and tortured (7: 17).

'Barbarian' was the term used by the Greeks to describe all those who failed to live virtuously. The author uses barbarian to describe the Greeks (15: 20).

'But do not think that God has forsaken our people. Keep on, and see how his mighty power will torture you and your descendents' (2 Maccabees 7: 17).

Commentary on 2 Maccabees 7

Read from 2 Maccabees 6: 18 to 7: 42 as this follows a single theme (7: 42).

The epitomist sets out his theological reasons as to why the Jews should suffer in 6: 12–17. The suffering of the righteous is 'not to destroy but to discipline our people' for their sins *now*. God punishes other non-Jewish people much more harshly after they have committed all their sins. Suffering now is God's merciful way of reducing his ultimate judgement. The story of the martyrdom of the mother and her seven sons was very popular with the rabbis and quoted in the Talmud.

Reward. The reward is resurrection for the righteous. The promise of new life after death was already contained in some of the Psalms (such as Psalm 73: 23–26), in Ezekiel 37 and Hosea 6: 2, but usually in a general and collective sense. In 1 Samuel 28: 18–19, the dead go to Sheol, but do not want to be disturbed. However, here resurrection is individual and something all the sons desire. In the new life the body is renewed (7: 11) and so present torture counts as nothing. The mother's courage (7: 20) is highlighted as an example of true Jewish behaviour because of her trust in God as the creator and giver of the breath of life (7: 23, where she refers to Genesis 2: 7).

Further reading

Read chapter 2 of *The Garden of Eden and Hope of Immortality* by James Barr (SCM Press 1992) for the development of ideas of immortality and resurrection in Jewish thought.

Further study

Consider how the mother is portrayed in this passage.

Punishment. For the wicked there is no resurrection (7: 14). In an audacious comment, the fourth son tells Antiochus, who was considered divine, that God would punish and torture him and his descendents (7: 17). All these ideas are summarised in the impressive speech of the youngest son (7: 30–38).

> **Further study**
> Learn the youngest son's speech. Is his explanation of suffering as individual and collective sin satisfactory?

Book of Amos

Authorship and historical setting

Scholars generally agree that the opening of Amos dates Amos as a prophet to the mid 8th century BCE – between 760 and 750. **Uzziah** was king of the southern kingdom (Judah) until 742; **Jeroboam II** was son of Joah and king of the northern kingdom (Israel) 786–746. The earthquake is probably the one mentioned in Isaiah 9: 8–10: 4 in the mid 8th century, for which there is archaeological evidence at Hazor.

> **Further reading**
> Read chapter 5 of *Propaganda and Subversion in the Old Testament* by Rex Mason (SPCK 1997) for a useful discussion of Amos, Isaiah, Micah and others.

Amos was writing at the end of a time of great stability. Jeroboam had ruled for 40 years and extended Israel's boundaries. Israel was wealthy and optimistic. Egypt was in decline and Assyria had only just begun to re-establish her power. The great Assyrian king Tiglath Pilesser II was shortly to defeat Damascus (in 738) and Syria (in 732). In 722–1 the Northern kingdom would fall to Shalmaneser V.

Although many consider that Amos' message has been revised in the light of the events of 722, there is general agreement that the present text retains the heart of his unusual prophecy. In many ways, Amos carried out the activities of the guild prophets of his time. He preaches about war (3: 11), considers himself part of the tradition of other prophets (3: 7), works at cult sanctuaries (4: 4–5), attends the court of the king (7: 10–13) and has ecstatic visions in which God speaks to him (7: 4–9). However, unlike the guild prophets, Amos has his own independent means of income as a 'sheepbreeder' (1: 1 – a herdsman of cattle and sheep) and as a 'tender of sycamore figs' (7: 14 – a small land owner). His ministry only lasted a year so he could support himself.

In the much discussed verse 'I am no prophet, and I am not a prophet's disciple' (7: 14), the meaning is probably that Amos considers himself to be a professional prophet only in the sense that he has been called by God to preach, not as a guild member.

Message

There are a number of characteristics of Amos' message that again make him quite different from earlier prophets. Unlike other prophets who aimed their message at one individual, Amos addresses the king, the priests, the judges, the rich, ordinary people and the nation as a whole. His message is essentially one of judgement, because at every level of society Amos sees corruption in worship, morality and the process of law. Another unusual aspect of Amos' teaching on judgement is that God judges Israel along with all the other nations of the world. God is no longer a national deity who protects and provides for his own people. God is the creator of the whole universe (4: 13); he is far greater than any temple or shrine set up to worship him.

Judgement and God

> **Further study**
> 'Thus said the Lord: for three transgressions of Judah, for four, I will not revoke it: because they have spurned the teaching of the Lord and have not observed His laws… I will send down fire upon Judah, and it shall devour the fortress of Jerusalem' (Amos 2: 4–5). However, contrast this with 9: 11–15 which looks at the restoration of the land, and consider to what extent this is part of Amos' original message.

There are four basic related symptoms of the nation's depravity:

Social teaching

1. **Oppression of the weak.** In numerous passages, the weak, poor and afflicted have all been exploited by the rich. Although the law permitted slavery (Ex 21: 2–11), the people who are being

Route H: Religious Ethics and contemporary issues. Compare Amos' ideas of social justice with those of Mill or Rawls (for example) and Route R (Judaism and contemporary issues).

Further reading

Look up 2: 6–8; 3: 9–10; 4: 1; 5: 11f; 6: 6; 8: 4–6 and read with a commentary such as *Amos* by James L Mays (SCM Press 1969).

'...using an *ephah* that is too small, and a shekel that is too big, tilting a dishonest scale and selling grain refuse as grain!' (8: 5). An *ephah* was a unit of dry measure and the shekel was a basic unit of weight. The merchants were corrupting their weights and measures. Amos contrasts city life with the old country life where money was hardly ever used.

'You who turn justice into wormwood and hurl righteousness to the ground!' (5: 7). Justice (Hebrew *mishpat*) and righteousness (Hebrew *tzedek*) are two key ideas paired together by Amos to refer to the heart of the Law and its right practice.

sold as slaves with 'just cause' – those who ought to be able to maintain their freedom. The implication is that the rich have corrupted the law courts in their favour to exploit the weak. The phrase 'a pair of sandals' (2: 6) might mean 'for land', in which case the needy are being dispossessed of their land and their means of livelihood through the greed and dishonesty of the rich and powerful. Furthermore, the rich not only take the land from the poor but charge them tax (5: 11).

2. **Corruption of the leaders.** By contrast the leaders live in luxury (3: 15; 6: 4–6) and acquire wealth by cheating and arrogance (6: 1).
3. **Corruption of the courts.** The corruption of the process of law is the sign that the Law of God has been abandoned in favour of human law, based not on the covenant but on greed.
4. **Corruption of universal justice.** One of the most memorable statements in Amos is 'But let justice well up like water, righteousness like an unfailing stream' (5: 24). Despite all external show of religious practice, the heart of the covenant lies in the universal application of justice. The great insight that Amos offers is that God is revealed in the weak and oppressed. In fact it is they who are sometimes described as the righteous.

Challenge and reversal of religion

Further reading

The Book of Amos by Susan Gillingham, Farmington Papers, number BS4 (January 1998).

Susan Gillingham highlights four areas in which Amos' message unusually reverses traditional religious expectation. The theme of reversal puts Amos' teaching on social justice in its theological framework – although the covenant is not referred to explicitly. By reversing the usual expectations of religion, Amos is able to turn the focus on what really matters.

1. **Curses**. It was traditional for a prophet to curse Israel's neighbours, but Amos curses Israel and Judah. He laments as if they are already dead (5: 1–2).
2. **Judgement**. It was usual to see great wealth as a sign of God's blessing, but it has become a sign of corruption, and therefore judgement, because the rich have failed to make the real sacrifices to God, only offering up ritual sacrifices which God rejects. They are not to 'Come to Bethel and transgress' (4: 4) but to 'seek God and live' (5: 6).
3. **Exodus**. The flight and exodus from Egypt to the promised land were seen by Jews as a sign of God's providential involvement in his people's salvation. But Amos uses it as a threat. In the past God had passed over the people; now he will not ('I will not pardon them again' 8: 2), but will judge them. The plagues that they escaped from will now be used to punish them.
4. **God as destroyer**. Not only does God create good (Gen 1: 31), he also destroys (Amos 5: 8–9).

'I sent against you pestilence in the manner of Egypt; I slew your young men with the sword...' (4: 10).

Messianic hope

There is no systematic view in Jewish scripture of the messiah, the messianic age or even the transformation of this world into the Age to Come. However, there is generally a hope that whatever sufferings Israel was going through, God would promise them some form of recompense. As we have seen in Amos, judgement on Israel would precede the 'messianic age', which would be a time when Israel could enjoy her independence, when the land would revive and the people live in justice (*mishpat*), in righteousness (*tzedek*) and in God's loving kindness (*hesed*). In some writings, the messianic age would be heralded by one specially chosen by God – perhaps a descendent of David (2 Sam 7: 13) or a judge or priest of outstanding moral qualities.

Route R: Judaism and contemporary issues. Read the chapter on Judaism, pages 161–163, and the debates about Zionism.

Isaiah 40–43

See page 53 for the question of authorship and date of Isaiah 40–55.

The theme of these chapters is salvation and reward after punishment. Deutero-Isaiah follows immediately in the tradition of the 8th- and 7th-century prophets that Israel's failure to worship God has resulted in punishment. This is an extraordinary claim compared to the general ancient middle-eastern view that the role of the nation's god was to protect and reward. But Isaiah's prophecy extends this: God's punishment of Israel is a sign that he is in control of history; any thought that their exile is due to the superiority of the foreign nations and their gods is completely false. Therefore, having saved Israel (that is, Israel and Judah) they are now entering a new period of history in which she is to be a 'light of nations' (42: 6). It is possible that 40: 6–7 is the call of the prophet. He is told to 'Proclaim' (40: 6a) and when he asks what to say, God tells him that he is to preach the weakness of people and (by contrast) the eternal word of God (40: 6b–7).

Punishment of the people. God's punishment of Israel has been excessive for her sins. Some suggest that the phrase 'double for all her sins' (40: 2) includes both the righteous and unrighteous who have suffered exile. These are the people whom Isaiah still refers to as the deaf and blind (Isaiah 42: 18–21).

The imagery of deaf and blind people is often referred to in Isaiah as a metaphor for Israel's sinful state (6: 9–10). Its reversal therefore comes to symbolise the new 'messianic' age: 'Then the eyes of the blind shall be opened…' (35: 5–6).

Servant. The servant is the instrument whereby God's rule on earth will be performed. The term is used 20 times in Isaiah 40–55 and in a variety of different ways. In 41: 8–14 Israel/Judah is God's servant and chosen one whom God protects with his 'victorious right hand', and who is witness to God's sovereignty (43: 10–12). However, most discussion is reserved for the servant songs. The first servant song (42: 1–4) appears to refer to Israel/Judah (after 41: 8). The servant or community is depicted in royal terms, having been anointed with God's spirit (42: 1a). The role of servant is to administer God's justice throughout the earth. Some find this difficult to equate with a people who are also 'blind' and 'deaf' and prefer to think of the servant as the faithful remnant. Furthermore, the servant here does not suffer as a means of atonement for others as he does in the fourth song (52: 13–53: 12). On the other hand, these are the people who have suffered in exile and are now forgiven by God, 'summoned…in My grace' (42: 6) to be 'a covenant people; a light of nations' (42: 6), and who have been used as a 'threshing board' for the nations (41: 15). Finally Isaiah suggests that his servant is the Persian king **Cyrus**. This extraordinary claim that a foreigner could be a 'chosen one' is part of Isaiah's wider vision of a God who is in absolute control of history (41: 4).

Further study

Compare 42: 1 with this psalm: 'I have made a covenant with My chosen one, I have sworn to My servant David: I will establish with your offspring forever' (Ps 89: 3–4). Isaiah appears to know the psalms very well. Does this parallel suggest he is giving the whole nation messianic status?

This continues the theme earlier in Isaiah of a future hope: 'Upon David's throne and kingdom, that it may be firmly established in justice and equity now and evermore' (11: 6).

Further study

It is Cyrus who is most clearly depicted as a messiah. God says, 'Cyrus, He is My shepherd, he shall fulfil My purposes!' and calls him his 'anointed one' (45: 1). Consider how likely it is that Isaiah considered Cyrus to be the chosen one/messiah.

Exodus, exile and restoration. If this part of Isaiah is read as a prophecy, then he presents more clearly an eschatological vision of

43: 14 is the first reference to Babylon since 39: 7 and one of the few factual details that place Isaiah 40–55 in the time of the exile.

For Ezekiel, the renewed Temple plays a vital role in the restoration of Israel.

Further study

Consider here the relationship between God and his servant. To what extent is the messianic age possible because of human action?

the land redeemed and the people restored to it. The people are exiled not only to Babylon (43: 14), but also to the four corners of the world (43: 4–8). Their return is a new exodus (43: 1–8); a sign of redemption and renewal of the covenant relationship. Interestingly, though Isaiah makes Zion (Jerusalem) the focus of the renewed land, he does not include the restoration of the Temple. The restored land flourished (41: 17–20) and the poor and needy are satisfied (41: 17).

God. God is twice described as 'redeemer' (41: 14b) because ultimately the 'messianic' age is the result of God's action in the world. A major theme of 40–42 is a law-court image that the 'nations' (non-Jews) should prove their case that their victories are the result of their gods. Isaiah knows that the Babylonians will suffer defeat and this will prove that their gods are useless and no more than human-created objects (41: 5–7 and 44: 9–20).

The nations. For the most part, the nations or foreign powers are depicted as being instruments in God's plan of salvation. But to what extent are they to be included in the new age? Is the transformation of the land and people of Israel part of a worldwide phenomenon? In later messianic thinking, this is an important consideration. 'The Presence of the Lord shall appear, and all flesh, as one, shall behold' (40: 5) supports a **universalist** interpretation, while being a 'light of nations' (42: 6) is no more than a command that the people should be a good example to the world.

Micah

Authorship and historical setting

Isaiah of Jerusalem is another way of referring to Proto-Isaiah, the author of Isaiah 1–39.

The opening of the book states that Amos was preaching from 750–692 BCE during the reigns of Jothan, Ahaz and Hezekiah.

Micah appears to have been a direct contemporary of Isaiah of Jerusalem, though neither seems to have acknowledged the other. Micah shares many of the social concerns of Amos and Isaiah, although his attack on the exploitation of the poor by the rich was not just due to the period of economic growth but also to fear of destruction by the Assyrians. It is possible that he had been preaching for some time. Most scholars consider that his reference in 1: 6 to the destruction of Samaria in 721 BCE formed the basis for his prediction for Jerusalem and the southern kingdom. This would correspond to Jeremiah's statement that Micah was writing only during the time of Hezekiah's reign (Jer 26: 18) when the king was preparing to rebel against the Assyrians, around 712–700 BCE.

Route H: Religious ethics and Route R: Judaism and contemporary issues. To what extent is Micah's teaching on judgement and social reform applicable in the world today?

Because Micah's predicted destruction of Jerusalem did not materialise, many argue that his predictions of judgement (Mic 1–3) were re-read in the light of 587 and the optimistic chapters of restoration (4–5) added post-exile. Certainly Jeremiah quoted Micah's prophecy (3: 12) as an example of the prophet's good effect on the monarch and used it for his own time.

Micah came from a rural town, Moresheth (1: 1) on the border of Judah and Samaria. He was probably a small landowner and a member of the *am ha eretz* – the ordinary people of the land. Some suggest that his keen awareness of justice – a key theme of his prophecy – meant that he was a local elder and judge. His message, though, is set in Jerusalem, and here he preached the contrast between the corrupt government and its officials, and those whom they had exploited. Chapters 6–7 broaden his attack on injustice to include all who fail to carry out the heart of the Law. This section is summarised: 'He has told you, O man, what is good, and what the Lord requires of you: only to do justice, and to love goodness, and to walk modestly with your God, then will your name achieve wisdom' (6: 8–9a). Ultimately Micah's message does not depend on its historical setting because, as John Marsh concludes, 'He was not, like his contemporary Isaiah, profoundly concerned with the theology of politics...his message is religious, not social; for he sees all life as a responsibility by man before God.'

John Marsh, *Amos and Micah* (SCM Press 1972) page 83.

Judgement. Chapters 1–3 outline the reasons why God will plough Zion 'like a field', leave Jerusalem as 'heaps of ruins' and the Temple 'a shrine in the woods' (3: 12). The officials of the government have coveted fields and seized inheritances (2: 2), and they have manipulated the judicial procedures to suit themselves (3: 1–4). Even the prophets have been paid to come up with the right answers (3: 5–8).

Route H: Religious Ethics and responsibility. Make sure you can compare and contrast Micah's social teaching with Amos.

Future hope. Chapters 4–5 work by reversing chapters 1–3 in favour of the remnant (4: 6–7). The remnant will be used for judgement of the nations (5: 7–9). In his vision of the future there is a universal hope that all nations will worship God and walk in his paths (4: 1–2). It will be a time of peace – 'they shall beat their swords into plowshares' (2: 4) – there will be no more war. The prophecy of 3: 9–12 is reversed. Finally, a renewed Jerusalem will enable God to reign through a restored member of the Davidic line (4: 8–5: 6).

The verses are repeated in Is 2: 2–4.

Further study

Consider to what extent Micah's universalism is the same as Isaiah 40–43.

Test yourself

1. Evaluate the importance of Jeremiah 7 and Job 18 for the study of reward and punishment in the Jewish scriptures.
2. To what extent does the book of Micah deal with the same social issues as the book of Amos?
3. 'Isaiah 40–43 is not concerned with messianic hope.' Discuss.
4. To what extent is it necessary to know about Jewish history to understand Daniel 12 properly?

Connections

Philosophy of Religion with Jewish Scriptures (Route B)

Jewish Scriptures and philosophical problems of evil and suffering. Consider to what extent the theology of Job corresponds to Augustine's free-will defence if Job makes no reference to the Fall. The same problem arises when considering Irenaeus, although the question of 'soul-making' is closer to Job's experience of God as his Redeemer. In answer to the biblical question 'why do the wicked prosper', look at contemporary interpretation of the Bible in the light of the holocaust (see pages 167–170 of the Judaism chapter).

See pages 70–72 of the *OCR AS Guide*. Remember to refer to your AS study of Job (pages 94–97 of the *OCR AS Guide*).

Authority of Jewish Scriptures. Consider the ways in which the Scriptures can be understood to be sacred texts by various Jewish traditions – Orthodox, Progressive, Conservative and Neo-Orthodox. Consider to what extent texts should be understood in their historical context; whether revelation is progressive/

See pages 170–173, plus pages 88–89 of the *OCR AS Guide*.

developmental; whether it is categorical or illustrative. Consider the levels of authority between Torah, Neviim and Ketuvim.

See pages 28–30 of the Philosophy of Religion chapter.

Use of symbol, analogy and myth. Consider the results of form criticism (*OCR AS Guide* pages 28–29). Should Genesis 1–11 be read as myth? Look at the poetic/metaphorical/analogical language of the prophets (e.g. basket of summer fruits, Isaiah and his sons, God's law court, judgement as 'ploughing' Israel). Advantages might include non-philosophical means of conveying the ineffable nature of God. Disadvantages might include problems of literalism and interpretation.

See the chapters on Philosophy of Religion in the *OCR AS Guide* and in this guide. Read also pages 98–106 of *The Original Story, God, Israel and the World* by John Barton and Julia Brown (DLT 2004).

Religious experience. Consider the relationship between revelation which is 'propositional' (God-given instruction) and religious experience which is 'existential' (human sense of the Divine but expressed in human terms). Consider how Adam and Eve 'saw' God (Gen 3). For example, is the suffering servant (Is 53) a collective experience of the exiles, anything similar to the Toronto blessing? Consider whether the sense of God's awesome holiness (*quodesh*) is the same as the sense of the numinous (Isaiah and Jeremiah) or whether Ezekiel 18's radical message to Israel about individual responsibility could be described in terms of 'conversion'.

Test yourself

1. 'The Jewish scriptures teach that human suffering is punishment from God.' Discuss.
2. 'The descriptions of God in Jewish scriptures are always symbolic.' Discuss.
3. To what extent are the Jewish scriptures the result of religious experience?

Religious Ethics with Jewish Scriptures (Route H)

Make sure you have re-read the texts studied for AS. See also pages 88–94 of the *OCR AS Guide*.

Duty and absolute systems of morality. Consider how the Torah is treated by different Jewish traditions – as absolute given by Orthodox Judaism to human-inspired historical document in Progressive Judaism. Compare and contrast Kant's duty ethics with the Torah's 613 mitzvoth: Kant's independence of human autonomy but a common view of reward and punishment (his 'Kingdom of Ends').

Read pages 79–81 of the *OCR AS Guide*, plus chapter 4 of *Ethics and the Old Testament* by John Barton (SCM 1998).

Free will and human responsibility. Consider the theme in the texts of why the wicked seem to prosper as an indication of freewill. Look at the texts in terms of hard and soft determinism: Ezekiel 18's teaching on individual and collective responsibility and Job's teaching on suffering, love and worship of God. Consider how humans behave when left to their own devices (for example, the torture of the Maccabees).

Further reading

Read pages 72–83 of *The Original Story*. This covers most of these issues very well.

Application of the specified texts to modern practical ethical issues. Consider the problems of environmental ethics in terms of *tikkun ha olam*, 'mending the world' of human, world or God relationships as expressed as covenant (especially the Noachide). In terms of issues of life and death, consider the intrinsic value of life and martyrdom in Daniel 7 and 2 Maccabees against suicide and euthanasia. Consider Micah and Amos' teaching on social justice, exploitation of the weak and God's justice (*mishpat*).

Consider the place of war and the eschatological hope for judgement peace (Micah). What kind of pacifism do these texts appear to be advocating?

Test yourself

1. 'The Jewish scriptures teach that the only reason for being good is for reward.' Discuss.
2. 'Ezekiel 18 and Kant have completely different views of duty.' Discuss.
3. To what extent does Micah teach that war is morally wrong?

Jewish Scriptures with Judaism (Route R)

Make sure you have re-read the texts studied for AS. Read pages 88–94 of the *OCR AS Guide*.

Use of scripture in Jewish worship. Consider the significance of reading Torah and Psalms in the synagogue and at home. For example look at the themes of suffering, redemption and hope in Pesach.

Read pages 162–167 of the *OCR AS Guide*.

Authority of Jewish scriptures. Consider the views of different groups (Orthodox, Progressive, Conservative, Neo-Orthodox) and the degree to which they incorporate contemporary views of science and philosophy when dealing with the Bible. Consider to what extent historical, archaeological and literary analysis of the texts has undermined or enhanced their authority.

Read pages 159–160 of the *OCR AS Guide* and pages 170–173 of this guide.

Theme of covenant for Jewish life and worship. Consider to what extent the Jewish scriptures present a developing view of the Covenant, from the legalism of Moses to the relational view of Jeremiah 31. Consider the individual-community tension, especially in terms of personal and collective sin as expressed in texts (Ezekiel and Jeremiah) and the festivals of Yom Tovim.

Read pages 89–94 of the *OCR AS Guide*.

Read pages 164–166 *OCR AS Guide*.

Theology of Job and post-Holocaust theology. Consider to what extent Job offers a satisfactory theodicy compared to the views of Rubenstein, Fackenheim, Berkovitz or Cohn-Sherbok.

See pages 57–58.

Look also at the question of suffering in the book of Jonah (pages 94–95 *OCR AS Guide*).

Texts and modern Jewish life. Consider the scriptural basis for and against Zionism with particular reference to messianic hope and the land. Evaluate whether dying as a martyr for Israel (Daniel 7 and 2 Maccabees 7) can be considered morally acceptable today. Consider also the significance of the prophets (Amos and Micah) on contemporary interpretations of *tsedeqah* (righteousness, charity, justice) in the community.

Test yourself

1. To what extent is Zionism based on the Jewish scriptures?
2. 'Jewish scriptures should be interpreted using knowledge of contemporary science and history.' Discuss.
3. 'The Jewish scriptures are not much help in post-Holocaust theology.' Discuss.

New Testament

You must continue to study whichever part you prepared for AS; *either* Early Church *or* Gospels.

You must make sure that you look up all the biblical passages referred to in this guide. Quotations here are taken from the RSV translation of the Bible.

Further reading

The question of dating and purpose of Galatians was covered at AS. See the *OCR AS Guide* pages 100–103.

Further reading

Paul's argument is often dense and very technical. You should use a good commentary such as *Epistle to the Galatians* by J. Dunn (Hendricksen 1995) or a shorter one such as G. N. Stanton in *The Oxford Bible Commentary* ed J. Barton and J. Muddiman (OUP 2001), see pages 1152–1165.

Early Church

Galatians 2–5

The key issue for Paul when writing Galatians was whether Gentile converts to Christianity also needed to become Jews living 'under the law'. In many passages in the Jewish scriptures, the prophets envisage a time when Gentiles would come to the Temple at the end of time and worship the God of Israel (Isaiah 2: 2–3, for example). However, a small group of 'Judaisers' had insisted that the Gentile converts should also abide by the laws of the Torah. Paul feels not only betrayed but also angry at the idea that Christianity should be reduced to certain entrance requirements such as circumcision and keeping to food laws, which are irrelevant compared to the crucial one: belief in Christ. Galatians 2–4 deals therefore with this issue, which Paul calls 'justification by faith' (the traditional phrase) or 'righteousness by faith'.

Commentary

Justification

Further study

E. P. Sanders has been influential in reinterpreting Martin Luther's 'justification by faith'. Luther's legalistic view of Paul posited that, whereas God forgave human sin through Christ's death, he did not remove human sin and guilt at an everyday level. Luther's conclusion was that a Christian is *simul justus et peccator* – 'at the same time righteous and a sinner'. Sanders concludes: 'But Luther's problems were not Paul's and we misunderstand him if we see him through Luther's eyes.' *Paul* (OUP 1991), page 49.

E. P. Sanders has made a good case for abandoning the old translation of the Greek word *dikaiosune* as 'justification' in favour of 'righteousness'. Righteousness contains the idea of being brought into right relationship with God, rather than a legal judgement, which justification implies.

Paul's complex argument was that righteousness by faith does not mean that Gentiles have to become Jews through circumcision. The Judaisers (or Jewish–Christians) argued that if Jesus is the Jewish messiah, then according to Genesis 17, those who wish to become part of the covenant must be circumcised. Paul's answer to this is a technical interpretation of the Abraham story from Genesis 12 and 15 – he carefully avoids Genesis 17. Paul combines this with Genesis 12: 3 as his second proof text to show the universal nature of God's covenant and righteousness.

Route T: Muhammad and Jesus. Consider the relationship between Abraham, Muhammad and Jesus. To what extent do Paul and the Qur'an consider Abraham to be the prototype for Christianity and Islam?

From these texts, Paul is able to make the simple conclusion 'so then, those who are men of faith are blessed with Abraham who had faith' (3: 8). Faith (or *pistis* in Greek) therefore becomes the *only* true mark of the Christian, not circumcision. But Paul does not rest his argument there. Having spoken of Abraham's blessing, he now considers its opposite, and this leads him to consider the law as a curse. The idea is picked up from Genesis 12: 3.

Law

Paul had already come to the conclusion in Galatians 2: 15–21 that if righteousness is achieved by keeping the law, Christ's death was for no purpose (2: 21). He then continues (3: 11) with his next proof text (from Deuteronomy 27: 26), which curses all those who do not keep *all* the commandments of the law. He quotes Habukkuk 2: 4, that faith is the only criterion for God's blessing of life. The 'curse' of the law is overturned by Christ's death. Abraham's blessing is now available to all (3: 13–14).

So is the law now redundant? Paul's answer is both yes and no (3: 17–4: 7). The law is described positively as something that can restrain people from sin (3: 23) and as a 'custodian' (3: 24–25) preparing people for the blessing promised by Abraham and fulfilled in Christ. In 4: 2–5 the law is a 'guardian' of 'children' (those young in faith) until they achieve maturity. Paul himself was very happy to act under the law (Deut 24: 10–12) by collecting money for the poor (2: 10). Some scholars have argued that Paul thought the law was the means of provoking sin as a 'curse' so that God's grace in Christ could be effective. Others reject this view, arguing that Paul considered the function of the law to be to condemn, whereas faith is to save.

Paul takes a very literal interpretation of Genesis 12 in 3: 15–16 because this suits his purpose. Earlier he interpreted offspring in the plural to mean Gentiles!

Further reading

This complex issue is discussed at length in E. P. Sanders *Paul, the Law, and the Jewish People* (Fortress Press, 1983) pages 65–70. This is not a book for beginners.

Second Adam

Despite the closeness of the themes in Galatians to Romans, Paul does not use 'Second Adam' imagery, but he does maintain the mystical idea that the Christians are united with God and one another through Christ's death and resurrection (3: 20). Being united with Christ means the transformation of the 'flesh' as the life of sin to the baptismal life, where having 'put on' Christ 'there is neither Jew or Greek; there is neither slave nor free; there is neither male or female; for you are all one in Christ Jesus' (3: 27–28).

Contrast this passage with Colossians 3: 16–24 and Ephesians 5: 21–6: 9.

Baptism

Baptism means living the life 'in Christ' and 'in the Spirit' (Gal 5). Paul draws a contrast between the freedom of living in the Spirit and the constraints of a life under the law. Baptism means receiving the blessing promised to Abraham (3: 29). In a sense, the whole of Galatians is about the baptismal life. Two passages indicate Paul's contrast of initiation by circumcision to the blessing of God and blessing by baptism:

In **5: 1–12** Paul reinforces his earlier point that the insistence of the Judaisers on circumcision for Gentiles means that in order to be 'righteoused' they must keep the *whole* law. This is not just an impossible task – it would be a life ceasing to experience Christ's love (5: 6). Neither circumcision nor non-circumcision mean anything in themselves. So why does Paul conclude that he is still persecuted for preaching circumcision (5: 11)? There is no clear answer to this, but perhaps Paul was preaching circumcision to Jewish converts and sending out a confusing message. His argument is not directed at Jewish converts but those who insist on the circumcision of Gentiles. In a moment of anger Paul suggests that if the Judaisers are so keen on circumcision, they should go all the way and castrate themselves (5: 12).

Love or *agape* in Greek is used very rarely outside the New Testament. It is used 75 times by Paul in his letters and refers to the sacrificial love of God shown in Christ.

Many translations are rather ambiguous. The RSV says: 'I wish those who unsettle you would mutilate themselves!' (5: 12). The actual meaning of this passage has caused a great deal of discussion.

In **6: 12–16** Paul reminds us that it is the symbolic insistence on circumcision that has provoked all his arguments so far. What matters is that Christ's crucifixion has enabled Paul to become 'a new creation' (3: 16) – this is the language of baptism, which he so clearly outlines in Romans 6: 1–11.

Redemption

In Galatians 4, Paul discusses redemption in terms of **two-age theology**: the present age and the coming age. Again he uses the story of Abraham's wives, allegorised so as to show that those who live under the law will never achieve salvation because the law represents the present evil age. However, those who believe in Christ have the vision of the age to come, and with it the blessing promised to Abraham.

The division into two ages is typical of apocalyptic Jewish writings, which considered that only a special revelation from God could look into the future. Apocalyptic writers often reinterpreted older stories in terms of allegories (stories with many hidden meanings) and Paul does just that.

In the allegory (4: 21–31), Paul explains that **Hagar**, Abraham's servant who bore Ishmael, represents the present age and the old covenant at Sinai, and the present earthly Jerusalem (4: 25). Paul makes the extraordinary claim that the Jews take their lineage from Hagar and Ishmael. As Hagar was a servant, so all her offspring (i.e. the Jews), and all those under the law, have been slaves.

2 Baruch 4 describes how God showed Adam, Abraham and Moses the vision of the heavenly Jerusalem. In Revelation 21: 1–2, John sees 'a new heaven and a new earth…new Jerusalem coming down from heaven'.

By implication **Sarah**, Abraham's wife who bore Isaac (4: 28), represents the true covenant of freedom and the heavenly Jerusalem. In some contemporary apocalyptic Jewish literature the heavenly Jerusalem already represented the age of redemption. Paul describes this as the Spirit-filled age (4: 29).

Spirit

Further reading

Read *The Theology of Paul's Letter to the Galatians* by James D. G. Dunn (CUP 1993) chapter 5.

Route J: Ethics and normative ethics. Paul draws up a list of vices (5: 19–21) and virtues (5: 22–23). Compare also to 1 Corinthians 13. To what extent is Paul a situationist or a virtue ethicist? Consider what he means by 'freedom'.

Galatians 5 and 6 especially illustrate Paul's own dependence on the life and example of Christ. The resurrected Jesus had enabled the promise of the Spirit to be released into the Christian communities. The promise of the coming age had now begun, and with it a freedom from the law and the positive new virtues (5: 23). Chapter 5 therefore draws a contrast between the life of the flesh and the law in the present age, and the life of the Spirit, freedom and the age to come. His attack is famously on those who 'bite and devour one another' (5: 15) – perhaps missionaries causing dissension, or those attacking Paul, or Jews who are infiltrating and destroying the Christian community. To 'walk by the Spirit' echoes the Bible's call to walk in God's law, but also to walk according to one's own baptismal experience of the Spirit.

Romans 2: 12–8: 39

Context

Authorship

Further reading

K. Barth *Epistle to the Romans* (OUP 1933), C. H. Dodd *The Epistle of Paul to the Romans* (Fontana, 1959), J. Fitzmyer in *The New Jerome Biblical Commentary* (Continuum 1990) and C. Hill in *The Oxford Bible Commentary* (OUP 2001).

There is very little dispute that Paul wrote Romans, with the exception of chapter 16, the authorship of which is debated. It is likely that he wrote Romans while on his final visit to Corinth before his visit to Jerusalem (15: 25). It is written to 'all God's beloved in Rome' (1: 7). Romans is generally regarded as the most mature of all Paul's writings. In terms of dating, as Paul's trip to Jerusalem was towards the end of his ministry (Acts 21) Romans was evidently written shortly after Galatians and 1 Corinthians in the mid 50s CE.

Historicity

Paul is writing to a well-established Christian community. If he was writing in the mid 50s then the shock of Claudius' expulsion of Jews in 49 CE (see Acts 18: 2), probably due to Jewish–Christian tensions, might explain some of Paul's concerns in his letter.

Purpose

He says he aims 'to impart to you some spiritual gift to strengthen you, that is that we might be mutually encouraged by each other's faith' (1: 11–12).

Further discussion

Read 11: 1 and 11: 11. Paul answers his own worry: 'Then what advantage has the Jew? Or what is the advantage of circumcision? Much in every way.' (3: 1–2). Discuss 3: 1–8 and compare this view with Galatians.

The purpose of Romans is the subject of much debate, and there is no one single satisfactory answer. Paul is not addressing a particular group of people on issues raised specifically in the community. Despite his stated aim, the complexity of his thought suggests that there are theological issues he wishes to address. Possible aims are:

- **Success of Gentile church.** The letter is an explanation as to why, due to the success of the Gentile church, God seems not to have acted righteously with the Jews. Paul is struggling to see Israel's place in this story of redemption ending in Christ, not the law. The theme of righteousness is basic in Romans.

- ✦ **Meeting at Jerusalem.** The letter is a rehearsal of his Jewish–Christian theology before meeting Peter and James in Jerusalem, although according to Galatians 2: 1–10 the Church in Jerusalem had already accepted the place of Gentiles in the Church.
- ✦ **Jewish–Christian tensions.** The letter addresses specific theological issues between Jews and Christians that might have been contributory factors to the Claudian expulsion.
- ✦ **Journey to Spain.** The letter reveals Paul's theological credentials so that the Roman church will back his proposed journey to Spain (15: 24) via Rome. It is written to show that Paul has a full and proper understanding of the Christian faith.

Some suggest that Paul gained knowledge of the situation from Priscilla and Aquila while in Corinth (Acts 18: 2) after the two had fled Rome – Paul mentions them specifically in 1 Corinthians 16: 9, and Romans 16: 3. 16: 7 suggests that there was friction between the different Christian house groups – but the letter is also aimed at the Jewish end of the Church and non-Christian Jews.

Commentary

Justification

Paul had begun to deal with the question of righteousness in his passionate self-defence in Galatians. The situation in Romans is less fraught and he is now able to expand on what it means to be 'righteoused by faith' much more extensively. Whereas Galatians had been concerned with the law and righteousness, Romans is concerned with the nature of faith and righteousness. In the first instance, God's righteousness is to be seen in his **judgement** or **anger** (they have the same meaning – see 2: 5–8) on Jew and Gentile as he puts a morally chaotic world to rights (3: 20). There is an essential equality between Jewish Christian and Gentile Christian because each is condemned: Jewish Christians because they have failed to keep the law, Gentile Christians because they have erroneously thought that if they are evil, God's grace will reward them (3: 8).

Further reading

Read again the notes above on justification in Galatians. Read also E. P. Sanders *Paul* chapter 7 for a very clear discussion.

Read 1: 18–32 where Paul describes how the natural order of society is turned upside down and conscience is rejected in favour of human passion.

This idea is developed in 6: 1–7: 25, beginning with 'Are we to sin so that grace may abound?' By no means!'

As in Galatians, Paul's key example from the Old Testament is Abraham – this time, however, to illustrate faith and righteousness. Paul's point is that Abraham's faith was righteoused by God *before* he was told to carry out circumcision (4: 10). In this way, circumcision (as a symbol of the law) is not a precondition of faith. Abraham is the model of the convert whom God creates anew, and he illustrates the common ground between Jew and Gentile Christian, being both a Gentile and the father of Judaism.

Abraham's body was 'dead' because he was old (4: 19). Deadness in Romans is a symbol of the life of sin. 'Life' is the renewed spiritual life that God gives.

The key term which Paul takes considerable pains to explain is given in 4: 3, and can be translated in various ways as 'reckoned' (RSV), 'credited' (NIV) or 'counted' (NEB). Paul has established a very important meaning of justification: those who are justified are those who are sinners, not those who earn it through good works. As Paul says, 'that is why it depends on faith in order that the promise may rest on grace and be guaranteed to all his descendents' (4: 16). Finally, justification is associated with God's gracious **act of redemption** – the theme of Romans 5–8.

In Judaism, Abraham is credited with righteousness because of his good works, but Paul gives it another meaning by quoting from Psalm 32: 1–2, where God forgives the sinful rather than counting their merits (4: 6–7).

Law

This is one of the most important ideas in Romans 1–8. The law is used in various ways to refer to the Torah and Judaism. Whatever the exact meaning that Paul had in mind, the contrast he wants to make is between the life under the old law and the life of grace made possible through Jesus' death and resurrection. Jews are condemned all the more because they have the law and fail to keep it.

The Torah here refers to the legal stipulations on ritual, moral and criminal affairs.

Further reading

Read chapter 9 of *Paul* by E. P. Sanders, or for more in-depth study see pages 29–43 of his *Paul, the Law and the Jewish People* (Fortress Press, 1983).

Paul's critics seem to be accusing him of terming the law as invalid (3: 31). Paul sees the law as a witness to God's righteousness. If law refers to the prophets, then they were witnesses to God's grace and judgement. However, what matters is faith, because just as Abraham's faith was 'reckoned' or rewarded with righteousness, so faith in Christ is rewarded with righteousness regardless of the law (4: 24).

Further discussion

To what extent is Paul antinomian (against the law)? How, for example, would you interpret 3: 21? Look at the question and answer in 3: 31.

Another implication Paul has to deal with is the idea that the law has caused sin (7: 7–25). In this complex passage, Paul argues that law was necessary because of human sin. Sin is the rebellious aspect of our nature, which cannot be restrained by mere willpower (7: 15–20). This is another kind of law, the 'law of sin'.

The Protestant Christian response of Luther focuses on the conclusion of the chapter that only Jesus Christ can save us 'from this body of death' (7: 24), which places the gospel above the law.

Second Adam

In 5: 10–21 Paul contrasts two types of humans represented by Adam and Christ. This is one of Paul's main uses of **typology**. The Adam of Genesis 2–3, who was disobedient to God, represents the rebellious nature of all human beings. Importantly, this rebellion marks the end of Paradise as a state of sinlessness and immortality. Adam's sin is punished in various ways including mortality and suffering. Jesus' life reverses the Fall: because of his obedience, innocent suffering and death, God removes Adam's punishment, and through his grace gives humans the possibility of immortality. The 'two Adam' typology is important for Paul's teaching on **atonement**: through baptism Christians have their sins removed.

Typology refers to the use of past examples of people or events as pointers to the future. For example, Paul uses the crossing of the Red Sea as a 'type' of baptism. Paul's use of typology assumes the significance and truth of the Old Testament.

See also 1 Corinthians 15: 45, where Paul makes the First Adam/Second Adam typology very clear in terms of the transformation from the old life/old Adam to new life in Christ – the new Adam.

Baptism

There is little doubt that baptism was essential in the early Church as the ritual that indicated a person's conversion to Christianity. Baptism means accepting the name of Jesus: in other words, accepting his lordship and protection (Romans 1: 5; 3: 21–36; 10: 13), but it doesn't guarantee against future sin (7: 13–20).

Further reading

See chapter 5 of *Pauline Christianity* by John Ziesler (OUP 1990).

The most important passage is **Romans 6**, where Paul describes the mystical union of the convert with the death and resurrection of Christ, so that he 'dies and rises' with Christ and experiences the fruits of the Second Adam's victory over sin. The person therefore becomes 'fully alive' (6: 11) to God, whereas in their old life they were 'dead to sin'.

Route P: Jewish Scriptures and religious experience. Compare the religious metaphor of living and dying with Ezekiel 18 and 36.

Paul's language works on three levels: the psychological, theological and metaphorical. Clearly, some thought that, given the abundance of God's grace through baptism, if they were actively to sin then God would bestow more grace. Paul opposes this very mechanical view of living the baptismal life.

Further study

Read 8: 1–9. How is Spirit being used? Contrast also the life under the law/flesh and in the Spirit/Jesus Christ. Compare to Galatians 5.

Spirit

In the Old Testament, the Spirit of God is often the way in which God's creative presence is described working in the world. It is responsible for the creation of the world (Gen 1: 2), is the inspiration of the prophets (Is 61: 1) and enables Israel to live at one with God (Ezek 37). The later prophets looked forward to a time when God's Spirit would be permanent and re-establish paradise, as the **messianic age** (Joel 2: 28). Paul teaches that it is the Spirit who at baptism brings a person into full union with Christ. Therefore, as the messianic age has begun, the Spirit is freely available to all those who have faith in Christ Jesus (Rom 5: 5, 8: 9). In Romans, the Spirit is holy and makes believers a holy people in Christ (1: 4, 5: 5), just as the Jews were a holy people through the Torah.

Route C: Philosophy of religion and religious experience. Consider Paul's views on what kind of religious experience being in the Spirit is. Compare to the Toronto Blessing.

See above for the contrast between life in the Spirit and life in the law. Note that following the discussion of the law in Romans 7, chapter 8 makes the contrast with life in the Spirit.

Read Romans 12–15 for a fuller description of the community or *ekklesia* living the life of the Spirit.

The Spirit of Christ (8: 9) gives the believer life free from sin (Romans 1) and brings him to peace (8: 6), righteousness (8: 10), and makes him their heir of Jesus' victory over death. (8: 17).

The image of **walking in the Spirit** (8: 4) recalls Galatians 5: 16–26 and highlights Paul's frequent contrast between Spirit and flesh. The contrast can be understood in various ways. Although Paul appears to be dualist in that he gives priority to the Spirit, he does not necessarily consider the 'lower' world of the flesh and material life to be inferior. The dualities contrast 'this age' versus the 'age to come', egoism versus love, law versus gospel and so on.

Augustine gave superiority of the spirit over the lust of the flesh. Read pages 119–120 of the *OCR AS Guide*.

> **Further study**
> Make a list of Paul's dualities contrasting spirit and flesh.

Redemption

As Paul argues in Romans 1, all have sinned, and all are judged and incur God's anger (3: 10–18). The heart of the gospel is that redemption is the process through which Jesus' life and death bring humanity back into right relationship with God. Although Paul rarely refers to the life of Jesus, he frequently alludes to Jesus' complete humanity, his suffering and solidarity with all people – but without himself falling into sin. As people share in his life (5: 17) they enjoy the first fruits (8: 23, 11: 6 and Num 15: 17–21) of his labour, namely God's blessing. Essential to redemption is the participation of the believer in Christ's death and resurrection through baptism (6: 1–5). The really complex aspect of Paul's theology is how the **cross** or Jesus' death can bring about atonement. His language is dependent on the Jewish Temple sacrificial process. The key Greek word often translated as **expiation** (3: 25) is *hilasterion*, meaning the 'mercy seat'.

> **Further reading**
> Chapter 4 of *Jesus and the Doctrine of the Atonement* by C. J. Den Heyer (SCM 1998) has a clear discussion of Paul's teaching on redemption.

> **Further discussion**
> The mercy seat was a gold covering over the Ark of the Covenant in the Holy of Holies. Only on the Day of Atonement could the High Priest offer a sin sacrifice that would be sufficient for God to wipe away sin for another year. There is much debate as to whether the term should be translated as expiation (meaning a sacrifice to remove sin) or propitiation (meaning a gift to please God). Consider why these should both be problematic.

In 3: 22–25 Paul describes Jesus' death as the ultimate sin offering. Jesus' death and resurrection are the signs that the punishment for sin and death has been conquered. Paul concludes the first part of Romans on the theme of 'hope unseen' (8: 24–25): the logical conclusion of faith in God's redemption and eternal life (6: 22). Whereas before he felt convicted/judged by the God of sin, now he is 'convinced' (8: 38–39) by God's love.

Read Romans 4: 24–25 and 8: 11. Note how Paul uses the language of the law court to describe how humans are acquitted ('reckoned') of their sins because of their faith in Christ and therefore 'justified'.

1 Corinthians 15

Context

Authorship

According to 1 Corinthians 1: 1, Paul and Sosthenes wrote the letter, although Paul took sole responsibility for it (16: 21). From the end of the 1st century CE, Clement accepted it as an authentic letter by Paul. Some scholars doubt whether Paul wrote passages such as 11: 2–6 and 14: 35–45. Noting sudden changes in subject matter and tone, some argue that it in fact comprises several letters, but most consider it to be one letter addressing a range of topics.

> **Further reading**
> *A Commentary on the First Epistle to the Corinthians* by C. K. Barrett (A&C Black 1971).

Date

According to 16: 8, Paul wrote the letter in Ephesus in spring or just before Pentecost. If Acts 18: 1–7 is right then Paul founded the church in Corinth in 50–51 CE. He was in Ephesus a couple of years later (Acts 19: 1–10), which means he probably wrote the letter between 52–53 CE.

Historicity

The historical context is important when looking at 1 Corinthians, especially chapter 15. Acts 18: 1–17 records Paul's visit to Corinth. The reference to the proconsul Gallio (Acts 18: 12) is confirmed by an inscription dated to 50–51 CE. More importantly, Acts 18 confirms that although the church's membership was comprised of many ordinary people, there were also several of wealth and intellectual standing such as the wealthy landowner Gaius (1 Corinthians 1: 14,

The rich refuse to share at the Lord's Supper (11: 17–34) and compete for power in the church (6: 1–8). Their teaching on sexual conduct is important (7: 1). Paul aims to correct such views.

see also Romans 16: 23) and the synagogue ruler Crispus (1: 14 and Acts 18: 8). This mix did not always work.

Purpose

Earlier Paul wrote: 'The body is not meant for immorality, but for the Lord, and the Lord for the body' (6: 13).

Route J: Religious ethics and ethical behaviour. 1 Corinthians provides a wide range of ethical teachings on the treatment of the body in terms of marriage (1 Corinthians 7) and sex (1 Corinthians 5).

1 Corinthians 15 stands apart from the main part of the letter and appears quite self-contained. Paul leaves the complex issue of the body/soul relationship to the end as a finale, and reinforces the various moral teachings that he has already covered. Paul's purpose is to show that having some kind of body is fundamental to Christian thought – even in the resurrected state. He has to explain to them that resurrection does not mean a disembodied state (a soul without a body) or an earthly 'resurrection' only of the mind. All this is covered in Chapter 15 by Paul's response to the Corinthians who say 'there is no resurrection of the dead' (15: 12).

Paul's own revelation of the risen Christ is very important in his theology. See Acts 9: 1–19, Galatians 1: 16 and Ephesians 3: 3.

1 Corinthians 15: 1–7 documents the earliest example of **creed** or *kerygma* in the New Testament. Paul reminds the Corinthians of his preaching that Jesus' death and burial were followed by his resurrection appearances, which were witnessed by the 12 apostles, 500 people and James. He even includes his own conversion experience some years later.

Commentary

Justification

Further reading

Life in the Face of Death by R. N. Longenecker (Eerdmans 1998). Gerd Ludemann *The Resurrection of Jesus* (SCM Press 1994) is more radical.

The *kerygma* (15: 1–7) should have made it plain that the resurrection of Christ is the basis for Christian faith (15: 7) because the promise of after-life is the indication of God's grace and reason for Jesus' death for our sins (15: 3) – if this were not the case, then the apostles who witnessed the resurrection of Christ would be liars, still living in a non-righteoused (non-justified) state of sin (15: 17).

Second Adam

Apocalyptic refers to 'revelation' of heavenly events in the future. Many apocalyptic writers divided history into two ages: the present age and the age to come.

Route T: Islam, sin, redemption, God as judge, eternal life. Note the close similarities between Islamic and Pauline apocalyptic views of the end. Consider the role of Jesus in Islam and note his subservient role in 15: 28.

Paul's reference to Adam and Christ (second Adam) fits neatly into his eschatology, particularly one strand referred to as **apocalyptic**. As seen in Romans 5: 10–21, the first Adam represents the present age of sin and death, while Christ represents the age to come, of life (15: 22). Paul sets out an eschatological programme: first Christ is raised as the 'first fruits' (a harvest metaphor for the first sign of the age to come), then at his **Parousia** all who believe in him will be raised (15: 23), and finally, when the Kingdom is fully established by God, all evil in the world will have been destroyed (15: 24–28).

Paul returns to the Adam typology (15: 47–49) having made the distinction between the physical body (like Adam created from dust, and therefore perishable and finite) and the spiritual body (the image 'of the man of heaven' 15: 49). The second Adam is not created from the dust but from heaven. So, just as humans were created like the first Adam, they now have the promise that in the resurrected state they will be created like the risen Christ.

See Mark 12: 25, where Jesus says people are 'like angels' in heaven.

Baptism

Route C: Philosophy of religion, life after death. Consider Paul's argument here with John Hick's defence in his 'replica theory' hypothesis. Read chapters 9–10 of *Philosophy of Religion* by Peter Cole (Hodder 1999).

In Romans, being baptised meant going through a mystical process of dying and rising in Christ. Here Paul points out their confused thinking. If it is only symbolic, why are some of them being baptised on behalf of those who have died unbaptised? If they believe this, then they must also believe in actual bodily resurrection.

The heart of the debate deals with the kind of body that a person will have in the resurrected state. The question is raised by the Corinth church (15: 35) and Paul is quick to dismiss any kind of literalism: the resurrected body is not the same as the present biological body. His language builds on the apocalyptic idea of the two ages and baptism. The argument concentrates on body (*soma* in Greek):

- There are many kinds of body distinguished by their 'glory' (15: 40–41).
- God gives each body its own kind of existence (15: 38).
- Some bodies can be transformed into other kinds of body – just as a seed becomes a plant (15: 37), so by analogy a person dies and is resurrected.
- So, there are two kinds of body (15: 44): the physical body (*psychikon soma*): a body that is animated by the soul or psyche; and the spiritual body (*pneumatikon soma*): a body animated by the spirit, presumably God's Spirit, as it is he who gives life.

By glory, Paul means the light produced by objects. Heavenly beings (stars and sun) produce more.

The final state of redemption is described in traditional apocalyptic terms – general resurrection of the dead and transformation of those alive and dead, the final trumpet followed by immortality. The term 'mystery' (15: 51) refers to a hidden truth. In keeping with apocalyptic tradition, Paul claims to have a revelation of the mystery: which is that Christ's death is a victory over death and therefore over sin and the law (15: 56).

Redemption

Route P: Jewish Scriptures with New Testament concepts. Compare ideas of resurrection as reward for the righteous, here and in 2 Maccabees 7.

4 Ephesians 1–4

Ephesians has been regarded differently by Protestant and Catholic Christians. For Roman Catholic commentators, the letter's value lies in the development of a concept of the one universal Church. Only recently has the letter become more popular among Protestant writers for its teaching on prayer and the moral life.

Further reading
P. Kobelski in *The New Jerome Biblical Commentary* (Geoffrey Chapman 1990) has a Roman Catholic interpretation. Also try J. D. G Dunn in *The Oxford Bible Commentary* (OUP 2001) and *Ephesians: A Shorter Commentary* by Ernest Best (T&T Clark 2003).

Context

The traditional view is that Paul wrote Ephesians, and the internal evidence seems to support this. The opening (1: 1) asserts that Paul wrote the letter to the 'saints who are faithful in Christ Jesus', and in 3: 1 Paul states that he is writing the letter while in prison. Ephesians 3: 1–13 especially develops some of Paul's more personal claims to preach specifically to the Gentiles. He refers to the **revelation** (3: 3): perhaps the Damascus experience (Acts 9) or a more general revelation (Galatians 1: 11–12) that authorised his special version of the gospel for Gentiles.

Authorship

Further discussion
Consider who the saints are to whom Paul compares himself in 3: 8. Is Paul claiming to be an apostle as in Galatians 1: 17?

However, the general consensus today is that Ephesians was written by a close companion of Paul, who, though well versed in his master's theology, wanted to develop certain aspects of it to new heights. The arguments for this are as follows:

- **Style.** The style is different from Philippians and Philemon. In contrast to authentic Pauline letters, the sentences are very long in the original Greek text. For example, 1: 3–14 is one sentence.
- **Closeness to Colossians.** There are many very close parallels to Paul's letter to the Colossians. This suggests that either one person wrote both letters at the same time to different

Ephesians' special emphasis on the universal Church marks a new development in Pauline thought. Dunn says: 'Its mood of elevated composure, sustained prayer and uninhibited confidence in God, its vision of the church, united, growing to maturity and lived have been uplifting and inspiring for countless individuals and communities over the centuries' (*The Oxford Bible Commentary*, page 1165).

recipients, or that the author of Ephesians has used Colossians as the basis for his more general letter.

Although Paul does sometimes boast of his achievements, there are some extravagant claims here. In particular, Paul is not just *a* prisoner of Jesus Christ (Philemon 1 and 9) but now *the* prisoner – the supreme example (4: 1). Compare Paul's 'boasting' in Ephesians to 1 Corinthians 14: 37–38 and 2 Corinthians 12: 1–13.

✦ **Second generation.** The author often refers back to the 'foundational' period of the growth of Christianity to the time of the 'apostles and prophets' (2: 20). He uses the metaphor of the building of the Church, which he now regards as being complete enough for God to dwell in (2: 21). Furthermore, the 'autobiography' of 3: 1–13 is better read as a **eulogy** to Paul.

✦ **Theology.** Scholars consider Ephesians to have a more reflective and developed theology than Colossians in terms of a cosmic Church (1: 22–23) and concepts of God's grace (2: 8–9), but with very little mention of the law which occupies much of Paul's own letters, and a realised rather than future eschatology (2: 5–8). There is no mention of the **Parousia** of Christ – the emphasis is on a community living in the presence of the Spirit and Christ's gifts *now*.

Further discussion

Is it morally deceitful of the author to write a letter pretending to be from Paul?

Date

If Ephesians is Paul's, then he probably wrote it during his imprisonment in Rome in the 60s CE. Alternatively, if written by someone quite close to Paul, it was likely to have been after his death, namely between 70–80 CE.

Historicity

The letter's historical accuracy also depends on its authorship. In the ancient world, **pseudepigraphal** writings (writings using someone else's name) were not uncommon. The historical value of Ephesians is that it reflects the development of Christian thought for second generation Christians at a time when Christianity was becoming more firmly established in Asia.

For example, it is unlikely that Jesus' disciple Matthew wrote the gospel that bears his name; the second part of Isaiah (40–66) is likely to have been written by a follower of the prophet sometime later

Purpose

Is Ephesians an actual letter or a theological essay? In most of the reliable ancient manuscripts, the reference to 'Ephesians' is missing in 1: 1. Therefore, unlike Paul's letters, it is not addressed to a specific community or people. Its purpose is much more general and it is thus not reasonable to see Ephesus as an example of a typical church community in Asia Minor. The author tends to talk in generalities rather than address specific issues, a characteristic of Paul's usual style. Some suggest that Ephesians was written as a 'covering letter' to be enclosed with Paul's letters as they were circulated round the new church communities, but there is no real evidence for this, and although many of Paul's ideas are found in Ephesians, it is strange that so little is made of the law and justification by faith. Two important features of the letter are:

Further study

Compare Ephesians with the letters to the Asia Minor churches in Revelation 2–3.

Gentiles and Jews. Ephesians 1–3 forms the first half of the letter, with a formal conclusion at 3: 20–21. Chapter 3 especially explains why God's **blessing** through Christ (1: 3–4), promised for eternity (3: 11), is for Gentiles as much as it is for Jews. Such inclusiveness is not in terms of Judaism but the unique revelation of God in Christ, which, as the author says, 'was not made known to the sons of men in other generations as it has now been revealed to his holy apostles and prophets by the Spirit' (3: 5). As in other Pauline letters, all things are to be brought to their **fullness** in Christ (1: 10), but for this author, this time has now been achieved due to Paul's own special revelation that 'this grace was given, to preach to the Gentiles the unsearchable riches of Christ' (3: 8). This is a bold

See also Galatians 2: 5–16; 3: 28.

claim, because until now this mystery remained hidden, not only to the Jews but even to the 'powers in the heavenly places' (3: 10). Therefore the Church is not a development from Judaism, but a new divinely ordered institution inclusive of all people with faith in Christ – Jew and Gentile.

The right functioning of the Church. The second part of Ephesians (4–6) follows the pattern of many of Paul's letters with a *paraenesis* or moral exhortation. So that this new insight of the Church might work, every member is to know their place in the social, moral and divine order. Only then will the truth of creation itself be established. The new order dominates the teaching of chapters 5–6: the family is presented as a microcosm of the Church in which husbands, wives, children and servants each know their place in relationship to each other but always in terms of acknowledging Christ as head of the Church (5: 23).

Head is an important metaphor in Ephesians and can refer to both 'source' of reality and 'authority'.

Commentary

Justification

There is no doctrine of justification by faith as presented in Romans and Galatians, but Ephesians continues the theme of the cosmic Christ in Colossians. Faith in Christ is rewarded by God's love and mercy in uniting the believer with Christ (2: 1–10).

> **Further reading**
>
> See *The Theology of Paul the Apostle* by James Dunn (Continuum 2003).

Law

Ephesians appears not to be as concerned as Galatians and Romans with the complex issue of the relationship between law and the gospel. Its primary interest is faith and salvation in Christ. What the author rejects is the law's discrimination against Gentiles because they happen not to be Jews: like the Pauline letters, Ephesians states that circumcision is no longer necessary for salvation, anymore than the law is in itself the means of grace (2: 8–9). The ambiguous phrase in this section is 'by abolishing in his flesh the law of commandments and ordinances' (2: 15). Although he appears to be rejecting the Torah, the author quotes the Ten Commandments with approval (6: 2) and develops his ethical commandments for the Church in 4–6, which are based on the Torah. Ephesians recognises that Gentile morality was driven by lower human desires (2: 1–3) but now *both* Jew and Gentile are to put on 'new clothes', namely 'new natures' (4: 22–24) driven by 'the spirit of your minds'. In this sense the internal law of Christ has replaced the external law.

Read Ephesians 2: 11–22 carefully with a commentary. This is an important passage.

> **Further discussion**
>
> Discuss whether Ephesians has a positive view of the law compared to what Paul says in Romans 7: 4, Galatians 3: 13.

Second Adam

Ephesians does not have an explicit Second Adam typology, although the author frequently develops the Pauline dualisms between the old and the new, the flesh and the spirit, which the death and resurrection of Christ have established. The author's jubilation at God's blessing given through Christ's resurrection (2: 20–23) is in every aspect of the letter. The author's prayer at the end of the first section (3: 14–21) is that all members of the Church will share in the same inner experience of love and faith that the 'saints' – the first generation of Christians – encountered.

These dualisms are also referred to as **antinomies**.

> **Further study**
>
> Compare 1: 10 and 1: 22–23. There appears to be some confusion here: does Christ unite all things or does he make things submit to him 'under his feet'?

Baptism

There is Pauline baptismal imagery throughout the letter. Just as in Romans 6 Paul spoke of dying and rising in Christ – the 'old man' of sin being resurrected to the life 'in Christ' – so Ephesians begins chapter 2: 'And you he made alive, when you were dead through trespasses and sins in which you once walked…' (2: 1). Baptism means allowing the Spirit to awaken the 'inner man' (3: 16) and to

The metaphor of planting is rare in the New Testament and stands parallel to the metaphor of regarding Christ and the saints as a building's foundation of faith.

> **Further discussion**
> What kind of love is implied here? Is it God's love as grace, or human love of God, that is the basis of salvation?

live a life 'rooted and grounded in love' (3: 17). Most importantly there is only one baptism (4: 5). The message of Ephesians 4 is for Christian **unity** – acknowledging one God and one Spirit. The church is growing to maturity and as such the time for squabbling is over (4: 13–16), to achieve 'fullness of Christ' (4: 13).

Redemption

Redemption can be interpreted to mean either a price paid for the release of a prisoner or general freeing from captivity (as in the Israelite's redemption from Egypt). Both meanings are possible here.

For the most part, redemption is not a future event but a present experience. However, in 4: 30 the author speaks of a future 'day of redemption' in his warning that without good moral conduct now they will forfeit God's love: they must 'put away all malice' (4: 31). Ephesians' message is otherwise quite Pauline: redemption is through Jesus' death, as 'redemption through his 'blood' (1: 7).

Spirit and the Church

The roles of the Spirit and the Church are closely linked, but Ephesians makes such close connection between God as Father, Christ as Son and the Holy Spirit that the theology has a strongly Trinitarian feel to it. The role of the Spirit is to 'seal' a person's faith – perhaps through baptism or more generally the Christian lifestyle – so as to provide access to God. The Spirit is a source of strength (3: 16) and controls worship (5: 19), leads prayers (6: 18) and 'grieves' when members of the Church live immorally (4: 25–32). The Spirit is the source of revelation (1: 17) that accepts Gentiles into the Church. The specific link between Spirit and Church is made through the link of body and Spirit (4: 4).

Ephesians differs from 1 Corinthians and Romans in that in 4: 7 it is Christ, not the Spirit, who gives grace. The Spirit's role appears to be reduced.

The body is used by Paul for **paraenetic** purposes (moral teaching) to encourage each member of the church to work according to the gift that has been given to them (4: 11–16). The metaphor allows him to address Christ as head of the Church.

> **Further discussion**
> Does Ephesians consider all members of the Church as equals?

The Church is presented as the **people of God**. The familiar building metaphor is used to describe Jesus in 2: 20 as the **cornerstone**. There is much dispute as to how this is to be understood. If Christ is the foundation stone, this implies that apostles and prophets are equally ranked. On the other hand, if the term is translated as 'capstone' then it implies that the building is not yet complete enough for the 'temple' of the Church to be the place where God's Spirit dwells.

Just as in late Judaism the 'saints' designated the people of God, here the saints are the new **household** (2: 19) built on the foundation of apostles and prophets.

A capstone is the centre stone in the middle of an arch that holds the other stones in place.

Test yourself

1. 'The most important idea in Romans is Paul's teaching on baptism.' Discuss.
2. Examine Paul's purpose in writing 1 Corinthians 15.
3. Discuss Paul's teaching on redemption in Galatians.
4. 'The theologies of Ephesians and Romans are completely different.' Discuss.

Gospels

Set texts: authorship and purpose

Matthew

> OCR's guidance to teachers states that 'for accessibility, the specified texts can be organised so that they are studied comparatively and in relation to the theological concepts outlined in the specification'. You must be able to discuss the set texts and *other relevant texts* according to the themes and concepts prescribed. The set texts for special study are Matthew 5–7, 13 and 25.

Authorship

If the solution to the synoptic problem is that Mark acted as a major source for Matthew, then Matthew must have been written between 70–100 CE. Internal evidence suggests that he was writing after the destruction of the Temple in 70 CE at a time of church-synagogue tension. There is some suggestion that this was particularly acute from 80–90 CE. The *Didache* (an early collection of church teaching and practice dated to 100 CE) appears to refer to Matthew quite frequently and Ignatius of Antioch (c. 35–107 CE) possibly quotes Matthew 3: 5 in one of his letters.

Further reading

For a thorough introduction to the gospel and modern scholarship read *Matthew – Evangelist and Teacher* by R. T. France (Wipf & Stock 2004).

Many scholars suggest **Antioch** as the place of writing because Paul witnesses the Jewish-Christian tensions characteristic of the gospel. Others argue for somewhere on the Palestine-Syrian border. As for who Matthew was: according to tradition, he was the tax collector who Jesus calls early in his ministry (Matthew 9: 9). In Mark's gospel he is referred to as Levi (Mark 2: 14).

Purpose

There is a general consensus that the gospel was written to alleviate the crisis in Matthew's community when his **Jewish-Christian** church was separating from the synagogue. Matthew's gospel appears to have the most intimate knowledge of Jewish theology and custom. His aim is to encourage his community and justify their gradual separation from mainstream Judaism. These are the bases of Matthew's theology:

Fulfilment of the Bible. Matthew often cites the Old Testament in order to show how Jesus is the fulfilment of Jewish expectation, such as in the birth stories (1: 23–24; 2: 22). Jesus is the Davidic Messiah, the Immanuel born to the young girl spoken of in Isaiah 7: 14, and in particular the new Moses who delivers a new law (in particular the Sermon on the Mount).

See page 54 of the chapter on Jewish Scriptures.

Language. His use of 'Kingdom of Heaven' is typical Jewish avoidance of referring directly to God. He often speaks of 'their/your' synagogues and scribes (4: 23, 7: 29, 10: 17, 13: 54), but he speaks positively of the Temple and what it represents (5: 23–24; 17: 24–27; 21: 23). A key term is **righteousness**, which Christians must thirst after to exceed the righteousness of the Pharisees.

J. A. Overman argues in *The Church and Community in Crisis* (Continuum 1996) that the claim to righteousness was characteristic of many sectarian Jewish groups in the 1st century CE (notably the Essenes and Pharisees). There is evidence that each group banned or expelled one another from their synagogues or communities. Read Matthew 18: 15–17.

The law. Matthew respects the Torah, lives in accordance with it, and sees his role as an interpreter of it as a Christian 'scribe'.

He quotes Jesus as saying that 'not an iota or dot shall pass from the law' (5: 18–19); and 24: 20 suggests they kept to the Sabbath laws. Whereas Mark 7: 1–23 rejects ritual laws, Matthew's version of this passage (15: 1–20) is less radical.

Mission to the world. Matthew develops his eschatology and notion of salvation to go further than Jesus' mission to 'the lost sheep of Israel' to include the Gentiles – those outside Israel. He prepares for this throughout the gospel, to his final command to 'make disciples of all nations' (28: 19).

Church/community. Matthew is the only gospel to use the Greek term *ekklesia* translated as 'church'. The organisation of his gospel into five discourses suggests that Matthew is interested in order and discipline for the new community. This means that when Jesus gives instructions to his disciples, Matthew redacts/interprets these to refer to his community.

10: 16–33 talks of discipleship in terms of suffering and reward, for the one 'who endures to the end will be saved' (10: 22). Peter is given prominence as the one who is given the keys of heaven (16: 19) with ability as an intermediary to forgive sins, just as the priests had done in the Temple.

Mark

The set texts for special study are Mark 1: 21–2: 12; 4 and 5.

Mark may well have been a travelling companion to Paul and later Barnabas, and may have visited Paul in Rome. As the earliest gospel, it was probably written before 70 CE and reflects a time of uncertainty and suffering, perhaps during the Neronian persecutions of 64 CE.

Authorship

See pages 108–109 of the *OCR AS Guide*. Read *The Gospel According to St Mark* by Morna Hooker (A&C Black 1991).

Purpose

If a Roman setting is accurate, then it may be possible to consider the characteristics of Mark's theology, although it is less easy to see how he has manipulated his sources compared to Matthew and Luke. Mark's theology has to be discerned largely through his **literary** construction and what form critics suggest the material had before Mark shaped it for his gospel. Key themes include:

Discipleship. Mark frequently presents the disciples in poor light: they need things explained to them (4: 13); Peter tries to dissuade Jesus from his path of suffering at Caesarea Philippi (8: 32–33); they are afraid in two storms (4: 35–41; 6: 45–52); and Jesus questions their understanding (8: 17–18). But Mark also sets out the virtues of discipleship: **humility** (10: 13–16); **detachment** from wealth and power (10: 17–31); **sacrifice** (3: 31–35), and **martyrdom** (8: 34) as also predicted for James and John (10: 35–45).

The James and John story about wanting to sit on Jesus' left and right side in the Kingdom of God gives an important insight into a lot of Mark's theology. Read pages 245–251 of *St Mark* by Hooker.

Conflict and suffering. After the first chapter, Mark collects **five conflict stories** (2: 1–3: 6), that illustrate Jesus' conflict with the Pharisees and scribes over authority and the law, the debate over Jesus' sanity with the scribes from Jerusalem (3: 20–30), and a series of Temple debates with the Sadducees, scribes and Pharisees (chapters 11–12). He is doubted by his family (3: 21), and by the inhabitants of his hometown (6: 1–6). Over a third of the gospel is dedicated to Jesus' passion and death.

New community. In the parable of the vineyard (12: 1–12), the vineyard (Israel) is given to new tenants (the Christian community) because Israel's leaders have consistently rejected God's covenant. Jesus is described as the cornerstone of a new building (perhaps the Temple). Jesus' death and resurrection establish the new community, which, like the Kingdom of God, develops and is revealed as a mystery (4: 27). Mark's community is inclusive of sinners (2: 16) and those previously excluded because of illness and impurity (1: 40–45; 5: 25–34), perhaps even some Gentiles (7: 24–30).

The parable of the seed growing secretly (4: 26–29) is only found in Mark and therefore might be a good indication of his own theology of secrecy.

Messianic secret. Wilhelm Wrede famously drew attention to Mark's secrecy theme as applied to the person of Jesus. He noted that Jesus often forbids evil spirits to speak and forbids those cured to say who he is. Wrede suggested that the secrecy motif was developed by the early Church to explain why Jesus never claimed to be divine during his lifetime. Alternatively, it is Mark's device to stress that Jesus is the **suffering servant**, whose sonship is revealed through suffering and resurrection.

Wilhelm Wrede, *The Messianic Secret* (James Clarke & Co 1971).

Even his response to the high priest's question 'Are you the Christ the Son of the Blessed?' is not a direct 'yes' (14: 61–62). He refers to himself as the 'Son of Man'.

The suffering servant of Isaiah 52–53 is influential on New Testament writers. See pages 53–55 on the Jewish Scriptures.

Luke

The set text is Luke 15.

Authorship

Luke is unique among the synoptic gospels because of his stated aims and readership in 1: 1–4, addressed to 'most excellent Theophilus'. A similar address occurs in Acts 1: 1–5, the clearest indication that Luke and Acts should be read as a two-volume whole. More importantly, however, there is much to indicate that the theology of both forms a coherent whole.

Further reading

You should read carefully the arguments about the purpose of Acts on pages 98–100 of the *OCR AS Guide*.

Most commentators agree on a time of composition between 70–90 CE. Eusebius (4th century CE) states that Luke wrote in Antioch, but there is no conclusive evidence for any particular place.

The first reliable statement about Luke is in the Muratorian Canon (late 2nd century), which says that he was a companion of Paul and wrote under his own name. Paul refers to Luke as his 'beloved physician' (Colossians 4: 14), and Kümmel argues he was not a Jew, because Paul excludes him from his list of fellow workers 'of the circumcision' (i.e. Jews). Some argue for Luke's knowledge of Paul's theology in his gospel and in the speeches in Acts, and argue that the 'we' sections in Acts refer to Paul and Luke. None of this is convincing. But Luke's knowledge of Jewish theology and the construction of Luke 1–2 based on Old Testament texts suggests a very knowledgeable Gentile, if that is the case.

Some have tried to date Luke-Acts before the mid 60s CE when Paul was executed, because Acts itself appears to be unaware of Paul's fate. However, for Luke 1: 1 to be possible, Mark and other sources need to be in existence. Luke 21: 21–24 appears to indicate a more detailed knowledge of the destruction of Jerusalem than Mark 13: 14–16.

Kümmel concludes: 'The only thing that can be said with certainty about the author, on the basis of Luke, is that he was a Gentile Christian' *Introduction to the New Testament* (SCM Press 1975).

Luke's stated purpose is to 'compile a narrative' of everything that has happened 'from the beginning' as an 'orderly account'. Luke acknowledges that he is using several sources but at the same time wishes to impose some kind of order on them. Source criticism suggests that when he uses Mark he does so with few alterations, but he often chooses parallel accounts that he considers to be closer to the overall meaning of the Christian story. These theological purposes include:

Purpose

This echoes Papias' description of Mark's account as 'not in order'. It is not clear what 'order' means, but if Luke is a historian writing to a well-to-do Gentile then it is possible that he has found Mark's arrangement unsatisfactory and limited.

Universalism. The gospel begins in Galilee and ends in Jerusalem. Acts begins in Jerusalem and ends in Rome, with the promise that the gospel will be preached to the 'ends of the earth' (Acts 1: 8) and to 'all nations' (Luke 24: 47). The gospel lays down the universal and inclusive message of salvation that is preached by the apostles.

Further reading

Read *The Theology of the Gospel of Luke* by Joel Green (CUP 1995) for a clear and comprehensive introduction to Luke.

Spirit. The sporadic outpouring of the Spirit in the Old Testament is now seen to be constantly present in the person of Jesus, first in his birth (1: 35) and then at his baptism 'in bodily form' (3: 22). The promise of the Holy Spirit is made in 12: 12 and 24: 49, and finally poured out on the Church at Pentecost in Acts 2: 1–4.

Salvation and the marginalised. Luke is the only synoptic gospel to use the noun 'salvation' and to refer to God (1: 47) and Jesus (2: 11) as 'saviour'. Luke is conscious that his history is **salvation history**. More than the other gospels he stresses Jesus' mission to the marginalised. Jesus' manifesto at Capernaum (4: 16–21) is a quotation from Isaiah 61: 1–2, which talks of liberation of the oppressed and the captives. Luke emphasises the place of women (8: 1–3, 10: 38–42), Gentiles, the poor – both literal and spiritual (4: 18, 6: 20, 7: 22), tax collectors (17: 18–14) and the Samaritans.

Salvation history (also referred to in the German as *Heilsgeschichte*) is achieved by Luke's very distinctive use of the Old Testament. Just as the Old Testament tells the story of Israel's relationship with God, Luke consciously links Jesus' family back to Adam – the father of all humans.

Samaritans were considered to be 'sinners' by the Jews and dangerous in religious terms.

Delay of the Parousia and the Church. Hans Conzelmann developed the most influential and controversial explanation of Luke's eschatology. He argued that as Jesus' second coming (the Parousia) had been delayed, Luke developed the Jewish two-age theology (see below) into a three-tier system: the old age of Israel, the middle time of Jesus and the indefinite time of the Church (as told in Acts), which fulfilled the ancient prophecies (notably Joel) of the age to come. Conzelmann argued that according to Luke 4: 13 and 22: 3, the middle time was free from the activities of Satan and that any of Jesus' future eschatological sayings were leftovers from an earlier tradition. The argument does underline the theological reasons for the establishment of the Church.

Further reading

The Theology of St Luke, Hans Conzelmann (Fortress 1982).

Concepts

Kingdom of God

The idea of the Kingdom of God was central to Jesus' ministry, but it is probably the most difficult to interpret. The first difficulty is relating it to contemporary Jewish ideas, and the second difficulty is disentangling Jesus' own words from the form that the Church or the evangelists gave them according to their own situation.

> **Further reading**
>
> Read Graham Stanton in chapter 4 of *Cambridge Companion to Jesus* ed. Markus Bockmuehl (CUP 2001), on the Kingdom of God, parables, miracles and sinners. Use a commentary to look up all the words contained in the summary of Jesus' ministry at Mark 1: 15

Jewish two-age theology

In the Old Testament, the phrase 'Kingdom of God' does not appear, although there is frequent reference to God's 'rule' or 'reign' as king of the world. As God's realm had been frequently opposed by other nations, by the 1st century CE a complex set of ideas had evolved whereby this age would give way to an 'age to come' when God would rule the whole world and his glory would be seen by all (Is 45: 23 and Dan 7: 13f). Some believed that there would be a messianic age preceding this final age, when the messiah would establish the Torah and cleanse the Temple. Others, such as the Essenes, imagined a more apocalyptic time when God would fight a cosmic battle with the earthly forces of evil, so that the world, cleansed of wickedness, could then enter the final age.

Imminent/future eschatology

> **Further reading**
>
> *Quest of the Historical Jesus*, Albert Schweitzer (SCM Press 1954).

Eschatology means 'discussion of the end time'. Scholars, such as Johannes Weiss, Albert Schweitzer and W. G. Kümmel have considered that Jesus held this 'pure' form of eschatology and argue that this core of his teaching was subsequently toned down and adapted by later Christian writers when the end did not arrive. The central saying of Jesus in Mark 1: 15 preserves the notion that the Kingdom was 'at hand' and that God's perfect reign was soon to break into the world. Therefore, the missionary activity of the Church (Matthew 10: 7 and Luke 10: 9) was to heal the sick and cast out demons in preparation. This view is reinforced by Jesus' special use of the term **Son of Man**, a term adapted from Daniel 7: 13 to refer to his future glorious role as God's judge. However, many scholars consider that as only very few Son of Man sayings deal with the future, these have probably been adapted by the early Church to reinforce Jesus' role as divine future judge – a role most unlikely to have been considered by Jesus himself. The bulk of Jesus' Son of Man sayings stressed his intimate relationship with God and role as one who was to suffer for others.

> **Further reading**
>
> See for example the arguments of Norman Perrin in *Rediscovering the Teaching of Jesus* (SCM Press 1967), Geza Vermes in *Jesus the Jew* (SCM Press 2001) or *The Religion of Jesus the Jew* (SCM Press 1993).

Realised eschatology

Dodd set out his argument in his *The Apostolic Teaching and its Developments* (Hodder and Stoughton 1936) and *The Parables of the Kingdom* (Fontana 1961).

'In other words, the "eschatological" Kingdom of God is proclaimed as a present fact, which men must recognise, whether by their actions they accept or reject it.' Dodd, *Parables of the Kingdom*.

C. H. Dodd argued that the best way of thinking of Jesus' eschatology is in personal or 'realised' terms. Dodd argues that at an early stage some Christians had adopted an apocalyptic understanding of Jesus' teaching that had caused considerable misunderstanding in the early churches. A realised eschatology means that Jesus' teaching emphasised the desire of each person to make God's eternal reign a reality on earth, just as the Lord's Prayer says, 'Thy will be done, on earth as it is in heaven' (Matt 6: 10). Jesus' growth parables in particular describe the mysterious process by which a person comes to encounter God's rule in their hearts. This is what made Jesus' teaching unusual. But Dodd's arguments reveal more about 20th-century existential philosophy and underestimate Jesus as a 1st-century Jewish preacher who had a strong sense of God's future intervention in Israel's history.

> **Further study**
>
> Read the parable of the seed growing secretly, Mark 4: 26–29, and give it a realised interpretation.

A middle-path eschatology (favoured by Joachim Jeremias and Norman Perrin, for example) states that Jesus did not attempt to give an apocalyptic prediction of when the Kingdom would arrive, but nevertheless taught that it would arrive as a **process**. He felt that those around him were now entering into a new phase of history and they were living on the threshold between the old and the new. The new order was already 'breaking into' the present and affecting the world. As Jesus performed many exorcisms and healing miracles, it is reasonable to suppose that all these helped to illustrate the beginnings of a new order.

Inaugurated/proleptic eschatology

The Lord's Prayer illustrates the proleptic 'now and yet to come': 'Thy Kingdom come, thy will be done.'

Take, for example, the following words of Jesus, generally regarded by many scholars as an authentic saying: 'But if it is by the finger of God that I cast out demons, then the Kingdom of God has come upon you' (Luke 11: 20).

Another saying that Perrin and others consider to be an authentic saying of Jesus is: 'The Kingdom of God is not coming with signs to be observed; nor will they say, "Lo, here it is!" or "There!" for behold, the Kingdom of God is in the midst of you' (Luke 17: 20–21). The purpose of the saying is to end speculation about the exact moment when the Kingdom would arrive, and it stresses that the Kingdom is already a present reality in the community of believers.

Further discussion

Discuss whether the inaugurated view deals adequately with important futuristic sayings such as: 'Truly, I say to you, there are some of you standing here who will not taste before they see the Kingdom of God come with power' (Mark 9: 1).

Judgement

The word for judgement in Greek is 'crisis'. In eschatological and apocalyptic literature, it describes the moment when the present age gives way to the age to come, when God will judge the world according to its goodness. In the late Old Testament/inter-testament Jewish tradition, after a period of political upheaval and cosmic disasters sometimes referred to as the **birth pangs**, God or his messiah appears to judge the nations of the world and welcome the elect or the 'righteous' into the Kingdom. Mark 13, sometimes referred to as the **little apocalypse**, is a good example of the programme of events describing the birth pangs, the arrival of the anti-Christ, 'the desolating sacrilege' (Mk 13: 14), and finally the Son of Man, who judges the world and chooses the elect (Mk 13: 24–27). Many assert that Mark has adapted a Jewish apocalyptic passage, so it is unclear just how much Jesus himself thought in terms of an eschatological programme, but the ending of Mark 13 reveals Mark's (or possibly Jesus') own ambivalence as to when these things would happen. Judgement, though, plays an important part in the synoptic tradition, and is linked closely with **repentance**. John the Baptist's apocalyptic imagery of the axe cutting down trees (Matt 3: 10) and sifting the wheat from the chaff (Matt 3: 12) warns people that they need a radical moral and spiritual change of lifestyle. Jesus' message follows directly on from John's (Mk 1: 15) – although to what extent Jesus taught an imminent judgement is an area of much dispute.

Mark 13

Route T: Islam and sin, redemption, God as judge. Compare and contrast eschatological and apocalyptic language, especially with *akhirah* and the earlier surahs of the Qur'an. See pages 150–151.

This depiction of judgement is part of the Q tradition. Read also Luke 3: 7–17.

An analysis of this chapter reveals Matthew's own theology in his redaction of Mark 13 – only then can parables of judgement in Matthew 25 be understood from the Matthean perspective. Matthew writes of Jesus' return as the Son of Man, but states it has been **delayed**. Matthew has 'calmed the apocalyptic enthusiasm' probably because the destruction of Jerusalem in 70 CE had not brought the end of the present age. He says the birth pangs *must* happen (24: 6) but it is still too early to expect the end. They must endure life by maintaining high standards. Endurance modifies Mark's 'alertness' and is the theme of Matthew 25. In typical

Matthew 24

David Hill, *The Gospel of Matthew*, page 317.

Matthew's themes of a master's journey and his delay convey the *Sitz im Leben* of Matthew's congregation and his warning that, as with the disgraceful behaviour of the servant left alone to his own devices, they too will be punished if they fail to be prepared for judgement day.

Matthew fashion, he teaches that the end will only occur when all things have been fulfilled – so they are to remain calm and practise the faith. He dispels the fear that the Parousia has already come but is hidden (24: 23–28). The discourse ends with the **Parable of the Householder** (24: 45–51), which acts as a introduction to the parables of 25.

Judge not

Route J: Religious ethics and reasons for ethical behaviour. Consider the place of eschatology in the discussion of nuclear war. Read pages 128–131 in *Issues of Life and Death* by Michael Wilcockson (Hodder 1999).

In the light of Matthew's delayed eschatology, **Matthew 7** shows how he deals with the daily issue of judgement. This part of the Sermon on the Mount begins: 'Judge not that you be not judged' (7: 1). The language is thoroughly eschatological; those who judge others will be judged by God in the same 'measure' (7: 2) now and at judgement day. The implication is that divine judgement will be far greater because God sees what we cannot. The theme of hypocrisy is important in Matthew and it relates to his demand for moral perfection (5: 48) at the heart of the Sermon on the Mount.

Salvation

Available to all?

The Jewish tradition on this was far from clear and appears to have divided the early Church: would non-Jews be saved? More problematic within Judaism was whether those considered 'sinners' were beyond redemption. There seems little doubt that from the perspective of the gospel writers, the chief characteristic of Jesus' mission was to offer salvation to the sinners and also the **amme ha eretz**, the ordinary 'people of the land'. For instance:

For example, in Paul's letters to the Galatians and Romans, a major issue was whether Gentiles had to adopt Jewish laws in order to become Christian. See pages 68–73. In the Old Testament books such as Jonah, a 'universalist' or inclusivist approach is adopted, but others such as Ezra and Nehemiah take a more hard-line view.

The opening of Mark (1: 21–2: 12) is a series of healings and exorcisms in which all the patients are ordinary people or outcasts. Mark's comments such as 'the people came to him from every quarter' (1: 45) and the comments of the Pharisees and scribes, 'why does this man eat with tax collectors and sinners?' (2: 16) are answered by Jesus: 'I came not to call the righteous but sinners'.

Some argue that Jesus' call for sinners to repent was so shocking because they were believed to be barred from salvation. Sanders, on the other hand, suggests that it was precisely because Jesus *did not* actually demand repentance that the religious leaders wanted to get rid of him. This is problematic, however, because repentance is fundamental to Jesus' message as a whole – certainly the early Church equated baptism with repentance. The conflict may have been because Jesus was offering repentance outside the official circles by offering the usual sacrifices (Mark 2: 7).

Further reading

Jesus and Judaism by E. P. Sanders, pages 200–208.

Did Jesus teach that there should be a mission to the Gentiles? So much depends on the interpretation of his eschatology. In the Q tradition of Matthew 8: 11 and Luke 13: 28, Jesus appears to hold the traditional Jewish view that in the Kingdom to come, Abraham and the patriarchs would reside and welcome in people from 'north and south, and sit at the table of the Kingdom of God' (Luke 13: 29). In the much-discussed passage concerning the 'sign of Jonah', Jesus compares this generation unfavourably with the repentance of the (Gentile) Ninevites. If Jesus saw himself like Jonah preaching to the Gentiles, then his message of salvation was certainly controversial.

However, consider how Matthew 15: 24 is to be interpreted: 'I came rather for the lost sheep of Israel'. Was Jesus' *primary* concern for the Jewish sinners and not Gentiles?

What is more certain is that, with the delay of the Parousia, Matthew envisaged a time after the resurrection of universal mission. Luke, on the other hand, prepares the way for a Gentile mission that sees its full-blown activity in Acts. This may well explain the **Mission of the 70** (Luke 10: 1–12), which is a parallel of the mission of the 12 to Israel. The shocking nature of even considering non-Jews as 'neighbours' who can enter the Kingdom is illustrated by Jesus' parable of the Good Samaritan (Luke 10: 25–37), which only Luke recounts.

Jesus' final words at the resurrection are: 'Go therefore and make disciples of all nations' (Matthew 28: 19).

The 70, according to Genesis 10, represent all the nations of the world, and the harvest that the 70 are to collect (10: 2) is the eschatological image of the coming of the Kingdom.

Luke 15 therefore has to be read on two levels: Jesus' own teaching on sinners and Luke's wider view of mission to non-Jews outside Israel.

Luke uses the term salvation more than any other gospel.

The new kingdom

How different will the Kingdom of God be from the present age? This question depends on the kind of eschatology Jesus had in mind. For those who consider Jesus' idea of the Kingdom breaking into the present, God's reign is already transforming social and spiritual relationships, typically in his **reversal theology** (the first will be last) and what Sanders has called his **restoration theology**: the concrete establishment of a renewed Israel.

See *Jesus and Judaism*, page 156.

Sanders' argument is that Jesus' teaching on the Kingdom was not radically different from contemporary Jewish hope for a restoration of Israel. At the heart of his theology, Jesus envisaged a cleansed Temple and a leadership of lay people (not priests and special holy people, because holiness would be possible for all). It is more than likely that it was Jesus who called Simon *kephas* ('rock' in Aramaic, Peter in Greek) to be the leader of the new community.

This is an idea especially important in Matthew, which is the only gospel to use the term 'church' or *ekklesia* as a contrast to synagogue.

However, there are some traditions in the New Testament that suggest that the final Kingdom will not be on this earth: see 1 Thessalonians 4: 16–17).

Further discussion

This is very similar to Jesus' words in Mark 9: 1. Read also Revelation 21: 1–8. What kind of final Kingdom do you think Jesus had in mind?

Further reading

Introducing The Gospels and Acts by D. Wenham and S. Walton.

Law

The idea of law or Torah in the 1st century CE was wide ranging. At its most fundamental, it referred to the covenant relationship between God and Israel through which the people could become a 'holy nation'. A positive version of the **Golden Rule** forms a summary of the law in the Sermon on the Mount (7: 12).

Although the heart of the law was summarised in the Ten Commandments, a number of stories in the first century recount how the rabbis were challenged to summarise the essence of the law. Rabbi Hillel was recorded to have said: 'Do not do to your fellow what is hateful to yourself – that is the whole Torah; the rest is merely commentary. Go away and study.'

- ✦ **Written and Oral Torah.** In the first century CE, the idea of the living Torah had developed to suggest that Moses had not only been given the Written Torah (in the first five books of the Bible), but also an Oral Torah or **halakhah**, which would slowly emerge from the teachings of the prophets and teachers. The Oral law allowed the Torah to be applied in new circumstances, to develop a dynamic covenant relationship.
- ✦ **Ethics and ritual.** Torah does not distinguish between what today would be called ethics and religious rituals (purity, food, worship and so on), although Aquinas considered that Jesus maintained the ethical teaching of the Torah and abandoned its teaching on rituals. This is most unlikely.

It is not clear exactly what Jesus taught concerning the law. A glimpse at the furious debates in Paul's letter to the Galatians suggests that some considered Jesus' interpretation of the law – although not controversial – as having laid the foundations for much more radical developments later on. Mark records Jesus

Read Mark 1: 40–44 and see Leviticus 14: 2–32.

See Deuteronomy 24: 1–4, Mark 10: 1–12 (who takes the tough line) and Matthew 5: 31–32 (the so-called 'Matthean exception').

Route J: Religious ethics and basic principles. Consider the present Roman Catholic debate about law in *Veritatis Splendor* (Catholic Truth Society, 1993).

sending the cured leper to the priest in accordance with the law, and Jesus taught that the law for divorce should either be abolished or permitted only on grounds of unfaithfulness. On the other hand, ritual laws of hand washing and food appear to have been less binding, perhaps because of the debate as to what was considered to be halakhah, especially for Mark as he presents them in 7: 1–23 because of his more gentile situation.

Parables, miracles, sayings, teachings

Parables

Further reading

Read chapter 12 of *Studying the Synoptic Gospels* by E. P. Sanders and Margaret Davies (SCM Press 1989), and pages 100–104 of *Introducing the Gospel and Acts* by David Wenham and Steve Walton.

An allegory is a story where each element has a symbolic meaning.

John Drury, *The Parables in the Gospels* (SPCK 1985).

The Parables of Jesus by Joachim Jeremias (SCM 2003), page 21.

Many regard Jesus' use of parables to be the most characteristic aspect of his teaching and probably the closest we get to his *ipsissima verba*. Jesus used an ancient Jewish form going back to the Old Testament, the **mashal** (in Hebrew). The mashal could take the form of a story, riddle, proverb, similitude (comparison), short pithy saying or allegory. **Adolf Jülicher** (1899) was one of the first to argue that Jesus' parables should not be interpreted as allegories but be stripped of the allegorical meaning that the early church attached to them, to get back to Jesus' original meaning. **John Drury** and others have argued that Jesus, like the prophets, often used exaggerated, unusual ideas and allegory. Jesus frequently used the parables to speak indirectly of the illusive nature of the Kingdom of God. **Joachim Jeremias** argues that the parables are not simple analogies but 'weapons of controversy'.

Mark 4

Mark quotes Jesus as saying that to the insiders the mystery of the Kingdom of God has been given but to outsiders 'everything is in parables' (4: 11). Jeremias argues that Mark has wrongly taken 'parables' here to mean *the* parables, whereas it simply means 'riddle'. Drury thinks this is wrong: Mark rightly understood Jesus to mean that he spoke in riddles and allegories as part of his challenging method.

It is found in all three Synoptic gospels and in the Gospel of Thomas, but not in John. Matthew 13: 3–8, Luke 8: 5–8 and Thomas 9.

The Sower (4: 1–8). Mark alone suggests that understanding this parable is the key to understanding *all* the parables (4: 13). Jeremias argues that as it stands this is not an allegory: Jesus uses an example from the everyday life of farming with the standard eschatological image of harvest time to illustrate that, though people will respond to teaching about the Kingdom in various ways, it will in the end flourish. But did Jesus intend the parable to be an allegory? Much depends on whether sowing before ploughing is realistic. Drury thinks not. If so, Jesus' parable is intended to be a riddle at each stage – this is a field of extremes, as it moves from no production to 100 per cent return. Drury suggests that Mark has redacted the parable to stress the oddness and mystery of the Kingdom. Therefore the allegorical explanation (4: 13–20) is the product of Mark or the early Church – although if Jesus intended the parable as an allegory then this explanation may go back to his *style* of teaching. Matthew (13: 19–23) also uses Mark's explanation but adapts the reason for the allegory. It is an allegory because Jesus is the key to its meaning, the revelation of the age to come.

Note the Marcan language: 'listen–behold–immediately–withered away–growing up–brought forth–hear'. Thomas' version lacks all these words.

'Many prophets and saints, I tell you, desired to see what you now see, yet never saw it, to hear what you hear yet never heard it' (Matthew 13: 16–17).

Mustard Seed (4: 30–32). Matthew exaggerates further the size of the plant and calls it a 'tree'. The mysterious growth of the seed can refer either to the development of preaching in preparation for the Kingdom or its gradual manifestation. The plant/tree represents the final Kingdom and inclusion of Gentiles (birds). It is far from clear in Mark or Matthew whether there is a Gentile mission here or not.

Matthew 13

Matthew 13 is regarded by some as the turning point in the gospel, and it certainly illustrates many of Matthew's theological concerns, both in his arrangement of the materials and his editing of them (mostly from Mark 4).

> **Further study**
> Compare Matthew 13 with Mark 4, on which he bases his collection. How and why has he developed the human element in all of them? Read chapter 14 of *Studying the Synoptic Gospels* on Matthew 13 and redaction criticism.

Wheat and Weeds (13: 24–30). Matthew substitutes Mark's 'seed growing secretly' with this parable, and while it illustrates something of the Kingdom, its focus is really on the mission of the disciples. From a redactional point of view it possibly reveals Matthew's view of his church/community. The allegorical interpretation (13: 36–43) shows that Jesus is the householder (master) who sows (preaches) good seed (the message of the imminent arrival of the Kingdom) in his field (the area of mission – the world, surprisingly not just Israel), and the enemy (the devil) sows weeds (people influenced by the devil). If the slaves represent the disciples, then in Matthew's church they must also be its leaders, and the wheat is the followers of Jesus/the ordinary members of Matthew's community. The teaching is a warning to the leaders not to judge – that is the role of the angels at judgement day.

> **Further discussion**
> Consider whether this parable can be interpreted with a realised or inaugurated eschatology.

The Leaven (13: 33). Some interpret this parable to be Matthew's means of saying to the Jews that the Kingdom has already appeared for his community in the person of Jesus, and that it is continuing to grow. But if the parables are about encouraging *preaching* about the Kingdom, then growth refers to belief rather than the Kingdom itself.

This is a Q parable (Luke 13: 20–21).

In Genesis 18: 6 the promise of a child to Sarah is represented by cakes.

Hidden Treasure and Pearl (13: 44, 45–46). It is not clear whether these parables stress the value of the Kingdom, its hiddenness, the sacrifice that has to be made or the search for it. If the treasure and pearl perhaps symbolise the state of the righteous after the final judgement, then these are parables of encouragement to the disciples to sacrifice all in this world for the Kingdom to come.

> **Further study**
> Consider whether Dodd is right to interpret the parables in a realised way: '...the Kingdom of God is the highest good: it is within your power to possess it here and now, if, like a treasure-finder and the pearl merchant, you will throw caution to the winds: "Follow me!"' *The Parables of the Kingdom*, page 86.

The Net (13: 47–50). This parable repeats most of the ideas in the Wheat and the Weeds, and may be the product of Matthew's own redaction as a means of emphasising the theme of 13. But there are new elements: if the 'bad fish' in the context of the gospel could refer to people such as Judas, then the warning of the parable for Matthew's community is not to judge them, but wait until final judgement.

Matthew 25

Coming towards the end of the gospel, this chapter looks forward to final judgement and the arrival of the Kingdom. The parables are essentially **hortatory**, warning the community that their present behaviour has future consequences.

> **Route P: Jewish Scriptures and concepts.** Look at the idea of the reward of the righteous and punishment of the wicked in 2 Maccabees 7. Read pages 102–107 of Drury's *The Parables in the Gospels*.

Ten Bridesmaids (25: 1–13). The setting of a wedding had eschatological significance in early Christianity, with Jesus as the bridegroom (Mk 2: 19). The command is to 'watch' and to be alert for the coming of the Kingdom because, like the last of the ten plagues, it will be sudden 'at midnight' (Ex 12: 29). The delay of the bridegroom represents the delay of the Parousia, but this is no excuse for lax moral behaviour.

This is a Q parable (Lk 19: 12–27). In Luke 19: 11 the parable refutes the immediate appearance of the Kingdom.

The Talents (25: 14–30). The parable may be based on Archelaus' bloody revenge on the Jews who tried to stop him becoming 'king' in 4 BCE. Matthew emphasises the warning to be prepared and wise with one's possessions because there is no room for complacency. Each person is left with a great deal of money. Compared to Mark 13: 34 where the servants are left in charge 'each with his work', Matthew envisages a time when the Church will have greater duties, and the consequence for failing to carry them out will be greater punishment (25: 29). The man who hides his talent is the reverse of those who discover or reveal the nature of the Kingdom in Matthew 13.

A talent was the highest currency denomination, worth 600 denarii.

The Judgment of the Nations. The parable brings together many of Matthew's themes elaborated from Mark 8: 38: concern for the 'little ones' (10: 42), reward for discipleship, role of the son of man as judge, the arrival of the Kingdom with angels. The emphasis is on good deeds – not just preaching. The reference to sheep and goats recalls the parable in Ezekiel 34. Sheep could refer to Israel but it is more likely to refer to the mixed community of Matthew's church.

This parable is fundamental for many liberation theologians who see it as the basis for Christian praxis to help the poor. Consider to what extent this gives an accurate interpretation of Matthew. See pages 125–131 of the *OCR AS Guide*.

Luke 15

Unlike Matthew and Mark, Luke's gospel is characterised by a series of great parables that are 'unallegorical, realistic stories which are rich in homely detail and characterisation'. Therefore according to the Jülicher/Jeremias view, these are closest to Jesus' own ideas. The parables in this chapter form part of Luke's biggest collection of 30 parables (10: 29–18: 14) and are grouped to deal with the theme of 'the lost' of Israel. As Drury argues, Luke's parables fit far better into the **wisdom** pattern of the Old Testament worldly advice (for example in the Book of Proverbs) than the mysterious, allegorical form found in Mark and Matthew.

John Drury, *The Parables in the Gospels*, page 111.

Further discussion

Compare Luke 15–16 with Mark 4 and Matthew 13. How and why has he developed his interest with people further than Matthew?

The Lost Sheep (15: 3–7). A comparison with Matthew 18: 12–14 provides a good example of a change of audience. In Luke, the setting is with the Pharisees, who criticise him (15: 2). The 'lost sheep' represent those who have abandoned Judaism: the startling message is that God actively seeks them out for his Kingdom. In Matthew, the audience is comprised of the disciples. Matthew 18 is about church discipline, and the sheep represents the 'little ones', who are the lapsed Christians or those very new to Christianity – an idea developed in the parable of Judgement (Matthew 25: 40, 45).

There is a great deal of discussion about what Matthew/Jesus meant by the 'mikroteroi' ('little ones' in Greek).

The Lost Son (15: 11–32) is an L source and, as is common in L parables, it centres on a crisis – in this case, the younger son who squanders his money, finds himself so hungry that he could eat the pigs' food and has to return home to ask for his father's forgiveness. Crisis, according to Hans Conzelmann, expresses Luke's mid-term eschatology: the indefinite historical period before the Parousia, when everyday life is a continual experience of human sin, repentance, judgement and forgiveness. This is what gives this parable its timeless feeling, like the great moral stories in the Old Testament. The two brothers' rivalry also has Old Testament parallels – Cain and Abel, Esau and Jacob and so on, all of which

L refers to material only found in Luke.

Further reading

See part two of Conzelmann's *The Theology of Luke* (SCM Press 1960).

Further study

Compare the parable with the story of David and Nathan (2 Samuel 12) or Joseph and Potipher's wife (Genesis 45).

illustrate a very real human experience and, on an allegorical level, express the relationship of Christianity (younger son) and Judaism (elder son). The lost son's act of repentance recalls Pharaoh's words to Moses: 'I have sinned against the Lord your God and against you' (Exodus 10: 16). So, Drury argues, the story *may* be read as an allegory, (the father represents God's great mercy) but it works just as well at an ordinary, realistic story level.

Further discussion

Consider to what extent Luke has constructed the parable using Old Testament stories. Jeremias considered this parable to be authentic.

Healing miracles: illness and sin

A characteristic of Jesus' ministry in all four gospels was his ability to perform miracles, in particular healings and exorcisms. But what exactly was their function? The question can be answered on two levels: firstly at the historical level within the *Sitz-im-Leben* of Jesus' life, and secondly as understood by the evangelists.

Route C: Philosophy of religion and the concept of miracle. To what extent are miracles presented as violations of the natural order? See *The Miracle Stories of the Gospels* by A. Richardson (SCM Press 1960) and *Reason and Religious Belief*, M. Peterson et al (OUP 2003).

Sanders sets out four important historical aspects 'which should be considered in studying the miracles and what they tell us about Jesus, his intention and significance of his career':

Jesus and Judaism, pages 172–173.

1. How Jesus understood his relationship with God and his role as messenger, messiah or even Son of God.
2. The impact of the miracles on the crowds as 'proofs' and an offer of repentance, and the challenge to the authorities that led to his arrest and execution.
3. The attitude of outsiders to Jesus and his miracles.
4. The relationship of miracles to Jesus' general teaching and their place in his eschatology.

The opening chapters of Mark indicate Jesus' success in preaching and teaching among the great crowds of ordinary people who consistently brought their sick and possessed to him for healing and exorcism (Mark 1: 32). However, although the healings are integral to Jesus' teaching on the coming of the Kingdom and certainly seem to have been a reason for the gathering of the crowds, it is less clear whether Jesus himself regarded them as integral to his mission – certainly Mark records the people as saying in the synagogue after his cure of the Man with the Unclean Spirit (1: 21–28) that Jesus employs a 'new teaching with authority' (1: 27). The conclusion is ambiguous: was his teaching authoritative because it was accompanied by a miracle or because of the nature of his teaching alone?

The crowds

His popularity is indicated, for example, in the curing of the Paralysed Man (2: 1–12), when there are so many people that there is no space 'not even about the door' (2: 2); equally, the Woman with Internal Bleeding (5: 24b–35) has to push herself through the crowds just to be able to touch his garments (5: 27).

Anthony Harvey argues that Jesus' exorcisms in particular indicated his battle with the devil and subsequent victory: this demonstrates that Jesus self-consciously saw himself as God's agent in the dawn of the new Kingdom. It was a potentially dangerous form of ministry as it allied him to magic and sorcery.

Eschatology and exorcisms

Jesus and the Constraints of History (Duckworth 1982) page 114.

The **Gerasene Demoniac** (Mk 5: 1–20) appears to support Harvey's eschatological reading. It is given considerable importance by Mark: the possessed man's state is built up to stress the violence of the demons and therefore the power and authority of Jesus' exorcism. Jesus not only cures a man who is mentally ill and rejected by society (he lives outside the village in the local burial ground) but also defeats Satan's army of demons in the establishment of the Kingdom of God.

Legion draws a parallel with Jesus' parable of the **strongman** (3: 27) who represents Satan. Legion/the evil spirits' recognition of 'Jesus, Son of the Most High God' (5: 7) is reminiscent of the Gentile term for the Jewish God and, as Jesus is in Gentile territory, evil recognises him as God's agent, and even worships him (5: 6).

Some interpreters of this passage comment that Jesus' power is so strong that the spirits give him their name immediately, while others think that they are trying to fool Jesus by giving him the man's nickname. Jesus ignores this and carries out the exorcism anyway.

To what extent is Jesus depicted as an ordinary exorcist? Scholars are divided. In other accounts of exorcisms, it was quite standard for demons to beg not to be sent 'out of the area' (5: 10). Jesus asks the spirits their name (5: 9) as part of the process. The twist in the story is that the spirits assumed they had tricked Jesus into allowing them to continue to exist in the pigs, but the pigs rush down the steep bank into the lake and are drowned (5: 13). Harvey argues that in comparison to other first-century exorcisms the story depicts Jesus acting with a good deal of restraint here and elsewhere, because it is not the actions that are important, but the eschatological action of casting out Satan.

Jesus and the Constraints of History, page 109.

See above on the discussion Luke 11: 20; read also Matthew 12: 28.

Jesus the Magician (Gollancz 1978).

Morton Smith on the other hand argued that Jesus' actions were not primarily about teaching or eschatology, but to establish himself as God's agent among the crowds. In this story, Jesus is a magician and plays on all the accepted superstitions of his day. The effect on the crowd is stunning (5: 17). Such stories confirm Jesus as God's son, who receives God's spirit at his baptism (Mark 1: 9), which enables him to carry out exorcisms. The tradition recalls several occasions on which Jesus is accused of being on the side of Satan/possessed due to 'abnormal behaviour on his part'.

According to Smith, being called a 'god's son' was attributed to many exorcists. *Jesus the Magician*, page 32.

Further study

Read Mark 3: 20–30 and consider what this story may originally have said about Jesus' reception as a healer. To what extent is Smith right to reject eschatology from Jesus' original mission?

For Mark, the man's spiritual and physical cure (5: 15) establishes Jesus' authority as saviour. The man wants to become a disciple, but Jesus sends him to preach in Decapolis, an area that was primarily occupied by Gentiles. The Kingdom is seen to spread abroad, overcoming evil and superstition. This may also be the reason why Mark so likes the story, as this was similar to the situation in Rome in the years 60–70 CE.

Eschatology and healings

Sanders concludes that Smith has underestimated Jesus as an eschatological prophet, which he considers a good description of Jesus' own sense of vocation. Harvey holds the stronger position that Jesus consciously chose to perform miracles that would fulfil the eschatological hope of Isaiah 35. There is no doubt that early Christian tradition links the healings with Isaiah: Matthew 11: 5 quotes Isaiah 35: 5–6. More contentious is the idea that the relationship of Isaiah 35 and miracles goes back to Jesus himself.

Let's look at the examples of healing miracles in the set texts:

Jesus heals Simon's mother in law (Mk 1: 29–31). This story from Mark's point of view has to be seen in the context of Jesus' proclamation of the coming of the Kingdom (1: 15) and its immediate successful effects.

Lepers constituted a broad category of those who were considered unclean by the law. According to the Torah (Leviticus 14: 2–32) lepers had to live apart from society.

Jesus cleanses a leper (Mk 1: 40–44). Mark's purpose in choosing this story is to illustrate the radical nature of the Kingdom, which places the last first, and the first last (Mark 10: 31).

A pericope is defined as a unit of traditional material passed on orally. The aim of the form critics was to establish the earliest form in which these pericopes took shape.

Jesus heals a paralytic (Mk 2: 1–10). The healing fulfils Isaiah's prophecy but form critics have long felt that there are two stories or **pericopes** here. The first conforms to the 'miracle' form (2: 3–5a, 10b–12), in which the conclusion ends with the amazement of the crowd. The second 'apophthegm' or 'pronouncement' form (2: 5b–10a) is the conflict between Jesus and the Pharisees over the question of forgiveness. Although the illness was often seen as an external manifestation of sin, Jesus' question 'which is easier to say, take up your bed and walk or your sins are forgiven?' is very difficult to answer.

A girl restored to life and a woman healed (Mk 5: 21–43). As it stands, the two pericopes show signs of Marcan redaction, with one story inside another. The eschatological purpose of Jairus' daughter may be to anticipate Jesus' own resurrection and the promise of resurrection to all those who have faith. Jesus' comment that the girl is not dead but 'sleeping' (5: 39) recalls the Pharisaic view that death is a transition period before being awoken prior to judgement and entry into the Kingdom. The woman's cure illustrates Jesus' concern for those rejected by society.

'Rise up, O sleeper rise from the dead and Christ will shine on you' (Ephesians 5: 14). Read 1 Corinthians 15 and look at the notes on pages 73–75. Matthew 11: 5 *adds* 'raising the dead' to Isaiah 35 as a specifically Christian eschatological sign (resurrection was not part of traditional Jewish thought).

According to Leviticus 15: 25–27, menstruating women were barred from all ordinary social relationships.

Sayings and teachings

The Sermon on the Mount (Matt 5–7) is the first of five discourses in Matthew's gospel that present Jesus as the new Moses, delivering a new law to the crowds (5: 1) and in particular to the disciples (5: 2). Matthew has constructed the material to unpack the phrase from 4: 23 that Jesus 'went in about Galilee, teaching in their synagogues and preaching the gospel of the Kingdom'. There are numerous problems of interpretation associated with the sermon, not least the question of for whom it was intended.

Sermon on the Mount

Route P: Jewish Scriptures and ethics. Consider teaching on justice in Amos. Look at ideas of the weak, justice and reversal.

There are three possible answers: the whole world; Christians (or Matthew's community) only; or Christian leaders (and those in Matthew's community) only, namely priests and monks. One solution is that Matthew intended the disciples to act as examples to all members of the community (the 'crowd'), who in turn would act as a 'light to the world' (5: 14) by their 'good works' (5: 16). The universal nature of the sermon appears in the very last verse of the gospel, where the disciples are told to teach the world 'all that I have commanded you' (28: 20). Here are three more important issues:

This influential view was developed by Martin Luther (1483–1546) and became an important part of Reformation theology.

Further reading

Read chapter 3 of *The Theology of the Gospel of Matthew* by Ulrich Luz (CUP 1995). A classic interpretation is *The Sermon on the Mount* by W. D. Davis (CUP 1966).

Law and ethics. What is meant by the problematic 'Think not that I have come to abolish the law and the prophets but to fulfil them' (5: 17), given that the **Antitheses** suggest that the old law *is* somehow to be modified? Luz argues that Matthew adds the phrase 'not an iota, not a dot, will pass from the law' (5: 18) to correct the view among some Christians that, as Jesus' teaching on the Kingdom was not derived from the Torah, he was therefore teaching an **antinomian** ethic. As we have seen, Torah was not a fixed idea in Jesus' or Matthew's day. Like the Pharisees and scribes, they all believed in the *living* Torah, which could continue to be interpreted. The ethical core of the sermon is a series of examples that amplify Torah. These are to be combined with the qualities set out in the **Beatitudes** (5: 1–12). As Matthew considers Jesus to be *the* teacher (23: 10), the sermon comes to be the interpretive tool of Torah. The Torah is not abolished but fulfilled.

The Antitheses (5: 21–48) each begin 'You have heard that it was said…' and continue 'but I say to you…'. They form the core of the ethical teaching of the sermon.

Antinomian, 'against the law', suggests a consequential or situational approach to ethics.

Route J: Religious ethics and principles. The sermon covers all aspects of Christian ethics, but consider how these might be understood as virtues in the 'polis' – i.e. the Christian community.

Perfection and righteousness. Just how are the disciples to exceed the righteousness of the scribes and Pharisees (5: 20) and be 'perfect, as your heavenly Father is perfect' (5: 48)? The sermon has often been criticised for setting a standard so high that very few could achieve it. Some have suggested that Jesus was teaching only about internal spiritual righteousness and the examples are not to be taken literally. Both views are in fact unlikely. Righteousness was understood in Jewish circles to mean good deeds, and Matthew balances good deeds in the Antitheses with the inward piety of alms giving, prayer and fasting (6: 1–18) as two sides of the same coin. Luz argues that perfection is to be understood as the goal of a righteousness superior to that of the Pharisees and scribes – not an impossible ideal but rather a path. The underlying principle of righteousness is love (5: 43–47).

The Lord's Prayer (6: 9–13) prays for active piety: 'Thy will be done on earth.'

Route T: Islam and ethical principles. Compare and contrast the teaching of the sermon on good works with Muslim teaching. See pages 152–153 of the Islam chapter.

Good works, grace and judgement. Some have argued that, in contrast to Paul's teaching on 'justification by faith', the sermon appears to have no teaching on God's grace, and salvation is entirely achieved by good works. As we have seen, good works are just one aspect of righteousness. Good works have to be accompanied by good intentions, which is why the Pharisees are accused of being hypocrites in their piety (6: 16). But this can be extended to false Christians, who are like wolves dressed up in 'sheep's clothing' (7: 15). Good works must be genuine acts. This is why the road that leads to hell is wide (7: 13–14) and the narrow path is achieved by a few. Those who achieve righteousness do so because they act according to an implicit understanding of God's love and justice. Matthew's characteristic theme of judgement concludes the sermon, with words similar to those in the parable of the sheep and goats (25: 41) and the parable of the two houses (7: 24–27) about works of sincerity and of superficial show.

Twice Matthew notes that it is the person who gives a glass of water to the thirsty 'little ones' – a seemingly small and trivial act – who on judgement day will be surprised by their reception into the Kingdom (10: 42 and 25: 40). God's grace is to recognise such acts, whether carried out by a Christian or not.

Route P: Jewish Scriptures and New Testament concepts. Compare messianic expectations in Micah and Isaiah 40–43 with the gospel presentations of Jesus, especially servant and kingly ideas.

Route T: Islam and status of Jesus and Muhammad. Consider the relationship of Jesus and Muhammad to the prophets. Consider the place of Jesus in Islam in the Day of Judgement.

Jesus' authority and status

From prison, John the Baptist sends a message via his disciples asking Jesus, 'Are you he who is to come, or shall we look for another?' (Matt 11: 3; Lk 7: 19–20). Interestingly, he does not use the term messiah, but a more general expression of hope. His request to know Jesus' credentials poses the basic question, what does the 'one who is to come' have to accomplish in order to be considered 'the one'? There is no doubt that as far as the early Church and the gospel writers were concerned, Jesus was 'the one who is to come' and they generally used the Greek term 'christ' to express this. Christ means 'anointed one' and translates to the Hebrew 'mashiah', hence 'messiah'. The historical and interpretative problems surrounding this are huge: was there a general 1st-century messianic expectation among the Jews? What kind of messiah was expected? Did Jesus think of himself as *the* messiah or *a* messiah? These questions are fundamental to looking at Jesus' authority and status.

Four portraits of Jesus

Further reading

Read Stephen C. Barton in *The Cambridge Companion to Jesus* (CUP 2001) on 'Many gospels, one Jesus'.

Does it matter that each gospel writer presents a different portrait of Jesus? For Matthew, Jesus is the 'only teacher' (Matthew 23: 8–11), a new Moses, and Davidic messiah. Mark's Jesus is a mysterious figure who frequently speaks in riddles, challenges authority and whose suffering is a 'ransom for many' (Mark 10: 45). Luke often refers to Jesus as the 'Lord' who is the liberator of the oppressed and the marginalised, both Jew and Gentile. John establishes that Jesus is the pre-existent Word of God, who has existed from the beginning (John 1: 1) and who becomes flesh (1: 14) to reveal God's glory in the world.

How did Jesus understand his mission? Since the 19th century, scholars have embarked on what has been called the 'quest for the historical Jesus' to answer this question. Ironically, the different Jesuses that have emerged are even more varied that the four portraits of the gospel writers. The fact that Jesus cannot be categorised may say something of the quality of his message, which was robust enough to be moulded for Jewish and Gentile audiences after his death.

The historical quest. Influenced by comparative religions of the 1st century, modern science and existentialism, the first-quest scholars made an important distinction between the **Jesus of history** and the **Christ of faith**. The Christ of faith as seen in the gospels is largely the construction of the Church after Jesus' death, to present him as a god to challenge other divine heroes of contemporary religions. The Jesus of history never claimed to be the messiah (Wrede), but taught a message of love (Renan) and hope against a meaningless world (Bultmann). Some scholars, like Schweitzer, portrayed Jesus as the final prophet hoping to herald in the eschatological Kingdom, but dying a broken man.

The new quest. These scholars assert that the Christ of faith could only have emerged from Jesus himself. Jesus' distinctive teaching on the Kingdom and its impact on the marginalised was true often because it was *different* from Judaism. Nevertheless, the new quest scholars conclude that there is very little that can be known of Jesus' own message for certain.

Jesus seminar. More recently in North America, the quest of Bultmann has been continued in the light of new discoveries, notably *The Gospel of Thomas* and work done on Q. By establishing the authentic sayings of Jesus, the seminar has most recently described Jesus as a **cynic teacher** who did not teach about an imminent Kingdom or his role as messiah, but non-violent wisdom for everyday life.

The third quest. This position is not an organised group like the Jesus seminar, but represents modern scholars who consider that the gospels give a reasonably trustworthy account of the historical Jesus, especially when understood against the Jewish background. Gerd Theissen presents Jesus as a popular wandering prophet. E. P. Sanders considers Jesus to be a **restorationist** prophet who looked forward to God's intervention in history to restore the Temple and Israel. N. T. Wright argues that Jesus saw himself as the messiah who would bring about the end of exile for God's people.

The key synoptic passage is the incident at **Caesarea Philippi** when Jesus asks the disciples who people are saying that he – Jesus – is. Peter replies that they say he is 'the Christ, the Son of the living God' (Matt 16: 16). Jesus' response is to insist that they do not tell anyone and then to explain his role in terms of suffering, death and resurrection. A similar episode takes place in front of the high priest at his trial (Mk 14: 61). In each synoptic account Jesus gives a form of 'yes', but qualifies it by referring to his role as the Son of Man. Could Jesus have thought of himself as the messiah?

The historical Jesus

Further reading

David Wenham and Steve Walton *Introducing The Gospels and Acts* pages 127–132, and James Carlton Paget in *The Cambridge Companion to Jesus* (CUP 2001).

Route C: Philosophy of religion and authority of the Bible. Consider to what extent these approaches have undermined the inspiration of the Bible. Read pages 37–40 of the *OCR AS Guide*.

Further reading

Günther Bornkamm, *Jesus of Nazareth* (Augsburg Fortress 1994).

The Cynics were a Greek philosophical school founded in the 4th century BCE. They adopted a simple lifestyle and rejected establishment traditions.

Further reading

See *Jesus: a Revolutionary Biography* by J. D. Crossan (Harper 1995).

Further reading

The Shadow of the Galilean by Gerd Theissen (SCM Press 1987) is written as a gripping detective story. *Who Was Jesus?* by N. T. Wright (SPCK 2005).

Jesus the messiah

Read all three versions: Matthew 16: 13–20; Mark 8: 27–33; Luke 9: 18–21.

Read and compare: Matthew 26: 63–66; Mark 14: 60–63; Luke 22: 66–71.

These texts do not necessarily mean that the idea of messiahship was widespread or consistent: the Essenes at Qumran spoke of two messiahs – one kingly and one priestly – being involved in the eschatological age.

Read *OCR AS Guide* pages 31–32.

Jewish views of the messiah. The Old Testament uses *mashiah* to refer to anyone who has a special relationship with God. In 1 Samuel 2: 10 the term is associated with the kings of Israel and the house of David in particular, and in 2 Samuel 7 Nathan promises that David's lineage will continue forever. But it is only after the end of monarchy in 586 BCE that some of the psalms begin to think in terms of a messiah. Daniel 9: 26 most specifically refers to a messiah who will aid God in bringing about his Kingdom – although the Hebrew does not term him *the* messiah. However, the **Psalms of Solomon**, composed sometime after Pompey's annexing of Palestine in 63 BCE, speak specifically of the messiah, the son of David, cleansing Jerusalem of Gentiles and establishing God's rule.

'Lo your king comes to you; triumphant and victorious is he, riding on a colt' (Zech 9: 9). Read also Matt 21: 1–12.

Jesus' view. Jesus' triumphal entry into Jerusalem certainly presents him in a kingly way in the fulfilment of Zechariah 9: 9, and his cleansing of the Temple symbolises the preparation of Israel for God's rule (Mk 11: 15–19). It may be possible that he thought of himself as the rejected stone of Psalm 118: 22 (quoted in Mk 12: 10–12), as the foundation of the new community. His stern rebuke of James and John (Mk 10: 35–44) suggests that he may have thought of himself as God's anointed, but not as a political liberator as depicted in the Psalms of Solomon.

Longenecker argues that no one could claim to be messiah until they had accomplished the works of the messiah. This may explain why Jesus himself never uses the term.

Son of Man

Further reading

Jesus Son of Man by Barnabas Lindars (SPCK 1983).

Jesus refers to himself frequently as the Son of Man. The history behind this phrase is complex but it appears to have two meanings:

Divine authority. Daniel 7: 13–14 refers to 'one like the son of man' who is given by God, 'dominion and glory and kingdom'. Later Jewish texts associate the Son of Man with God's revelation of the Kingdom or age to come. In the synoptics, Jesus' authority to heal and to forgive sins is associated with his role as Son of Man (Mark 2: 10). In his response to the High Priest, Jesus uses the language of Daniel 7: 13, depicting himself as God's agent at judgement when God vindicates Israel (or the world).

For example 1 Enoch 37–71 and 4 Ezra 13.

The suffering servant. It is possible that Isaiah's suffering servant (Is 52–53) had come to be interpreted in messianic terms as the one who would redeem Israel through his vicarious suffering. Son of Man or 'bar enasha' (in Aramaic) could mean 'I' in the sense of one who is a member of mankind. This suggests that, if the term is part of Jesus' *ipsissima verba*, he may have seen his role as one who was to suffer 'yet he bore the sin of many and made intercession for the transgressors' (Is 53: 12).

Further study

Consider what kind of eschatology best fits Jesus' teaching and how this affects your judgement of his authority and status.

Test yourself

1. 'The purpose of Matthew's gospel was to reject Judaism.' Discuss.
2. 'Jesus taught that the Kingdom of God was yet to come.' Discuss.
3. 'The purpose of the healing miracles in Mark was to show that Jesus was the messiah.' Discuss.
4. To what extent are the parables in Luke 15 about the lost intended to challenge the scribes and the Pharisees?

Connections

Route C: Philosophy of Religion with New Testament

Life after death. How coherent can New Testament ideas be considered to be when held up to philosophical criticism. **Early Church:** Consider the relation between moral behaviour and life after death in the New Testament (e.g. the realised eschatology of Ephesians 4 and Galatians 4–5 and the use of paraenesis). Compare 1 Corinthians 15 teaching on the body/soul relationship with Plato, Aristotle, Freud and Hick. Consider the effectiveness of Paul's metaphors. **Gospels:** Consider what the gospels have to say about the future Kingdom and the resurrection miracles. Contrast this with ideas of reincarnation. Compare the resurrection narratives, the empty tomb and resurrection appearances, and what these mean either as history or myth/symbol.

Further reading

Read chapter 2 of *Survival?* By David Lorimer (Routledge 1984) or part three of *Death and Eternal Life* by John Hick (Westminster John Knox Press 1996).

See pages 113–116 of the *OCR AS Guide*.

Inspiration and authority of the Bible. Consider the extent to which the New Testament can be considered the direct word of God, and the implications of different understandings of its authority. **Early Church:** Consider the claim in Ephesians 3, Galatians 3 and 4 of a special revelation that has been hidden until the coming of Christ and then revealed only to Paul. Consider what kind of authority this gives Paul's letters in relation to the gospels. **Gospels:** Consider modern approaches to the quest for the historical Jesus, and to the gospels as reliable witness or record of Jesus' life. Consider what is meant by inspiration and to what extent source criticism has contributed towards the authority of the Bible.

The concept of miracle. Early Church: Consider why Paul never speaks of Jesus' miracles in his letters except indirectly, concerning God's special providence in his call and the nature of the resurrection of Jesus. **Gospels**: Consider the importance of defining 'miracle' and whether Hume's idea of violation accurately applies. Consider the various ways in which miracles function in the gospels as illustrations of the Kingdom and as authoritative signs of Jesus' divine status and scholarly interpretations.

Religious experience. Consider the ways in which religious experiences are described in the New Testament. **Early Church:** Consider the importance of Paul's 'Damascus experience' in Galatians 1 and impact of his revelation in Ephesians 3, along with the noetic (knowledge-giving) dimension in each case. Compare and contrast the significance of the mystical experience of the Spirit and of dying and rising 'in Christ' in Romans 6 with other mystical experiences. **Gospels:** Consider the healing miracles in terms of religious experience and their noetic value. Consider the importance of the resurrection in terms of being a personal experience of 'ransom' (Mk 10: 45), atonement and salvation. Could parables be considered a means of conveying religious experience by challenging the world-view of their listeners?

Test yourself

1. 'Miracles in the New Testament are best understood as symbols.' Discuss in relation to the texts you have studied.
2. 'The New Testament has no accounts which could be considered religious experience.' Discuss.

3. 'The New Testament does not intend the idea of life after death to be taken literally.' Discuss.

Route J: Religious Ethics with New Testament

Further reading

Read *either* chapter II on the synoptic gospels *or* III on Paul in *Ethics in the New Testament* by Jack T. Saunders (SCM Press 1986).

Practical ethics. Consider the possibilities and difficulties of applying your specified texts to the ethical issues studied. **Early Church:** Consider Paul's teaching (for example, 1 Corinthians 15) on the body and sin, and its treatment of sexual ethics especially. Consider Paul's eschatology and its application to war, peace and nuclear war. **Gospels:** Consider the Sermon on the Mount on sexual ethics, violence, war and pacifism, especially in terms of eschatology and perfectionism.

Further reading

Chapter 14 of *Understanding Paul's Ethics* ed. Brian S. Rosner (Eerdmans 1995). See chapters 4–5 of *Strenuous Commands* by A. E. Harvey (Xpress Reprints 1996) on the practical demands of Jesus' teaching in the Sermon on the Mount.

The reasons for and consequences of ethical behaviour. Early Church: Consider whether Pauline ethics are deontological or consequential. For example, Ephesians 4 appears to be to take a situational/virtue view and also a natural law view of the idea of order. Consider Paul's teaching on ethics to counter sin (see Romans 7) and therefore his attitude to the deontology of the Torah. Consider Pauline teaching on Christian freedom and the Spirit (see Gal 5) and compare to theories on freewill and determinism. **Gospels:** Consider differing scholarly eschatological interpretations of the Kingdom of God (and judgement) and their implications for ethical behaviour and freewill. Consider whether Jesus is presented as having a strong or a weak deontology in his attitude to Torah and halakhah.

Further reading

Read pages 355–372 of *Ephesians: A Shorter Commentary* by Ernest Best for a good discussion of morality in this letter.

New Testament ethics and normative ethical systems. Early Church: Consider the teaching in Galatians 5 and Ephesians 4 in terms of situationism and virtue ethics. Consider Romans in terms of natural/revealed law. **Gospels:** Consider the Beatitudes as the foundation for Christian virtues and compare with the virtue theories of Aristotle or McIntyre. Compare the parables – as examples of Christian principles of neighbourly love, mercy, forgiveness – with Kant's practical imperative. Compare Jesus' criticisms on the law with utilitarianism. Consider what Jesus meant by love and whether he was a situationist.

Further reading

Love is a basic principle of Christian thought and ethics but is often given a very narrow meaning. Read chapter 1 of *Friendship: A Way of Interpreting Christ* by Liz Carmichael (T&T Clark 2004).

Basic principles of New Testament ethics. Early Church: Consider Pauline teaching on love: is it subjective (utilitarian, existential) or revealed and uniquely Christian? Consider Paul's principle of freedom as a life free from sinful human nature in accordance with the Spirit (Gal 5: 22–26). **Gospels:** Consider love of neighbour (as expressed in parables of Lk 15), justice (Matt 25) and forgiveness (Mk 2): compare with utilitarian and natural law principles.

Test yourself

1. 'The New Testament teaches absolute pacifism.' Discuss.
2. 'The ethical teaching in the New Testament allows no place for freewill.' Discuss.
3. 'Love is the only virtue needed in Christian ethics.' Discuss.

Route P: Jewish Scriptures with New Testament

The specification makes an unlikely link here. In practice, it is unlikely that questions will be set on this.

Form and source criticism. Make a comparison between the usefulness of form criticism in interpreting the Jewish Scriptures, with that of source criticism in interpreting the gospels. **Early Church:** Compare and contrast 1 Corinthians 15 and Daniel 12 as examples of apocalyptic literature. **Gospels:** Compare how scholars have treated the parable form in the gospels with the psalms. Compare how important the treatment of sources and forms is in the quest for the historical Jesus with the historical setting of the various Jewish scriptures.

New Testament use of the Jewish Scriptures. Consider the ways in which the New Testament passages studied have made use of the concepts of the Jewish Scriptures (covenant, reward and punishment, messiah, sin and sacrifice). **Early Church:** Compare the idea of the Abrahamic covenant (Gen 12 and 15) with Paul's interpretation in Galatians 3–4 and Romans 4. Consider the idea of reward and punishment in Daniel 12, 2 Maccabees 7 and 1 Corinthians 15. **Gospels:** Consider to what extent the Jewish Scriptures support the idea of a messiah and the ways in which the gospel writers have interpreted them – in particular Isaiah 53 (the suffering servant) and Micah (Davidic messiah). Contrast different ideas of Jewish sacrifice with Jesus' death as sacrifice for sin.

These are concepts covered at AS and A2.

Ethics. Compare the ethics of the Jewish scriptures and New Testament passages. **Early Church:** Compare and contrast teaching on the law in Ephesians and Romans: is it sufficient for salvation? Consider Paul's view of the halakhah in Galatians 5 (walking in the Spirit) and compare with Jeremiah 31's new covenant of love. Compare and contrast Amos' teaching on justice, order and reversal with Romans. **Gospels:** Compare and contrast Amos' teaching on justice, order and reversal with the ethical teaching in the Sermon on the Mount, Luke's parables and Matthew 25.

Revelation. Compare Jewish Scriptures and New Testament understanding of revelation and of religious experience. **Early Church:** Consider the claim in Ephesians 3 and Galatians 2 of a special revelation that was 'hidden' until Paul preached the message of Christ to the Gentiles, and compare this with Daniel's apocalyptic/pesher method of understanding God's revelation. Compare ideas of suffering and God's grace in Job, Jonah, 2 Maccabees, Romans and Galatians. **Gospels:** Contrast the idea of the Kingdom of God as a revelation of what is now and yet to come (especially parables and miracles) with the apocalyptic imagery of Daniel 12. Compare the place of suffering and God's grace in Job, Jonah, and 2 Maccabees with the Beatitudes and Matthew 25.

Read pages 94–97 of the *OCR AS Guide*.

Test yourself

1. Compare and contrast how the idea of **either** covenant **or** sacrifice is presented in the Jewish Scriptures with the New Testament texts you have studied.
2. 'The ethics in the New Testament continue the same ideas as those found in the Jewish Scriptures.' Discuss.
3. Compare and contrast the place of religious experience in the Jewish Scriptures and the New Testament texts studied.

Route T: New Testament with Islam

Status of Jesus and Muhammad. Compare Jesus' status in the New Testament with the status of Muhammad in Islam. **Early Church:** Compare the sunnah of Muhammad as the seal of the prophets and

Remember to bear in mind different aspects of Islam according the Sunni, Shia and Sufi traditions.

See pages 55–57 of the *OCR AS Guide*.

as statesman with Jesus as fulfilment of the Abrahamic covenant (Romans and Galatians) and as the cosmic Christ who is 'head' of the cosmos and of the Church (Ephesians). **Gospels:** Compare the sunnah of Muhammad as the seal of the prophets and as statesmen with Jesus as the new Moses and Davidic messiah (Matthew's gospel) and founder of a 'church' (Matt 16: 18). Compare and contrast scholarly views of the historical Muhammad through hadiths and *sira* (biographies) with the various quests for Jesus.

Ethical principles of the New Testament and the ethical principles of Islam. Early Church: Consider whether the Pauline teaching on love is comparable to the Sufi mystical teaching of *fana* (dying and rising in God). Compare Paul's principle of freedom as a life free from sinful human nature in accordance with the Spirit (Gal 5) with Muslim notions of Shari'ah. **Gospels:** Compare the Christian principles of neighbourly love (as expressed in parables of Lk 15), justice (Matt 25), and forgiveness (Mk 2) with the Muslim notion of Shari'ah. Consider the place of inner intention in Jesus' Sermon on the Mount with the Muslim teaching on *niyyah* and *fard.*

Sin, redemption, God as judge, and eternal life.
Early Church: Compare Pauline teaching on 'original' sin through Adam (Rom 2–8) with Muslim teaching on sin as failure to comply with Shari'ah. Consider the implications of this for Paul's teaching on atonement and the resurrection with Islamic teaching on freewill and responsibility. Consider whether Paul has an internalised view of the end time (realised eschatology) and if this is a possible interpretation of Judgement Day in Islam. **Gospels:** Compare Luke's parables of forgiveness of 'the lost' with Islam's teaching on mercy. Consider whether Jesus taught an internalised view of the end time and if this is a possible interpretation of Judgement Day in Islam. Compare teaching on reward and punishment in Matthew 25 with Muslim views of the *Al Qadr.*

Authority of the New Testament for Christians and the authority of the Qur'an for Muslims. Consider the nature of revelation in the New Testament and in Islam. Bear in mind the general Muslim notion of the Qur'an as *nazala* or direct revelation, with the Injil (Gospel) as incomplete revelation. **Early Church:** Consider the place of Paul as an interpreter of the kerygma (1 Cor 15: 1–4), or as one who has special revelation of the risen Jesus (Gal 1: 12), and compare with traditionalist, Islamist and modernist views of the composition of the Qur'an. **Gospels:** Compare scholarly views of the sources of the gospels with traditionalist, Islamist and modernist views of the composition of the Qur'an.

Test yourself

1. Compare and contrast the status of Jesus in the New Testament with that of Muhammad in Islam.
2. Assess the ways in which Islam and the New Testament texts you have studied establish their ethical principles.
3. Compare and contrast the ways in which Islam and the New Testament texts you have studied teach about sin.

Black theology in North America

Why a black theology?

At a basic level, black theology is the articulation of African Americans, who, having laboured for almost 300 years as slaves and then treated as racially inferior citizens, have developed their own distinctive religious beliefs. Black theology is a self-conscious attack on white philosophy and theology by academics who feel that western European culture has perpetuated a racist notion of society and justice.

The examination paper is divided into two parts. You will write two essays. You must answer one question on black theology and one question on Christianity in a multi-faith society.

Further reading

For a good overall view, read *Black Theology of Liberation* by Dwight Hopkins (Orbis 1999).

Historical context

The key question is why, despite a constitution that is based on a combination of Christian values of equality and natural law notions of human rights, America continued to perpetuate systematic discrimination against its black population well into the mid 20th century. The development of black religion and – more recently – black theology is intimately linked with America's history. As **contextual theology**, black theology is rooted in a particular history and in black experience. There are four phases:

The **Declaration of Independence** (1789) states: 'We hold these truths to be self-evident, that all men are created equal, that they are endowed by their Creator with certain inalienable Rights, that among these are Life, Liberty and the pursuit of Happiness.'

Slavery

Black theology is the product of North America, as it relates directly to American history, from the introduction of slaves from west Africa to the end of slavery in the USA in 1865. The experience of ancestral roots in Africa, of slavery, of working in the plantations, of segregation, of deprivation and poverty defines 'blackness' historically in terms of human suffering, oppression and solidarity. Black theology acknowledges that religion is always culturally determined.

During this time, it is estimated that some 14 million black slaves were transported from Africa to America, and 60 million more died on the journey.

In **1619** the first black Africans were employed to work on the tobacco plantations in Virginia, and the Southern colonies began to thrive economically. Northern colonies also had slaves but laws such as those of **1641** in Massachusetts made bond slavery illegal.

Although the slaves adopted the Protestant Christianity of their slave masters, scholars argue that **Africanisms** were preserved and adapted by the black slaves. Remaining African was an important part of the slave culture. The slaves from Africa brought with them their own pantheistic tribal religions. Pantheism makes very little distinction between nature and spirit, and although many of the religions had notions of a supreme deity, what is important for black religion is that it rejected or at least greatly modified the western **dualism** between matter and spirit.

Jesus for the slave was not an abstract idea, but a person like themselves who, despite his suffering, preached liberation. For God to be among them in this way gave them real hope. The slaves also grasped the New Testament image of the **New Jerusalem** (Revelation 21) as a fundamental aspect of Christianity. Through Jesus' suffering and death, as a servant and slave, his resurrection established the hope for a transformed world.

Most important for black religion was the transformation of the African village priest into the **preacher** and eventually the minister. To begin with, when independent organised religion was banned among slaves, the preacher was simply the person who knew the Bible well and was able to sing.

> **Further study**
> The popular song *Swing Low, Sweet Chariot* is an example of a Negro spiritual. Find out the titles of some more. How many do you recognise?

Protest was a characteristic of slave life. The underlying belief was that God would bring about freedom but only through human effort. Protest was expressed through: **Negro spirituals**; **rebellions** (Nat Turner in 1831 and Denmark Vesey in 1822); the **Invisible Institution** (the Negro church, which often met in secret); the **Underground Railroad** (secretly helping slaves escape to the north).

Emancipation

Article 4 Section 2, for instance, recognised the public obligation to return runaway slaves.

The constitution enshrined the notion of slavery, but the anti-slave trade movements in Britain and Europe, and the influence of the Quakers began to change attitudes, especially in the northern states. The key moments in the history of emancipation and civil rights are outlined below:

- In **1808** the constitution outlawed trading in slaves and in **1860** Abraham Lincoln's promise to abolish slavery was a major cause of the Civil War. On 4 April **1865** the Civil War ended, resulting in the abolition of slavery and emancipation of all slaves in the south.
- The 13th and 14th Amendments and Civil Rights Acts (1866–1875) made slavery illegal, but the US Supreme Court declared the 1875 act unconstitutional, opening the door to the '**Jim Crow**' laws that forbade intermarriage and required separate schooling, transport and so on for black Americans.
- Many blacks moved to the northern States to find jobs as domestics and cleaners; the early 20th century saw the development of black organisations working for rights and working conditions.
- **The bus boycott in Montgomery**, Alabama (1955) triggered the Civil Rights movement, led by Martin Luther King Jr of the Southern Christian Leadership Council. In 1963, 200,000 blacks and whites demonstrated for equal rights by marching on Washington. In 1964, under President Lyndon Baines Johnson, Congress passed far-reaching rights legislation forbidding public segregation.

Black theology: first generation

Black *religion* had been developing since the time of the first black preachers but black *theology* was the realisation that the white liberal and academic establishment was only interested in black integration on white terms. Black theology is an attempt to articulate a distinctive theology that is just as rigorous as white western/ European theology but based on a different set of experiences.

During the 1950s and 1960s, three people prepared the way for the birth of black theology. **Martin Luther King Jr**'s campaign for equality and civil rights revived the idea of the American Dream, but his liberal inclusivism failed to take into account the cultural divide between blacks and whites. **Malcolm X** (1925–1965) provided the anger and sense of 'blackness' which inspired first generation writers – even though he spoke from a Muslim perspective. **Joseph**

Washington's *Black Religion* (1964) argued that black religion was often more to do with culture than true faith and that white theology was where truth lay because it was based on authentic truth. The book proved explosive and in forming their answer to it, black leaders were forced to formulate their own black theology.

In June 1966, Stokely Carmichael first used the phrase '**black power**' in public, out of his frustration with the white liberal establishment. The National Committee of Negro Churchmen (NCNC) wrote a full-page article for the *New York Times* outlining the main aims of black theology. In 1969, **James Cone** wrote his seminal *Black Theology and Black Power*. The formation of Society for the Study of Black Theology in 1970 marked the moment when black theology became an academic discipline.

Make sure you know the following quotation:
'Black theology is a theology of liberation. It seeks to plumb the black condition in the light of God's revelation in Jesus Christ, so that the black community can see the gospel is commensurate with the achievement of black humanity. Black theology is a theology of 'blackness'. It is the affirmation of black humanity that emancipates black people from white racism, thus providing authentic freedom for both white and black people. It affirms the humanity of white people in that it says No to the encroachment of white oppression.'
National Association of Black Churchmen, June 13, 1969

Black theology: second generation

Second generation Black theology developed during the 1980s. The main concerns of the first generation had been rights and black power, but it had overlooked other important issues facing society that were also implicit in black culture. By now, many women had studied black theology at university. An interest in the pioneering work of 19th-century black women and criticism of white middle-class American feminism gave birth to **womanism**. Womanists argue that first generation black theology is sexist, classist and too exclusive. They embrace many of the postmodern ideas of religion and culture. Recent black theologians have also tackled other areas of sexual identity, notably homosexuality and transexuality, and many are influenced by the work of the Latin-American liberation theologians on class.

Further reading
Read *King Among the Theologians* by Noel Erskine (Pilgrim Press 1994).

The main concepts of black theology: Martin Luther King Jr (1929–1968)

Trained as a baptist minister, with an academic background in liberal Protestant Christianity, King believed that human beings are essentially good, given the right conditions to think and act rationally. King's frequent reference to the American constitution and to common human rationality appealed to both blacks and white liberals.

James Cone said of King that he was a 'prophet with charisma never before witnessed in the 20th century'. *A Black Theology of Liberation* (Orbis 1986), page 37.

Key influences

King was affected by the American philosophical tradition of **personalism**, which holds that people cannot be reduced to physical processes because each person is more than the sum of their parts. God's existence can be known through human personality. In Christian doctrinal terms, this is expressed by the principle of *imago Dei*, that all humans are created in the likeness of the creator. The second important source for his theology was Paul Tillich (1886–1965) and his idea of **correlation** – a theology which considers that God acts through human agency in so far as humans are only really free when they act according to God's will. King often used Tillich's way of expressing sin in terms of human psychological alienation and estrangement. The third influence on his theology was his life as a black man and black pastor. King may not have considered himself as a black theologian but his writings, speeches and sermons make constant use of black history and religion: in protest that the slave would eventually defeat his oppressor, in the hope that justice would eventually prevail and the eschatological dream of the New Jerusalem where the black person would gain his freedom and enter the 'promised land'.

Route D: Philosophy of religion and revelation. To what extent does King consider revelation is merely human experience of God?

'This personal idealism remains today my basic philosophical position... it gave me metaphysical and philosophical grounding for the idea of a personal God, and it gave me a metaphysical basis for the dignity of all human personality.' *The Autobiography of Martin Luther King Jr* ed. Clayborne Carson (Abacus 2000) pages 31–32.

An example of an 8th-century BCE prophet is Amos, whose message strongly criticised the exploitation of the weak. See pages 61–62.

Many would argue that King is not a 'black theologian' as such but more like an 8th-century BCE Hebrew prophet, working tirelessly to strike at the political heart of American life to create what he famously called the **beloved community**.

Human nature

Further reading

Read *The Great Sermons of Martin Luther King Jr.* eds. Clayborne Carson and Peter Holloran (Abacus 2000). Consider to what extent King really can be considered a black theologian or a theologian who happened to be black.

Despite King's optimistic view of human nature, his own experience of racism presented the paradox of human nature that most liberals find hard to reconcile. King's 'black theology' expresses the contradiction he sees in American life: a nation built on rational principles of freedom and rights for all but yet curiously blind to its own racism. In his famous sermon, *The Drum Major Instinct* (1968), King illustrates the duality of human nature by using the metaphor of the drum major. Humans are egoistical, but egoism can be channelled to fight for justice. Like many later black theologians, King often suggested that one of the main reasons for black suffering was to allow others to go free, the inspiration for which comes from Isaiah's Suffering Servant (Is 53) and Jesus' vicarious death on the cross. King's preoccupation with the nature of social sin illustrates that he was more than just a civil rights campaigner.

'Yes, if you want to say that I was a drum major, say that I was a drum major for justice. Say that I was a drum major for peace' *The Great Sermons*, page 185.

See the chapter on Jewish Scriptures, pages 53–55.

Eschatology

Route D: Philosophy of Religion and after-life. Compare King's eschatology with the this-worldly view of liberation theology. What does he teach about heaven?

King's prophetic 'dream', as he frequently called it, is a direct product of his black religious background. Spirituals often speak of freedom and a life free from pain and misery. But King doesn't take the Christian notion of the Kingdom of God simply to mean heaven; he is far closer to the way in which the gospels consider Jesus to be referring to a decisive moment in history itself. It is the **kairos** (Mk 1: 15) – the time, the right moment in history to act. King sees the nation still caught in Egypt but preparing to escape to the promised land. In his sermon, a *Knock at Midnight* (1963), based on Jesus' parable (Lk 11: 5-6), midnight represents the moment when the social order will be transformed unexpectedly and when humans will respond fully to God's call. King retains the black hope that God will establish the **New Jerusalem**. King's theological insistence – that human action for good will prevail through God's action at the 'right time' – creates his optimistic view that history *will* shortly change. King considered that the Kingdom of God must become a political reality as well as the transformation of the individual.

'And He's allowed me to go up to the mountain. And I've looked over, and I have seen the promised land. I may not get there with you. But I want you to know tonight, that we, as people, will get to the promised land.' *Autobiography*, page 365.

Praxis and Black Power

King brought theology from the privacy of the church into the public arena. His theology of praxis therefore marks an important departure from Tillich's theology. Whereas Tillich derives universal 'answers' from the general human condition, King derives universals appropriate to the particular moment. For King, if God's will can only be actualised through human action, then religion must be politically involved. King developed his notion of Christian praxis well before it became the mainstay of Latin-American liberation theology, but he was very cautious about linking it with Stokely Carmichael's idea of **black power**. King regarded this as a negative term born out of 'despair'. Reluctantly King accepted that 'black power' could be used if it meant giving black people their dignity and sense of identity.

Reconciliation and peace

The primary focus of King's black theology was reconciliation. In theological terms he considered it to be the restoration of the human *imago Dei* and the original God-human covenant. It forms the foundation of all his rights campaigns. Well before he became a rights leader, King had developed the idea that the heart of the Christian covenant is to be understood as **love**. Love cannot condone any use of violence; violence makes reconciliation impossible. In eschatological terms, reconciliation means the inclusive reconciling of blacks and whites, not in the master-slave relationship (or the I-It relationship as Martin Buber termed it) which has been the history of racism and black oppression, but in the 'I-Thou' relationship, where true freedom enables each person to express themselves as an individual. King's language is reminiscent of Tillich when he says, 'The essence of man is found in freedom'. The catchphrase of the movement was **we shall overcome**. King considered it to refer to the religious eschatological hope of justice flowing down to wipe out injustice, hate and poverty, as well as political action to get the churches to challenge the *status quo*. King is aware of the tension. Christians are told to submit to the authorities and pay Caesar what is due to Caesar (Mk 12: 13–17) but they are also called to sacrifice themselves to the higher law of God just as Shadrach, Meshach and Abednego did when they refused to obey Nebuchadnezzar's laws and were placed in the lion's den (Dan 6).

Route K: Religious ethics and war/peace. Compare King's views with Cone's and other forms of pacifisim. Find out about his views on the Vietnam war.

'As we go back to the buses let us be loving enough to turn an enemy into a friend. We must move from protest to reconciliation. It is my firm conviction that God is working in Montgomery.' Martin Luther King *Stride Toward Freedom* (HarperSanFrancisco 1990) page 172.

King's idea of protest through non-violent means would have meant very little to the black slaves in the 19th century. Is this aspect of his theology alien to black theology? Some have argued that non-violence can also cause injustice, suffering and excuse inaction. The question is whether King's campaigns really did bring about the fundamental changes in social attitudes that he hoped for.

Further discussion

Consider whether King failed to develop a distinctive theology – is it fair to say that his theology was neither 'black' nor politically coherent?

The main concepts of black theology: James Cone

James Cone was an academic who self-consciously developed a black theology drawing on several sources.

Key influences

Further reading

Read chapter 3 of *God of the Oppressed* by James Cone (Orbis 1997).

- **Malcolm X** (1925–1965) was a Muslim preacher in the Nation of Islam. Whereas King called for integration, Malcolm knew this would always be on the white man's terms; he preached separation and revolution. What Malcolm grasped better than King was that being black was more than just skin colour: it was a whole cultural identity and history.
- **Martin Luther King** (1929–1968). Cone admired King because his 'faith was primarily in his *preached word*... he was a theologian of action, a theologian of liberation (in the best sense) whose thinking about God was developed in his efforts to achieve freedom and dignity for black people'. However, Cone found King's message of reconciliation and universal justice confused and contradictory. His idea of justice reflected what his own experiences as a black *middle-class* American.

Martin and Malcolm and America, J. H. Cone (Orbis 1992), pages 122–123.

'King was caught in two worlds – one was made up of whites and middle-class blacks and the other was composed of poor blacks'. *Martin and Malcolm*, page 149.

- **Albert Camus** (1913–1960). Cone admired Camus' argument that human existence is properly defined in a protest against the 'indifference' of the universe and the absurdity of society. Cone could see that black power is a protest against the indifference of a society that has made black existence invisible.
- **Karl Marx** (1818–1883). Cone's writings are influenced by the Marxist idea that a revolutionary theology of liberation must take into account the economic power structures of society. Cone frequently calls for the overthrow of existing white structures because white theology perpetuates white ideology, however inclusive it thinks it is being.

Route D: Philosophy of religion and revelation. Cone appears to struggle between traditional and liberal protestant views of revelation. Has he undermined traditional Christian teaching on revelation?

Revelation and black consciousness

'Theology is not universal language about God. Rather, it is human speech informed by historical and theological traditions, and written for particular times and places.' Cone, *A Black Theology of Liberation*, preface page xi.

'Our theology must emerge consciously from an investigation of the socio-religious experience of black people, as that experience is reflected in *black* stories of God's dealings with black people on the struggle for freedom.' *God of the Oppressed* page 15.

Further reading

Read James Cone *The Spirituals and the Blues* (Orbis 1992).

'There is no revelation of God without a condition of oppression which develops into a situation of liberation... God not only reveals to the oppressed the divine right to break their chains by any means necessary, but also assures them that their work in their own liberation is God's own work.' Cone, *A Black Theology of Liberation*, pages 45-46.

Cone argues that theology is **dialectical** in so far as it is the human attempt to articulate a God who is both beyond human knowledge and yet who is known through human experience and history. Black experience has taught that God is not an abstract idea but is involved specifically with the plight of the oppressed. More than King, Cone stresses the **contextual** nature of theology. In *God of the Oppressed* Cone uses the distinction between existence and essence. If black **existence** (experience) precedes **essence** (theology) then black suffering is even more important than the Bible as the starting point for black theology:

- Black experience is the source of God's revelation through sermons, prayers, spirituals, secular stories, the blues, novels and poetry – all important sources for black theology.
- Black consciousness, whether it is Christian or not, is a primary source of God's revelation because it has developed out of **suffering**. God is available through human suffering. Any special moments in a history of suffering and liberation – whether it is the Exodus or Jesus' life and resurrection – are special illustrations of general revelation. Using a phrase from Tillich's existential theology, being black requires 'the courage to be' fully human against a hostile white world.

God is black

Route D: Philosophy of religion and God. Bear in mind the philosophical debates about language and God. Read chapter 5 of *Philosophy of Religion* by John Hick (Prentice Hall 1973).

Cone challenges the white idea of God. Discussions about God's existence or non-existence, argues Cone, are possible only in an affluent, white, bourgeois society where people have time to ponder such things. The challenge is to say, 'God is black'. The reaction of white theologians inevitably is to reject such a claim – all language about God is equivocal and to say that God is anything is not to say what God actually is. But that is Cone's point. 'Blackness' is a summary term that describes a God who is active in human oppression, who is a God of both judgement (Old Testament) and love (New Testament). A theology which claims that God is love fails to recognise that God also demands justice. God is not impartial; those who are racist are not equally loved by God and should never believe that what they do is condoned.

'If this is true, then Jesus Christ must be black so that blacks can know that their liberation is his liberation'. *A Black Theology of Liberation*, page 12.

'Black theology cannot accept a view of God which does not represent God as being for oppressed blacks and thus against white oppressors. Living in a world of white oppressors, blacks have no time for a neutral God.' *A Black Theology of Liberation*, page 70.

Cone argues that Jesus should be given a new title besides those found in the New Testament. Not only is Jesus the Son of God, he is also the **Black Messiah**. Jesus is 'black' because he sides with the oppressed (baptised, he acknowledges his place with sinners) but as the Black Christ, the Church recognises that his resurrection marks a triumph of justice over oppression. Black theology teaches the necessity of combining the Jesus of history and the Christ of faith. Cone's theology, more so than that of Latin-American liberation theologians, deals with the mind of the oppressor.

Justice

Route K: Religious ethics and ethical principles. To what extent is Cone advocating a consequentialism (that the ends justify the means)?

Although Cone and the other black theologians were initially developing their theology independently of the South-American liberation theologians, black theology shares the same principle that theology should be, as Guttierez called it, '**second act**'. Second act theology is the process of reflection, study and **conscientisation**. Here, Cone's contribution to black theology is far more significant than King's. King developed his theology through his sermons and speeches but it lacked intellectual rigour. Cone on the other hand acknowledges that King and Malcolm X were 'first act' practitioners. There is a danger that Cone's black theology might well be considered as just another academic intellectual exercise. Nevertheless, Cone is adamant that the existential 'passion' aroused from centuries of black oppression will ensure that the gospel will continue to inspire liberation from oppression.

'The sin of American theology is that it has spoken without passion. It has failed miserably in relating its work to the oppressed in society by refusing to confront the structures of this nation with the evil of racism.' *A Black Theology of Liberation*, page 18.

One of the least satisfactory aspects of his early writings is his teaching on eschatology. In the final chapter of *A Black Theology of Liberation*, Cone deals with the Christian notion of eschatology – the discussion of the final things or the consummation of history:

- **Heaven** is a metaphor for this world, transformed through human struggle for freedom. But in a black struggle it is unclear how whites will undergo the spiritual and moral change or **metanoia** in order to be included in this new 'black society'.
- On the other hand, Cone appears to argue that history has no foreseeable end and so the afterlife is still a reality and reward for those blacks who have fought for justice and died in the process.
- Yet he also argues that the 'heaven' of the spirituals was a white man's 'lie' to explain why blacks are suffering now. In the final pages of *Black Theology and Black Power*, Cone argues that the Christian notion of reconciliation means firstly that blacks must recognise with pride their own blackness and demand 'respect' from whites and secondly that whites must reconcile themselves to accepting blacks as blacks and ultimately becoming 'black' themselves. But can whites ever become 'black' given their very different historical experiences?
- Cone's eschatology appears to preserve white/black difference and yet he condemns white attitudes as inherently racist.

Eschatology and liberation

Route D: Philosophy of religion and after-life. Compare Cone's, King's and liberation theologians' teaching on the afterlife.

'Only blacks can speak about sin in a black perspective and apply it to black and white persons. The white version of reality is too distorted and renders whites incapable of talking to the oppressed about their shortcomings.' *Black Theology of Liberation*, page 51.

Black theology and other contextual theologies

The basic problem is whether theologies of liberation are compatible with one another. All appear to share two common ideas:

- Theology is developed out of a specific context of oppression and exploitation.
- The 'exodus' experience serves as a theological symbol of liberation, whereby an oppressed group is conscientised and liberated from injustice. Full humanity is achieved through a belief in a God of love and justice.

Black theology and feminist theology

Is black theology sexist? Black women comprise over 80 per cent of black worshipping communities and yet black theology, until the second generation writers, had been developed almost entirely by men. The development of white feminism undoubtedly acted as a catalyst for many black women to express their criticisms of black theology, yet they are also equally critical of feminism. The term **womanism** is used by black women to distance themselves from feminism and is borrowed from the black phrase 'to act womanish'.

Alice Walker defined being womanish as: 'wanting to know more and in greater depth than is good for one... outrageous, audacious, courageous and wilful behaviour' and 'responsible, in charge, serious.' *In Search of our Mothers' Gardens* (Women's Press 2000).

Feminism has been regarded with suspicion by black men and women. Black men considered that feminism was the reaction of bored white middle-class wives and was a means of avoiding their responsibility to the family. Initially, feminism was overwhelmingly white, middle-class, educated and secular, and did little to address issues of race, class and religion. For black women, the church, its liturgy, songs and fellowship provide the basis for solidarity that is lacking not only for white women but also in society as a whole. Womanism therefore offers a critique of black theology and white culture.

Black Theology eds. Cone and Wilmore (Orbis 1993), volume 2, page 268.

Womanists argue that black theology has failed to acknowledge the place of women in African-American identity and history: 'If Rosa Parks had not sat down, Martin King would not have stood up.' Womanist ethics oppose homophobia, because the notions of sex and gender are fluid terms; no 'colourism', because all people are coloured; no classism because this is based on a male idea of competition and leads to violence.

Route D: Philosophy of religion and God. To what extent have womanists undermined the traditional view of God?

Womanist theology is even more radical than black theology in its attack on white theology's dualism of matter and spirit. Despite what Cone professes, his depiction of God is one who judges the world between black and white. God's justice is exclusive only for the oppressed, and Jesus' death is a victory over the present evil society. On the other hand, womanist theology often presents God in pantheistic terms – as the Spirit who is neither male nor female but is the empowering animating force from within.

Further reading

Read *The Color Purple* by Alice Walker (Woman's Press 1983) and look at the way she develops the notion of God as Spirit.

The experience of God as Spirit is to be found in:

Bible. God is described as the Spirit creating the world, inspiring and supporting women like Hagar and Mary. It gives life (Jn 6: 63) and is the source of truth (Jn 14: 17).

Jesus. Womanists criticise white women for making Jesus too remote and an abstract idea, whereas they think of Jesus in personal terms as one who shares in their lives: 'Black woman's Jesus and white woman's Christ.' Jesus is 'womanish' because he was the source of strength and love in the family (Mk 3: 31–35).

Stories. Womanism offers the postmodern idea that truth is not to be found in historical facts but in narratives. Black literature, especially novels by black women, provide the means by which the Spirit may be encountered, reflected upon and used as inspiration.

'God's response of survival and quality of life to Hagar is God's response of survival and quality of life to African women and mothers of slave descent struggling to sustain their families with God's help…' Dolores Williams in *Sisters in the Wilderness: The Challenge of Womanist God-Talk* (Orbis 1993), page 6.

Hagar. The story of Hagar provides a good summary of womanist theology. Being a story it loses nothing if its historical validity is questioned. Secondly, as a paradigm it challenges the black theologians' emphasis on the exodus-liberation model. It is not an external fight between oppressors and the oppressed, but the story of spiritual courage and victory. Thirdly, Hagar is oppressed because of her race (as an Egyptian), class (as a servant) and sex (as a concubine and surrogate mother). Finally, Hagar is the first person in the Bible who directly encounters God's messenger.

Black theology and liberation theology

Route K: Religious ethics and ethical principles. Consider their criticisms of Kant or even Aquinas. Do these pose a problem for Christian ethics?

The origins of black theology's reluctance to develop a radical view of economics can be traced to Martin Luther King's and Malcolm X's common mistrust of Marxism. Despite the fact that black theology and liberation theology share so many ideas and themes there is a tension between them. Latin-American theologians are accused of being institutionally racist by many black theologians. This hesitancy highlights some fundamental problems of contextual theologies:

- Racism is not an issue for liberation theologians in South America; harsh poverty is. Black theologians ought to recognise that liberation in that context has nothing to do with racism.
- If racism, poverty and class are all institutional sins (spiritually and physically) of *any* society then liberation theologies are dealing with *universals*. But contextual liberation theologies are very suspicious about theological universals and consider them to belong to western (white) bourgeois academic societies.
- A confusion often caused in liberation theology is the balance between the secular and the spiritual. Although both Latin-American and black theologians try to treat history as an expression of both human and divine will, nevertheless there is a danger that they in fact reduce God too much to the human level and make religion just a cultural expression of human hopes.

Christianity in a multi-faith society

Exclusivism

Exclusivism posits that only Christians will be assured salvation. In traditional Protestant Christian terms, exclusivism is derived from the idea that Christianity alone satisfies all the necessary conditions for salvation. These views are typically expressed by **John Calvin** (1509–1564) when he says that salvation is only through personal faith in Jesus Christ and God's grace, as a 'share in the life of God'. But for Calvin, even those who are committed to Jesus Christ and who live exemplary moral lives are not assured salvation, as this always depends on the unknown will of God.

Traditional Protestant exclusivism

Route D: Philosophy of religion and authority of scripture. Traditional exclusivism is very dependent on a conservative reading of the Bible.

In the early Church many held the **ecclesia ab Abel** view that salvation was possible to those who lived before Jesus. In 1 Peter, Jesus, after his resurrection and before his ascension into heaven, preached the gospel to all those who had died before the incarnation. **Augustine** (354–430) argued that God knew who would or would not receive and reject the gospel, and **Aquinas** (c. 1225–1274) argued that special revelation would be given only to those in extraordinary situations (such as a child brought up by wolves). Aquinas makes the important point that although God is revealed in creation to all, this is not sufficient to secure salvation but only to prepare a person so that when they finally encounter the gospel their minds will be ready to embrace it fully.

Traditional Catholic exclusivism

'Ecclesia ab Abel' refers to those who through faith in God put themselves in a position of salvation before the coming of Christ.

Look up 1 Peter 3: 18–20 and 4: 5–6.

John Hick doubts whether there are any real exclusivists in the mainstream churches today. The traditional Catholic dogma of **extra ecclesiam nulla salus** (there is no salvation outside the Church) appeared to be quietly dropped at the time of the Second Vatican Council (1968). The most recent Vatican declaration – **Dominus Iesus** (2000) – begins by reiterating the message of Vatican 2 and goes on to make the following points:

- Other religions provide a human 'treasury' of wisdom but only the quest for, not the finality of, truth.
- The eternal Word of God and Incarnate Word are one and the same but God's Spirit extends to all humanity.

Modern Roman Catholic teaching

Further reading

The Rainbow of Faiths by John Hick (SCM 1995).

Further discussion

Consider whether you would judge modern Roman Catholic teaching exclusivist or inclusivist.

'The Catholic Church rejects nothing of what is true and holy in these religions. She has a high regard for the manner of life and conduct, the precepts and teachings, which, although differing in many ways from her own teaching, nonetheless often reflect a ray of that truth which enlightens everyone.' *Dominus Iesus* (Catholic Truth Society) page 4.

- ✦ The Catholic Church represents the best path to salvation, as even other Christian denominations may lack sufficient elements of faith – those which have no apostolic succession, or fail to represent the sacraments properly, for example.

Dominus Iesus, page 31.

It concludes that 'the church has a 'sincere respect' for the religions of the world but there is no place for 'a religious relativism' which holds that 'one religion is as good as another'. Although followers of other religions 'can receive divine grace… objectively speaking they are in a gravely deficient situation in comparison with those who, in the Church, have the fullness of the means of salvation'.

Karl Barth (1886–1968)

Rejection of liberal theology

Further reading

Read chapter 3 of *Barth* by John Webster (Continuum 2000) on the purpose of theology.

Route K: Religious ethics and relationship with God. What kind of ethics is Barth presenting? This is a difficult aspect of his theology.

Barth's neo-orthodox theology developed as he rejected the liberal Protestant tradition in which he had been brought up. The first world war illustrated the failure of human reason to create a good society. Barth argued that Christians must rediscover the basic idea that revelation is *God*-given and that as humans we can only imperfectly apprehend and act upon it. He therefore rejected the liberal Christian view that theology begins with human religious experience. It is very difficult to classify what kind of theologian Barth is:

Pre-modernist. His theology is traditional and appears to reject modern critical thinking. But Barth is fully aware of modern thought. He argues that science and philosophy are all human activities and can never do more than point to God's revelation, which is, by definition, outside human comprehension.

Postmodernist. His suspicion and rejection of history as a source of reality combine with his concern that too much emphasis has been placed on human reason as a means of truth. But Barth is not postmodern in the sense that he is assimilating religious experience into a world where absolutes and certainties have ceased to mean anything. Barth's suspicion of human experience is derived from his overwhelming sense of the objective infinite God and finite man.

Modernist. He is concerned to rescue God from those like Feuerbach who had argued that if God is an expression of human religious experience then that is *all* he is. According to Barth, God is 'wholly other'. So he is a neo-orthodox theologian re-expressing traditional Christian doctrine in the light of modern experience.

Doctrine of the Word

Route D: Philosophy of religion and scripture. Barth is not a literalist or a fundamentalist. How is the Bible the Word of God?

What makes Christianity unique? The answer, argues Barth, is its central epistemological (knowledge-based) notion of the **Word**. Barth sets out his central themes and methods in the 'Prolegomena' (volumes I.1 and I.2) of *Church Dogmatics*: 'The Doctrine of the Word of God'. God's 'existence' is beyond all knowledge but he is knowable to humans through his *Logos* or Word. Barth offers no one definition of the Word, for the whole of the *Church Dogmatics* is an attempt to unpack and illustrate the Word as experienced and perceived by humans. The Word may be encountered in three ways: revealed in Jesus Christ, in the written Word and in the preached Word. Barth's task was to unpack what this means.

Look up John 1: 1 and 14; Hebrews 1: 2; Revelation 19: 13.

Revealed Word in Jesus Christ. Several texts in the New Testament make the unique claim that God's Word was revealed absolutely and completely in the person of Jesus Christ. As Barth says: 'Revelation in fact does not differ from the Person of Jesus Christ… To say revelation is to say "The Word became flesh".'

Written Word of God in scripture. The Bible is the witness to God's Word; it is the one fixed given notion on which Christianity can draw timelessly from generation to generation. But the Bible must not become the object of reverence, as this is 'bibliotry'. So, Barth was not a biblical fundamentalist or literalist. He makes it clear that the Bible is not itself the Word of God but witness to the Word.

'The Bible is God's Word, so far as God speaks through it.' Karl Barth.

Preached Word of God. Barth follows reformers such as Luther and Calvin when he states the power and importance of preaching the Word of God. He criticised liberal Protestants for their over-subjective claim that it is the individual's rational encounter with God that is authentic. God's Word is not generally available through reason, but exclusively through the Christian Bible.

The revelation of God

The core of Barth's theology is the exclusive revelation of God in the person of Christ with the Bible as the unique witness. Through it, revelation offers a concrete knowledge of God, initiated by God. All philosophy falls short because it fails to observe the datum of revelation. A constant phrase of Barth is, '**through God alone may God be known**'.

The Trinity. No one since the Reformation had revived the doctrine of the Trinity as comprehensively as Barth. For Barth, the Trinity is a fact *a priori*; it is the unique defining revelation of the Christian God (*Church Dogmatics* I: 1). Many theologians have criticised the doctrine because it is unbiblical, but this is one of the very reasons why Barth finds in it an authentic expression of God, because God's revelation must necessarily be greater than that of the Bible. The Trinity is about the oneness of God; God who operates as 'revealer, revelation and revealedness'. No other religion expresses God in this way. Barth's comment, while not elaborating on other religions, makes it quite clear that Christianity alone has exclusive access to this knowledge.

'It is the doctrine of the Trinity which fundamentally distinguishes the Christian doctrine of God as Christian – it is it, therefore, also, that which marks off the Christian concept of revelation as Christian.'

The Incarnation. In *Church Dogmatics* I.2 Part II, Barth concentrates on the person of Christ and the incarnation – God, as *Logos*, who becomes human. The incarnation reveals the second mode of the Trinity. For in Jesus Christ, God freely reveals himself to us as fully man but he does not 'empty' himself of his divine attributes; he only reveals himself to humans and not to any other part of creation. In Jesus Christ, God's Word is most completely revealed.

The Spirit. So how can God's revelation be experienced by humans? Barth accepted that there *could* be general religious experience, but he differed from the liberal Protestants and what he called their 'self-centred I-piety' (over-emphasis on human subjectivity). Properly understood, religious experience is the result of God's **grace**. Theoretically the Spirit can be active in other religions but only as the third revealing person of the Trinity. The Spirit is the means by which the human mind is opened to accept the particular reality of the incarnation, the teaching of the Word found in the Bible and Church tradition. The Spirit is the subjective dimension of God creating a community of believers through whom the Word of God is actively preached and lived. Unlike the God of the

'According to Holy Scripture God's revelation occurs in our enlightenment by the Holy Spirit of God to a knowledge of His Word. The outpouring of the Holy Spirit is God's revelation. In the reality of this event consists our freedom to be the children of God and to know and love and praise Him in His revelation.'

philosophers, God as Spirit is ever active, involved and present in the world. But the Spirit is not sufficient in itself for salvation, for the Spirit *must* be understood in terms of the Trinity.

A theology of religion

Route K: Religious ethics and relationship with God. To what extent does Barth acknowledge moral cultural relativism?

Read Romans 1: 18–2: 1. It is often cited as an example of natural law and conscience.

'We know that God is He whom we do not know, and that our ignorance is precisely the problem and the source of our knowledge.' *Epistle to the Romans* (OUP 1968, second edition), page 45.

Barth had begun his academic career with a controversial commentary on Paul's letter to the Romans. *The Epistle to the Romans* (1921) provides us with Barth's analysis of what constitutes authentic religion. The first issue he had to deal with in *Romans* is where Paul appears to be talking about God's goodness revealed generally in nature and known through conscience and reason. The paradox that Paul sets up is that if God can be known through human reason, what makes Christianity significant? Barth's reading of Paul is that, although hypothetically reason may be a necessary condition for faith, it is not sufficient for salvation, particularly given human subjectivity and sinfulness.

Exclusivism: rejection of natural theology. The debate about natural theology had, in 1934, been the catalyst for Barth's famous 'No!' to his colleague Emil Brunner, by which he made clear his belief that human reason and human experience is never sufficient to know about God. Barth felt Brunner (and others) had made revelation too objective and faith too rational, whereas Barth argued that they have a **dialectical** relationship: just as the world is wholly different from God, so faith is wholly different from revelation. It is in the tension between the two that we may say God can be known. However, although it is true that Barth distances himself from the liberal Protestant notion that revelation is a condition of the world, his claim that revelation is always a special active event of God makes it quite possible that God might choose to reveal himself outside Christianity.

Further reading

Read J. A. Di Noia in *The Cambridge Companion to Karl Barth* ed. John Webster (CUP 2000), chapter 15.

The test for true religion. Di Noia argues that the only place where Barth actually tackles the question of the truth outside Christianity in other religions is found in *Church Dogmatics* I.2 section 17, entitled 'The Revelation of God as the Abolition of Religion', and this has often been misunderstood. The term 'abolition' as it appears in translation suggests to many that Barth considered Christian revelation to abolish the claims of other religions. This would indeed make him an exclusivist. But Di Noia argues that Barth's argument is to warn against those who have made religion more important than revelation. This is reinforced by the translation of the German word *Aufhebung* as 'abolition'. A much better word is 'sublation' or 'untruth'. Barth is arguing that it is not religions that are true, because they are human institutions. The only truth is revelation. Revelation is defined by the active Word. By implication a religion (including Christianity) is only true insofar as it embodies revelation.

Unbelief. Further confusion is caused by Barth's striking claim that: 'Religion is unbelief. It is the one great concern… of godless man.' 'Unbelief' appears to present a form of exclusivism because religions other than Christianity are not true and are godless. However, the German *Unglaube* can be translated as 'faithlessness' – a less harsh judgement meaning that religions remain that way unless redeemed by God's grace.

Inclusivism

The Christian inclusivist argument is simply that if God is a God of love then all people of good will, whatever their religion, may be included in God's saving grace. Inclusivism concedes that if religious experience is possible outside Christianity, then there is much to be gained in enriching Christianity with the diversity of other great religious traditions. Whereas Barth, and exclusivists in general, talk of Christianity in terms of revelation, the inclusivist perspective is driven by experience. Inclusivism attempts to justify from the Bible and tradition the idea that there is a universal human religious experience, while preserving the uniqueness of salvation through Jesus Christ. The Church of England report *The Mystery of Salvation* (1995) acknowledged that one of the greatest challenges to Christian belief in the late 20th century, along with feminism and science, is the presence of other religions. The report cautiously adopts an inclusivist position.

'It is incompatible with the essential Christian affirmation that God is love to say that God brings millions into the world to damn them. The God of Love also longs for all to come into relationship with him, and this is his purpose in creation. When he chooses certain peoples, such as Israel, or certain persons such as the prophets or the Apostles, he chooses them not for exclusive privilege or salvation, but for a purpose in the expression of God's self-revelation and showing of his saving love for all.' *The Mystery of Salvation* (Church House Publishing 1995), page 180.

Understanding the sociological origins of the New Testament means realising that passages that may sound as if they are making exclusive claims are often the response to situations in which the early Christian groups were trying to assert their identity. A particularly dramatic example of the ways in which exclusivism appears to have developed in early Christianity is in **John 8**. Many sociologists consider this passage to reflect an extreme moment of tension between one group of Jews (the in-group) and a group of heretical Jews i.e. 'Christians' (the out-group). As the in-group seeks to reassert its dominance and identity, the smaller out-group fights back. Their identities or 'badges' both depend on Abraham (Jn 8: 32–41, 52–59) as their ancestor and symbol of faith. In John 8, the writer develops Jesus' words so as to show that the Jews have a totally distorted view of commitment to Abraham and that only those who follow Jesus can know the truth. This is the context to understanding the often quoted phrase, 'I am the way, and the truth, and the life; no one comes to the Father, but by me' (Jn 14: 6). In its context it overstates the claims of Christianity against Jewish hostility, so although it may sound exclusive it has to be understood in terms of the common Jewish/Christian roots.

Understanding the origins of Christianity

Route D: Philosophy of religion and authority of scripture. If inclusivists stress the contextual nature of the Bible as a repository of religious experience, what kind of authority does it have?

Further reading

Read *After the Evil* by Richard Harries (OUP 2003). Harries uses this kind of analysis to show how Christian anti-Semitism has resulted from an exclusivist reading of the New Testament.

Karl Rahner

Karl Rahner (1904–1984) was a German Roman Catholic Jesuit who argued for an inclusivist view of Christianity. Rahner is known for developing the twin ideas of **anonymous Christianity** and the **anonymous Christian** – that is the person who through goodwill is able to respond to God's grace, unaware that this indeed is the God of love central to Christian doctrine. His task was to balance this notion against the Catholic doctrine of the Church and her place as the institution through which salvation is possible.

General outlook

Rahner's inclusivism is based on his interpretation of Aquinas and Kant – that as human knowledge is finite and limited no one can have exclusive claims to truth. Yet there is a universal human 'openness' or desire to gain knowledge that will lead to ultimate knowledge of salvation. Rahner notes that throughout history humans from every culture have constantly searched for grace. But for him, Christianity is the most explicit and clear expression of what humans experience the world over whenever they act selflessly, lovingly and charitably to one another.

> **Further reading**
>
> Rahner's argument is set out in an essay in *Theological Investigations* Volume 5 (1966).

The argument works by developing four interlocking areas:

- defining Christian exclusivism and the *Solus Christus* claim
- analysing experience of what Christians call grace in history
- defining anonymous Christianity
- considering the role of the Church and the idea of the Christian community as a means of salvation.

Solus Christus: Christian exclusivism

Rahner makes it clear that Christianity is a revelatory religion and that humans cannot know God through reason alone. Even though Christianity has a 'pre-history', which can be seen in the story of Israel in the Old Testament and the teaching of the prophets, it properly begins at a *particular* moment in history. This has implications for the role and function of the Church. The knowledge of Christ is mediated through the history of the church (teaching, mission, sacraments). Rahner argues that even exclusivists have to acknowledge that there are times when a culture could not have been Christian (i.e. before Christianity existed) and a culture must have been religionless before it encountered and converted to Christianity. Christian exclusivism has to be questioned because it assumes that God doesn't wish all humans to be saved. Exclusivism leads to the uncomfortable realisation that the Christian God is not a god of love, but is selective. Rahner argues that it makes more philosophical – and Christian – sense to conclude that what really matters is being open to God's will through different cultures.

Based on his claim that humans desire grace, Rahner develops Aquinas' notion of the **votum ecclesiae** – that even *wanting* to be a member of the Church can constitute sufficient faith sometimes to receive God's grace. God's grace is to be observed in Israel's history, the creation, conscience, and the social and historical conditions of every age. Therefore, although the incarnation occurred at a particular time and place among a particular people, its significance was a universal and timeless expression of God's active place in history and creation.

History and the experience of grace

> **Route K: Religious ethics and relationship with God.** Consider the influence of Kant's universalism in Rahner's theology.

> **Further reading**
>
> Read Acts of the Apostles 17 and note how Paul uses both natural theology and revelation in Christ to persuade the Athenians.

For example, read pages 61–65 on Amos and Micah in this guide.

Rahner argues firstly that all humans are ignorant to some extent according to the doctrine of original sin. Secondly, all humans are loved unconditionally by God according to the doctrine of grace. Rahner disagrees with traditional Catholicism that all religions are invalid unless they embrace historical Christianity. After all, St Paul chose the altar to the 'unknown god' at the Areopagus in Athens (Acts 17) as a basis for his argument that, although the Greeks worshipped what they could not see, Christians know this unknown God through their encounter with Christ. However, not all religions are equally legitimate. For a religion to be legitimate it must be judged by the quality of salvation that it offers. It needs an organisational authority by which to regulate truth and falsehood. Even so, there are some individuals who do live morally and religiously good lives *outside* the institution – how should they be judged? The Old Testament prophets existed outside the cult and yet are regarded as the main proponents of Israel's doctrine of grace.

Rahner is now able to use the idea of the anonymous Christian: 'If the second thesis is correct, then Christianity does not simply confront the member of an extra-Christian religion as a mere non-Christian, but as someone who can and must already be regarded in this or that respect as an anonymous Christian.'

Anonymous Christianity

Theological Investigations (Crossroad Publishing Company 1970), volume 5 page

Finally, Rahner discusses the Church's role in salvation. From what he has said so far, the church cannot be an 'exclusive community' but an expression of what Christianity means in the wider world. In an increasingly secular world, the role of the church is therefore all the more significant. This may appear presumptuous to non-Christian religions and to non-religious people. But a Christian has a duty to make God (who is greater than the Church) known to the world. The requirement to mission is summarised by Paul's speech at Athens.

Role of the Church

Further reading

Read *Karl Rahner* by William Dych (Continuum 2000), in particular chapter 6 on the Church.

Pluralism: John Hick

The pluralist position is often arrived at through the simple conclusion that people of other religions live virtuous lives. This is true for John Hick, whose conversion to a plural view of Christianity developed over a number of years despite his conservative evangelical conversion to Christianity while at university. The first stage of his conversion to pluralism began when he was a lecturer and church minister encountering other religious traditions in Birmingham. This led him to two conclusions. Firstly that it was clear to him that being Christian did not necessarily make people morally better than those of different faiths. Secondly, it appeared incoherent to him that a God of love could damn those who simply by the quirk of history, geographical location and cultural upbringing had not experienced Christian revelation.

Further reading

Read chapter 1 of *God has many names* by John Hick (Macmillan 1980).

'But whilst there cannot be a world religion, there can be approaches to a world theology. For if awareness of the Transcendent Reality that we call God is not confined to the Christian tradition, the possibility opens up of what might be called (for want of a better term) a global theology... The project of a global theology is obviously vast, requiring the co-operative labours of many individuals and groups over a period of several generations. The increasing dialogue of world religions is basic to this work.' John Hick in *God Has Many Names*, page 8.

Influenced by the great liberal Protestant theologian **Friedrich Schleiermacher** (1768–1834) and by **Rudolf Otto** (1869–1937), Hick argued that revelation should be considered primarily in terms of religious experience. His aim has been to create a 'global theology'. His vision of the world is one in which religion will play a much more active political and moral role in society by increasing a common awareness of great universal themes which unite religious traditions in their aim to create a better world.

Hick begins by defining God or the Absolute. In the tradition of the liberal Protestants, Hick argues that Christianity must first rethink itself in **theocentric** and not **Christocentric** terms. Its failure has been to turn its early religious experiences into facts. These facts (incarnation, atonement and resurrection) are really 'myths' or metaphors about the experience of God. In his controversial *The Myth of God Incarnate* (pages 167–185) Hick draws a parallel between the way in which the Buddha in Mahayana Buddhism was gradually transformed from the great enlightened teacher to be revered as the incarnation of the eternal Buddha. Hick observes that it is human nature to wish to elevate a person to become their personal saviour. The earliest strands of the New Testament stress that Jesus was God's Son in the sense that he was the specially chosen prophet, and the resurrection demonstrated God's love, not Jesus' divinity. Jesus' claim that, 'no one comes to the Father, but by me' (Jn 14: 6) was the result of much later reflection by the

Theocentric not Christocentric revelation

Route D: Philosophy of religion and afterlife. Read *God and the Universe of Faiths* by John Hick (Oneworld 1973). Consider whether Hick's de-mythologised Christianity has turned it into a form of humanism.

'The need arises from growing knowledge of Christian origins, and involves a recognition that Jesus was (as he is presented in Acts 2.22) "a man approved by God" for a special role within the divine purpose, and that the later conception of him as God incarnate, the Second Person of the Holy Trinity living a human life, is a mythological or poetic way of expressing his significance for us.' John Hick in *The Myth of God Incarnate* (SCM 1977), page vii.

author, not the actual words of Jesus himself. Hick concludes that the uniqueness of Jesus lies in his own remarkable effect on others but, properly understood, Jesus' divinity is a myth.

Hick proposes that Christianity must rid itself of the ancient doctrines laid down at the great councils of Nicea (325) and Chalcedon (451) that defined the divinity of Christ and established the idea of the Trinity. Once it has done so, then Jesus' social teaching and example can be appropriated by other religions as a gift to the world – to 'enlarge the relationship with God to which they have already come within their own tradition' (*Myth*, page 181).

Kant and non-personal universal truth

Route K: Religious ethics and relationship with God. Read chapter 5 of *The Universe of Faiths: A Critical Study of John Hick's Pluralism* by Christopher Sinkinson (Paternoster Press 2001) for a very good analysis of Hick. Consider whether Hick's use of Kant has in fact developed a different kind of exclusivism and moral absolutism.

Critics have accused Hick of assuming a unified Kantian view of reality that religions tap into. How does he know this? Is the Kantian world-view necessarily one that, for example, a tribal African religion would recognise?

Kant argued that knowledge of a thing may be considered in two ways:

- **Phenomenal** existance is the world as we experience it
- **Noumenal** reality of a thing is its essence or its *an-sich* (in German). It can only be inferred or postulated from what we experience; the *an-sich* therefore remains unknown to us.

From this, Hick argues that although each religion has a very different experience of the phenomenal world, all postulate a shared noumenal reality which Hick calls the **'Eternal One'**. Where Hick goes further than Kant is by saying that the religious experience of the great world religions provides concrete evidence for the noumenal reality of the universe that Kant can only postulate according to reason. Some religions express their sense of the Eternal One in personal terms – such as Christianity, Judaism and Islam. Others, such as Buddhism and certain forms of Hinduism, present the Eternal One as a non-personal reality.

Morality and reality-centredness

Hick (following Kant) argues that authentic religions are those that turn self-centred moral behaviour to reality-centred existence. In a reality-centred life people become more generous by seeing their place in the universe. Although at the historical and cultural level there may seem to be conflicting claims, each religion produces enough 'saints' to illustrate that there are those who live up to the ultimate moral reality. This means that all the great religions have something to teach one another. Critics consider Hick to have developed a modern form of agnosticism, through which – though he tries to avoid becoming attached to a particular tradition – he simply adopts another tradition of western liberalism.

Further reading

Read part IV of *The Case for Religion* by Keith Ward (Oneworld 2004) in which, although he shares some of Hick's ideas, Ward develops a 'soft' pluralism that aims to respect the integrity of each religion more.

Test yourself

1. 'James Cone's black theology of liberation is full of contradictions.' Discuss.
2. 'Black theology and feminist theology are incompatible.' Discuss.
3. 'A plural theology of religion is another form of exclusivism.' Discuss.
4. Assess the view that Karl Rahner's inclusivist theology offers the best solution to the relationship between Christianity and other religions.

Connections

Philosophy of Religion with Developments in Christian Thought (Route D)

Black, feminist and liberation theologians' reinterpretation of belief in God. Consider the **black** theologians' emphasis on the immanence of God in history, as one who is known through suffering but with tension between male and womanist interpretations (God as Spirit and avoidance of patriarchy). Consider the **feminist** challenge to traditional male/rational arguments for the existence of God, the problem of male language and the sex/gender embodiment debate – bear in mind the reconstructionist and radical remodelling of God (Goddess theology). Consider the **liberation** theologians' view of God who actively sides with the poor in history, with problems of the transcendence of God and causal arguments which avoid making God a cause among causes – compare to traditional arguments, especially the Russell-Copplestone debate.

'Immanence' means God's involvement in the creation and human affairs.

> **Further reading**
>
> Read pages 121–123 of the *OCR AS Guide* and chapter 3 of *Cambridge Companion to Feminist Theology* ed. Susan Parsons (CUP 2002) on feminism and philosophy of religion.

See pages 63–68 of the *OCR AS Guide*.

Worldly interests of liberation theology in comparison with views of the afterlife. Consider the emphasis on the dialectical process of praxis, which places the needs of the poor prior to orthodoxy. Look at the place of God in history and the suffering of Jesus as a model of God's justice now. Consider whether the influence of Marxism/Feuerbach has diminished the afterlife and undermined Christian teaching on the resurrection.

See pages 127–131 of the *OCR AS Guide* and see the section in this guide on philosophy of religion (pages 16–19).

> **Further reading**
>
> Read chapter 16 of *Systematic Theology* eds. Jon Sobrino and Ignacio Ellacuría (SCM 1996) on hope, utopia and resurrection.

Ways in which feminist and black theology have challenged the concept of revelation. Consider the challenge of feminists that philosophy is patriarchal in the way it has undermined personal experience, rationalised revelation and become obsessed with evidence. Consider whether it has made religious experience too dependent on sexuality. Consider whether Cone's dialectical view of revelation is coherent. Has he undermined the Bible and placed too much emphasis on black experience? Has womanism emptied revelation of any propositional value for Christians?

Implications of Christian attitudes towards religious plurality for an understanding of the authority of scripture. Consider the distinction between liberal Protestant and traditional attitudes to scripture. Uncritical exclusivists tend to give the Bible high authority. Hick, on the other hand, sees it as a cultural repository of religious experience (which needs de-mythologising). Consider Barth's views on revelation and dislike of 'bibliotary'.

Read pages 37–40 of the *OCR AS Guide* and see the section on philosophy of religion in this guide (pages 19–22).

Exclusivist, inclusivist and pluralist understandings of salvation, and beliefs about life after death. Consider whether 'goodness' is a 'necessary or sufficient condition' for salvation. Consider God's grace, the role of the Church, sacraments and faith as other necessary conditions (especially for Barth and Rahner). Compare and contrast Hick's pluralism with his notion of the 'replica theory' of personal resurrection – are they compatible?

Read the chapter on philosophy of religion, pages 16–19.

Test yourself

1. 'Heaven is just a metaphor for social justice.' Discuss.
2. 'If God sides with the poor he cannot be universal.' Discuss.
3. Discuss the view that being a good person is not enough to be saved.

Religious Ethics with Developments in Christian Thought (Route K)

Read pages 125–129 of the *OCR AS Guide* and the chapter in this guide on religious ethics (pages 46–50).

Jon Sobrino summarises his view of political holiness in this way: 'In spite of the difficulties they encounter, they always maintain the primacy of life, justice, obligatory struggle, the revolutions and structural reforms seen to be necessary.' *Spirituality of Liberation* (Orbis 1988), page 85. Is he a contingent pacifist?

Liberation theology and ethical issues of war, peace and justice. Consider the different aims/types of war. Consider the place of martyrdom/altruism and dying for justice as a central theme and their relationship to Just War arguments. Consider the tension between desiring the eschatological peace and harmony of the Kingdom of God with the practical concerns of siding with the poor and making a political stand. Compare different views of justice – from the distribution of goods (Mill/Rawls) to reward (Aristotle), to retribution – with those of the 8th-century prophets and the view that justice requires human action as well as God's judgement.

Further reading

Read pages 75–84 and 121–122 of the *OCR AS Guide* and *Feminism and Christian Ethics* by Susan Parsons (CUP 1996).

Ethical principles underlying feminist theology and black theology. Consider how each type of feminist theology emphasises a different ethical basis. For example, liberal feminists share the same concern of Kant and Mill about human rights. Reconstructionists aim to rethink freedom in terms of economic power (Marx) and question institutions such as marriage. Note the considerable debate among radicals over 'natural law' (sex/gender/sexuality tension) and production/reproduction/motherhood views. Consider the liberal influences on Martin Luther King's 'black' theology such as equality of rights, natural law assumptions of justice, Christian love/agape doctrine and non-violent direct action. Compare with Cone's (and others') utilitarian/Marxist consequential view that in 'black power' ends justify means in the use of violence to combat injustice.

Further reading

Read the very clear essay by James Cone in *The Risks of Faith* (Beacon Press 1999), pages 28–39.

Read pages 75–84 of the *OCR AS Guide*.

Absolute and relative morality and humanity's relationship with God. It is too simple here to equate exclusivism with absolute ethics and pluralism with relativism. Consider the place of morality within salvation and the doctrine of justification by faith. Consider Barth's suspicion of natural law, and Hick's use of Kant and the good-will as the absolute basis of religion. Do they all consider religions to be examples of cultural moral relativism?

Test yourself

1. 'Liberation Theologians place justice before peace.' Discuss.
2. To what extent do feminist theologians consider marriage to be outdated and patriarchal?
3. 'Christianity teaches that there is only one acceptable form of moral behaviour.' Discuss.

New Testament with Developments in Christian Thought (Route S)

Make sure you revise all the AS New Testament set texts (Gospels or Early Church) as well as the A2 texts (Gospels or

Read pages 112–116 and 125–131 of the *OCR AS Guide*, and the chapter in this guide on New Testament (pages 68–98).

Note how black theologians focus on Paul's description of the human condition as 'the slavery' of sin (Romans 8: 21).

For example, Archbishop Romero and Martin Luther King Jr. This is an important theme in Jon Sobrino's writings.

Suffering, death and resurrection of Christ in the light of liberation theology and black theology. Consider how the various writers in the New Testament understand Jesus' death: as a victory over the slavery of sin (Rom 6: 5) or over death (1 Cor 15), as example (Mk 8: 31–34), as glorifying God (Jn 17: 1–5) or as triumph over evil. Consider how liberation/black theologians have presented sin as the result of structural poverty and racism/slavery. Consider the death of Jesus as a prototype of martyrdom, and suffering as a means of establishing the 'new Jerusalem'/'Kingdom of God'. Consider Jesus as the Liberator or Black Messiah whose resurrection marks a triumph over the existing order – but to what extent is the promise of afterlife important to liberation/black theologies?

Gospels or Paul as interpreted by feminist and black theologians. Consider the prominence given to women in the Gospels and the overcoming of ancient body-related taboos of Levitical law. Consider the revisionist/reconstructionist feminist views especially of the woman at Bethany (Mk 14) and women at the resurrection. Consider feminist interpretations of Paul, from those who see him limited by his Jewish patriarchal background, to those who consider his more radical vision of equality (Gal 3: 27),to radicals (such as Daly) who consider his vision of equality to diminish women's identity. Consider black theologians' view of Jesus in the Gospels as one who sides with the poor and the oppressed as an act of political praxis, and consider to what extent Cone is right to reject the view that Jesus offered freedom only in a personal spiritual sense. Consider the ambivalence of Paul, who sees Jesus as a servant (Phil 2: 5–8) who dies to free humans from the slavery of sin (Romans 6: 5), yet seems to teach that slaves should be obedient to their masters (Eph 6: 5–9).

Read pages 121–123 of the *OCR AS Guide*.

Further reading

A useful survey of women in the Gospels is by Luise Schottroff: *Lydia's Impatient Sisters* (SCM 1995).

Consider the debates about the authenticity of Ephesians and feminist interpretation of the household lists.

Further reading

Read chapters 4 and 6 of *God of the Oppressed* by James Cone. Consider how the Gospels have led to racism (for example, Matthew 27: 24–26 and John 8: 39–47).

Gospels or Paul as interpreted by liberation theologians. Consider the important passages in the Gospels of Luke 4 and Matthew 25, especially the theme of reversal (first-last) understood as the continuation of Old Testament justice. Consider how successful they have been in the use of the hermeneutic of suspicion to liberate texts from western European interpretations of (for example) the Sermon on the Mount and the place of the oppressed (Matthew 5: 1–11), or to see the parable of the Prodigal Son (Luke 15) in terms of class oppression. Consider the interpretation of Paul as an example of the continuing journey or exodus from the Old Testament. 'Walking in the Spirit' transforms a world of law, sin, flesh and death into a world of freedom and justice.

Further reading

Read the chapter on Romans 8 and Galatians 5 in *We Drink from Our Own Wells* by Gustavo Guteirrez (SCM 1984).

The Gospels' or Paul's teaching on non-Christian religions. Consider Jesus' treatment of Gentiles as presented in the Gospels – especially in Luke (and Acts) and Matthew 25. Consider the Gospels' use of and dependency on Judaism, and modern views about the emergence of Christianity and Judaism. Consider Paul's attitude to Judaism – especially to circumcision, the Law and the covenant – from his letters (Galatians and Romans) and presentation by Luke in Acts (Acts 13 and 17). Consider how consistent the idea of universalism is and to what extent it can be incorporated into inclusivism.

Further reading

Read pages 111–112 and 116 of the *OCR AS Guide*, plus chapter 7 of *The Mystery of Salvation* (Church House Publishing 1995).

Further reading

David Rensberger is a good example of a writer who explains very early Jewish/Christian relationships in sociological terms. See *Overcoming the World: Politics and Community in the Gospel of John* (SPCK 1989).

Test yourself

1. 'The bodily resurrection of Jesus is not an important aspect of Liberation Theology.' Discuss.

2. 'The New Testament teaches that only Christians will enter the Kingdom of God.' Discuss.

3. Assess the view that feminist theologians have given an unbalanced interpretation of the New Testament.

Eastern religions

You may only study **either** Buddhism **or** Hinduism for the examination.

Theravada Buddhists used Pali, whereas most Mahayanist scriptures are in Sanskrit. Sanskrit will be used here.

Route E: Philosophy of Religion with Buddhism. Compare Buddhist views about rebirth with Christian beliefs about resurrection. Read chapters 15 and 18 in *Death and Eternal Life* by John Hick (Collins 1976). For a summary of Buddhist teaching on samsara and nirvana, see pages 134–136 of the *OCR AS Guide*.

Buddhism

After the death of Gautama the Buddha, his followers established sanghas or monasteries, where they followed a monastic code (vinaya) and lived according to the teachings of the **Pali Canon**. Over time, numerous vinayas emerged, resulting in a range of different schools of Buddhism. **Theravada** was one of the early Buddhist schools and the only one that still survives today. Eventually, a new spiritual movement began to take hold within Buddhism, which became known as **Mahayana**, meaning Great Vehicle. For various reasons, the Mahayanists saw their movement as superior to non-Mahayana schools such as the Theravada, which they negatively termed as Lesser Vehicle (Hinayana).

Theravada and Mahayana Buddhism

Nirvana and samsara

The Heart Sutra is an important source of Mahayana teaching on emptiness. Nagarjuna (150–250 CE) also developed the idea in his 'Middle Way' philosophy. See page 125 for more on the Heart Sutra.

'The conditioned and the unconditioned cannot, then, be differentiated because "both" are found to "be" emptiness.' Peter Harvey, *An Introduction to Buddhism* (CUP 1990), page 103.

Whereas the Theravadins contrast nirvana with samsara (the cycle of life and rebirth), the Mahayanists suggest that ultimately there is no difference between them. According to the **Heart Sutra**, it is misguided to endow nirvana with certain qualities that differentiate it from samsara. Rather than viewing nirvana as an unconditioned and permanent absolute, and samsara as conditioned and impermanent, Mahayanists believe that they are in fact the same.

The Buddha

Another important difference concerns the Mahayana view of the Buddha. While Theravadins believe that the historical Buddha, Siddhatta Gautama, lived and died like any other mortal, the Mahayanists believe that he is somehow still alive, communicating to beings in various ways. Furthermore, they tend to give him a semi-divine status. According to the Mahayana, the Buddha has **three bodies** (trikaya), which exist in three distinct realms. Not only does he have an earthly, human body (nirmanakaya), he also has a heavenly or enjoyment-body (sambhogakaya) that exists in a paradise removed from this world. The dharma-body (dharmakaya) is absolute reality, the essence of the Buddha. Over time, it became common to believe that all Buddhas, not just Gautama, existed in these three bodies or forms.

Further reading

Pages 125–128 of *An Introduction to Buddhism* by Peter Harvey has a helpful account of trikaya. For more on Buddhism in general, see *Buddhism* by Denise Cush (Hodder 1994).

Mahayana dharma

Further reading

Read the discussion of Upaya-kausalya and the Parable of the Burning House in the *OCR AS Guide*, pages 138–139. See too the section on Lotus Sutra and Buddhist ethics on pages 124–129 of this guide for a further discussion of skilful means.

The Mahayana lays great emphasis on **skilful means** (upaya-kausalya). It helps to explain the view that Gautama did not reveal the whole dharma at once, but taught only what could be understood at the time, skilfully adapting his message to suit his audience. Owing to the trikaya doctrine, the Mahayanists believed that the Buddha still existed and continued to inspire and guide his followers. Centuries later, the Buddha's dharmakaya communicated the full extent of the dharma to those whom he thought capable of understanding it. Over time, an enormous and diverse body of literature grew, collectively known as the **Mahayana Sutras**. The Mahayanists developed many ideas that were already present in the older traditions, and saw themselves as completing the original, incomplete dharma contained in the Pali Canon. The diversity of the Mahayana Sutras means that unlike Theravada Buddhism, it is difficult to describe the Mahayana as one single school of thought. Zen Buddhism and Pure Land Buddhism may be called 'Mahayana', even though they differ substantially from many earlier Mahayana schools, and have their own textual traditions.

Route E: Philosophy of religion and ultimate truths. Consider Mahayana Buddhist views about the authority of the Mahayana sutras and compare with Christian views about the divine inspiration of the Bible.

The arhat

In the Theravada tradition, the arhat is highly respected. Having completed the noble eightfold path, they are enlightened and have attained nirvana. They are thus detached from this life; their thoughts and actions generate no karma and as a result they do not suffer rebirths. Arhats are considered to be like saints: compassionate and virtuous. They are a role model for all wise, Theravada Buddhists: for members of the Sangha who hope to become arhats during this life; and for lay Buddhists, for whom arhatship is a goal towards which they will continue to strive over a period of lives. In the Mahayana tradition, however, becoming an arhat is not the ideal. Those who attain their own enlightenment without helping others along the path may even be thought of as selfish. For Mahayanists, then, the ideal of the arhat is replaced by the bodhisattva ideal.

The bodhisattva ideal

The idea of the bodhisattva is present in the Theravada tradition, but it was the Mahayana that really exalted the bodhisattva path. Whereas Theravada Buddhists try to attain their own enlightenment (the path to arhatship), the Mahayanists seek to help other living beings realise it first (the ideal of the bodhisattva). In order to become a bodhisattva, one must first develop **bodhicitta**, which is the initial intention to 'become a Buddha, for the sake of all living beings'. This altruistic commitment to help others is the basis of the bodhisattva path. Bodhicitta is not easily achieved, but requires repeated meditations to help cultivate compassion and loving kindness. The bodhisattva will then seek to:

Route L: Religious ethics with Buddhism. Consider the purpose of the bodhisattva path.

Develop the six perfections. The six **paramitas** are: generosity (dana), morality (sila), patience (ksanti), courage (virya), meditation (dhyana) and wisdom (prajna). Generosity is demonstrated by the giving away of possessions for the benefit of others. This generates good karma that can then be transferred to other beings to help them on their way. Morality is perfected by living an ethical life, and encouraging others to do so, because immorality generates bad karma, leading to undesirable rebirths. Patience is helpful because explaining the dharma to ignorant beings can be a trying process. Courage gives one the strength required to grow in compassion; meditation enables the bodhisattva to recognise and fully understand the Four Noble Truths. Finally, wisdom itself is perfected, giving the bodhisattva knowledge of dependent origination. They are now equivalent to an arhat in terms of wisdom and compassion.

Further reading

See page 204 of *Mahayana Buddhism* by Paul Williams (Routledge 1989). See pages 121–123 of this book for more on meditation

Further reading

It is essential that you understand the Four *Noble Truths*: start with pages 45–46 of the *OCR AS Guide*. For a more detailed account, read pages 44–56 of *Buddhism: A Very Short Introduction* by Damien Keown (Oxford 1996).

See page 127 for more on the bodhisattva and Mahayana ethics.

Demonstrate compassion to all living beings. This is shown by helping others, in various ways, to get closer to nirvana. The priority of the bodhisattva is to save others before himself. This is made easier by the fact that all beings have a Buddha-nature (tathagata-garbha) within them, giving them the potential to attain Buddhahood. As they ascend the stages towards Buddhahood, they must continue to help sentient beings, using the great powers they have developed.

Attain perfect Buddhahood. Once wisdom is perfected, there remain four stages before ultimate Buddhahood. At the seventh stage, they become a 'Great Being', and are no longer reborn according to karma. By the tenth stage, they dwell in a special heavenly realm, and are on the threshold of Buddhahood. Finally, having helped other beings for countless eons, they may realise nirvana for themselves.

Zen Buddhism

Ch'an Buddhism arrived in Japan from China in the 13th century, and became known as Zen. It is a type of Mahayana Buddhism. 'Ch'an' and 'Zen' are derived from the Sanskrit word **dhyana** meaning trance, or deep state of meditation. The origins of the school lie in the teachings of Bodhidharma, who established a meditative school of Buddhism. There are two main divisions of Zen Buddhism – Rinzai and Soto – but many Zen practices are common to both.

Zen meditation

Further reading

Read page 270–279 of *An Introduction to Buddhism* for a full explanation of the different forms of Zen meditation.

Meditation is at the heart of Zen Buddhism. Its purpose is to awaken the Buddha-nature present within all of us. This is made possible when the mind is purified of all distractions and focused on one particular object. In this way, samsara can be seen in its true light and experienced as nirvana. Various forms of meditation are practised that have been developed by Zen teachers for the benefit of their students:

- **Just sitting**. The meditator focuses on the process of sitting, nothing else. This technique is known as *zazen*. They keep their mind on the task in hand, and do not worry about what the practice achieves. By doing so, they are able to achieve **samadhi** (total concentration). This technique can be extended to any day-to-day activity: just walking, just drinking tea and so on.

'What is the sound of one hand clapping?' is an example of a Koan exercise. To find out the answer, read the story called 'The Sound of one Hand' on pages 79–80 in Clive Erricker's *Teach Yourself Buddhism* (Hodder 2001).

- **Asking difficult questions**. This technique, called *koan*, involves asking oneself a specific question repeatedly. Under the guidance of a master, the student offers responses, but these are rejected time and again. Eventually, the student realises that reality as we perceive it cannot provide answers to these questions. This is the breakthrough and the goal of the exercise. According to Harvey: 'There is no longer anyone to ask or answer the question, but only a blissful, radiant emptiness beyond self or other, words or concepts. In this state of dhyana (zen), insight of various levels can be present.'

Peter Harvey, *An Introduction to Buddhism*, page 275.

- **Sudden insight**: This is a moment of blissful realisation (*kensho*) when the meditator realises their true Buddha-nature. It is an experience of pure consciousness, which often directly follows samadhi. Sudden kenshos are more common in the Rinzai tradition; followers of Soto Zen believe that kensho needs to be achieved gradually.

Less emphasis on dharma

Zen places less emphasis on Buddhist teaching than most other forms of Buddhism. Prajna (wisdom) is not to be attained by study of the scriptures, but by meditation. Thinking too much about whether one's beliefs are correct is considered an unhelpful distraction from the main purpose of the religion, which is to realise one's own true nature.

One important Zen aim is to act naturally, according to one's inner Buddha nature. This is possible when one has no sense of 'I' – without concern for the ego, one acts spontaneously, not motivated by any personal rewards that the action might generate. It is then possible to focus on daily tasks and perform them with a clear mind, fully concentrating on doing the job well (whatever it may be). In this way, actions can be a form of meditation too.

Ethics

Further reading

For an illustration of the importance of ethics in Zen, read the story of the Happy Chinaman on page 78 of *Buddhism* by Clive Erricker (Teach Yourself 2001) .

Zen Buddhists believe that it is possible to experience the true nature of things through contemplation of objects in the world. The arts have long been recognised as a means of capturing reality. Simple forms of poetry (haiku), zen paintings, flower arrangement, theatre and landscape gardening are just some of the art forms that have been explored. Matsuo Basho (1644–94), Japan's most famous poet is a good example. He had an experience of the true nature of things while in a quiet garden and turned the experience into a haiku.

Creativity

Further study

Read pages 277–279 of *An Introduction to Buddhism* for the principles of Zen art forms. Now try to compose a Zen haiku yourself.

Pure Land Buddhism

Pure Land Buddhism, a form of Mahayana devotionalism, can be traced back to the 2nd century CE, with the writing of the Larger and Smaller *Sukhavativyuha Sutras*. These scriptures depict a heavenly realm created by the sambogakhaya body of a Buddha, Amitabha, meaning 'Infinite Light'. Amitabha presides over the remote Happy Land (sukhavati), which is free from the dukkha that characterises the world of samsara. Pure Land Buddhism, centred on Amitabha, became an organised movement around the 6th and 7th centuries CE, and has been popular in the Far East.

Amitabha

Route E: Philosophy of religion with Buddhism. Consider the similarities between Buddhist and Christian ideas of heaven. Read pages 251–276 of *Mahayana Buddhism* by Paul Willliams (Routledge 1989) and compare with the description of heaven in chapter 10 of *Death and Eternal Life* by John Hick.

Pure Land Buddhists see certain Buddhas as **divine saviour-figures** whose favour is essential in order to escape from samsaric suffering. One gains entry into the Pure Land by showing great faith in the Buddha who presides over it; praying to Amitabha and repeatedly chanting his name will often be sufficient to secure his grace. There is therefore less emphasis in Pure Land Buddhism on correct ethical behaviour. This is particularly the case for a sect of Pure Land Buddhism called **Shin Buddhism**. Shin Buddhists believe that good ethical behaviour generates no merit whatsoever: faith in Amitabha is all that is required. Those who are not able to practise the bodhisattva ideal in this life will nonetheless have their faith, if not their actions, rewarded by being admitted into a Pure Land.

Aims of Pure Land Buddhists

Further reading

Read pages 137–139 of *Buddhism* by Denise Cush (Hodder and Stoughton 1993) and pages 269–275 of *Mahayana Buddhism*. Do you think Shin Buddhism is true to the spirit of the Buddha's original teaching? Explain your view.

Once in a Pure Land, it is much easier to discover the truth of the dharma and attain nirvana through practising the bodhisattva path. Pure Land Buddhism, like Zen Buddhism, has proved very popular, particularly because it does not require careful study of the dharma. It also does not require observance of a disciplined monastic lifestyle in a Sangha. As such, it has appealed to many people who have wanted to gain salvation through faith rather than action.

Further discussion

'In the 1930s, between 60% and 70% of Chinese Buddhists were of the Pure Land variety. Denise Cush, *Buddhism*, page 137. Why do you think this was the case?

Meditation

Meditation is the English term for the Sanskrit *bhavana*, which means 'culture' or 'development', and refers to various ways of disciplining the mind. It is extremely important in both Theravada and Mahayana Buddhism. It was through quiet meditation that Gautama realised the Four Noble Truths and became the Buddha (enlightened one). The Buddha's own experience helps to illustrate

Further reading

For an excellent account of the methods and aims of meditation from a Theravada point of view, read pages 67–75 of *What the Buddha Taught by* Walpola Sri Rahula (Oneworld 1997).

what meditation is: an attempt to calm and control the mind in order to gain insight into the true nature of things. According to the Buddha, there are eight aspects of the Noble Eightfold Path to nirvana. These are: right understanding, right thought, right speech, right action, right livelihood, right effort, right mindfulness and right concentration. Meditation forms a substantial part of the path: the last three aspects are all meditative. There are two main meditative techniques in Buddhism, although some practices do vary between schools.

See pages 46–47 of the *OCR AS Guide* for a summary of the Noble Eightfold Path

Calm meditation

Calm meditation is known as samadhi, and is largely a Theravadin practice. Otherwise known as *samatha*, it involves developing a still, calm mind that is fixed on one object. According to the *Visuddimanga*, there are 40 different objects suitable for meditation. Two possible types of samadhi meditation are:

Further reading

See pages 246–253 of *An Introduction to Buddhism*, for a more detailed treatment of samadhi.

- **Meditating on breathing**. This is a popular form of meditation, involving sitting straight and becoming aware of breathing.
- **Meditating on loving-kindness**. For example, the meditator might focus on a person they greatly respect, then a person they feel indifferent to, then a person they dislike. The aim is to practise genuine, non-discriminatory loving-kindness to all living beings.

The aim for the meditator as they try to develop inner calm is to eliminate the **five hindrances**: sensual desire, ill-will, laziness, anxiety and fear of commitment. This enables the meditator to ascend the **four jhanas** or levels of trance. Once the fourth jhana is attained, the mind is one-pointed: a deep inner peace is experienced. The process of calming continues with the development of the four formless attainments. The mind becomes increasingly pure and radiant, and it ultimately shuts down entirely – at this point, one is very close to nirvana. Practice of samadhi is not the same as experiencing nirvana, nor is it vital for attaining it. It is nevertheless important as way of suspending attachment to the five hindrances, clearing the mind and cultivating morality. All this aids progression along the Noble Eightfold Path.

Insight meditation

Samadhi meditation is essentially a preparation for insight meditation or **vipassana**. This form of meditation was developed by the Buddha, and refers to insight into the way things really are. Whereas samadhi requires the cessation of intellectual activity, vipassana demands great intellectual concentration. Examples of vipassana techniques include meditating on actions, feelings, the mind, theories and forms.

Focus	Process	Aim
Actions	The meditator focuses on whatever they are saying or doing at the present moment, and is not concerned about past or future actions or events.	To become aware of **acting**, but not of *oneself* acting.
Feelings	The meditator scrutinises their own sensations, whether good, bad or indifferent. They try to see them not as their own feelings, but simply as things that are experienced. Knowing that the sensation itself a product of dependent origination, they become aware of its impermanence.	To become detached from one's **feelings**.

The mind	This involves examining the mind critically, as one would examine someone else's mind. This helps the individual to see that personal experiences of frustration should be viewed in the same way, from a critical distance.	To observe the **mind** as one would someone else's mind. This reinforces the notion that the mental states which make up the mind, such as frustration, are simply objects of experience.
Theories	The meditator studies an intellectual topic or body of ideas, such as the theory of dependent origination or the Six Elements of the body (matter, liquid, fire, air, space and consciousness). One might also meditate on the Seven Factors of Enlightenment, or the Four Noble Truths.	To increase in wisdom and understands things the way they really are by studying various Buddhist **theories** of existence.
Forms	This is known as visualisation, and is particularly popular in Mahayana Buddhism. A person seeking to become a bodhisattva may meditate on a great bodhisattva such as Avalokitesvara.	To be inspired to pursue the bodhisattva ideal, through the visualisation of the **form** of a great bodhisattva such as Avalokitesvara.

All methods of insight meditation help the meditator to gain understanding of the true nature of things. By becoming fully absorbed in the object of their meditation, and not at all conscious of themselves meditating, the meditator realises the profound truth that 'they' do not really exist as an independent being. This is the doctrine of anatta (no-self), one of the three marks of existence of all conditioned phenomena. This is a vitally important stage along the path to nirvana, because it frees one from all selfish attachments and cravings. Connected with insight into one's own true nature is the realisation that life is dukkha. The aim is to understand, as the Buddha himself did, that the world is impermanent. Consequently, there is no point in clinging to one's life. This kind of penetrating insight is true wisdom (prajna), and it enables one to appreciate fully the meaning and significance of the Four Noble Truths.

Route E: Philosophy of religion with Buddhism. Consider the different ways in which Buddhists gain insight into the nature of reality through meditation. Read chapter 3 'Religious Experience and Authority' in *Philosophy of Religion for A Level* by Jordan, Lockyer and Tate (Nelson Thornes 2002) for western approaches to ultimate truth.

See page 133 of the *OCR AS Guide* for an overview of the three marks of existence.

Bodhisattva meditation

The forms of meditation indicated above help the aspiring bodhisattva to develop **bodhicitta**, which is the willingness to pursue the path towards Buddhahood. Particular meditations are practised that aim specifically to induce great compassion towards others. These include 'six causes and one effect', during which the meditator tries to develop loving-kindness towards all beings. He may also practise 'exchanging self for others', which helps develop an attitude of altruism. As the bodhisattva pursues his path, he continues to meditate in various ways in order to generate both calm and insight. By the fifth stage of the bodhisattva path, he masters the perfection of meditation; it is at this moment, too, that he fully understands the Four Noble Truths. In Mahayana as well as Theravada, then, meditation is a vital means of developing compassion and wisdom.

Buddhist scriptures

Buddhism has a diverse range of scriptures, written over many centuries. This variety is largely due to the enormous geographical spread of the religion across much of Asia. As a result, texts have been composed in a number of languages, including Pali, Sanskrit,

Further reading

A useful collection is selected and translated by Edward Conze: *The Buddhist Scriptures* (Penguin 1959).

Chinese, Japanese and Tibetan. Many of these texts reflect aspects of the particular culture or period in which they were written. The main division is between those belonging to the Theravada tradition and those belonging to the Mahayana tradition.

The Pali Canon

The Pali Canon is also known as Tipitaka or Tripitaka, meaning 'the three baskets', because it was originally written on palm leaf manuscripts that were kept in baskets.

Route E: Philosophy of religion with Buddhism. Consider how and why the Pali Canon is considered to be sacred and authoritative scripture by Theravada Buddhists. Denise Cush notes that 'ancient scriptures are considered to be relics of the Buddha, and are to be found buried in stupas'. Read pages 47–53 of her *Buddhism* for a clear and helpful presentation of the content and the significance of the Pali Canon.

The Pali Canon is widely believed to be the most ancient collection of texts, inspired by the Buddha and written down by Theravada monks in Sri Lanka in the 1st century. For Theravada Buddhists, it is their holy scripture and is treated accordingly. There are three parts to the Canon. Each is important for different reasons:

Vinaya Pitaka. This means 'discipline section'; it is particularly important for Theravadin monks, who follow the 227 rules dealing with how to live in the Sangha. They include four rules that, if broken, will result in expulsion from the Sangha: no stealing, no killing, no sex and no false claiming of supernatural powers.

Sutta Pitaka. The sutta pitaka is the most important part of the Pali Canon for lay Buddhists. It is divided into five distinct sections and contains the sermons, discussions and sayings of the Buddha, and a few of his disciples. It provides guidance for many aspects of day-to-day life: how to meditate, behave appropriately and escape from the world of dukkha. It also illuminates different aspects of the life of the Buddha, and as such provides rich material for storytelling and for communicating the truths of Buddhism to different groups of people, including non-Buddhists and children. The **Jataka** tales, for example, describe the Buddha's past lives. And the **Dhammapada** is also very popular; it contains sayings that are sometimes used as devotional aids.

Abhidharma Pitaka. These texts are concerned with Buddhist views on the nature of reality. They explore both philosophical and psychological ideas. Abhidharma deals with Buddhist thought about the nature of dharmas that make up the phenomenal world. It does not come directly from the Buddha, but from later Buddhist scholars who analysed his teaching; it is nonetheless in the spirit of his original message. The texts are important because they serve as a systematic defence and explanation of the Buddhist world-view. Although largely the preserve of academic circles, the Abhidharma philosophy underpins much Buddhist teaching.

The Lotus Sutra

The quotation is from *Mahayana Buddhism* page 141. Read pages 141–155 for a detailed account of the teaching and sacred significance of the Lotus Sutra.

See page 128 on Mahayana ethics for more on skilful means. As the Buddha declares in Lotus Sutra 2: 'I use different means to raise each according to his own character. Such is the might of my knowledge.' (quoted in *Buddhism* by Clive Erricker, page 72).

The **Saddharmapundarika** ('Lotus of the Wonderful Law'), commonly known as the Lotus Sutra, is a hugely important and sacred text for Mahayana Buddhists. According to Paul Williams, 'For many East Asian Buddhists since early times the *Lotus Sutra* is the nearest Buddhist equivalent to a bible – one revealed work containing the final truth, itself sufficient for salvation'. Indeed, recitation of the sutra may guarantee entry into a Pure Land. It is an object of devotion, believed to be the holy teaching of the eternal Buddha: as such, it is widely venerated and revered. The Lotus Sutra is a key source of teaching on **skilful means**, the doctrine that allows for various ways of preaching the dharma. The sutra is believed to have been given by the heavenly being of the original Buddha, known here as Shakyamuni. Though appearing to enter nirvana, he returns repeatedly to samsara in order to save countless living beings by skilfully revealing the dharma to them.

Before the Lotus Sutra became influential (the earliest surviving manuscript dates from 286 CE), it was generally accepted that there were three Buddhist ideals: arhathood, pratyekabuddhahood (a Buddha who does not help others to achieve nirvana) and perfect Buddhahood (involving the bodhisattva path). However, the Sutra reveals that there is in reality only **one vehicle**: the path to perfect Buddhahood. This is something that all beings can and will attain. Previously, the Buddha had set the goals of arhathood and pratyekabuddhahood, but these are mere stepping-stones to the one true goal. This is an example of skilful means used by the Buddha; he was concerned that the path to Buddhahood would be considered too demanding by his original followers, so he taught them inferior alternatives. The Sutra therefore epitomises the Mahayana belief that it teaches the superior form of Buddhism.

Route E: Philosophy of religion with Buddhism. Compare the Christian belief in the divine inspiration of the Bible with the Mahayana view that the Lotus Sutra represents the word of the Buddha.

Further discussion

Consider why the Lotus Sutra is so important for Mahayana Buddhists.

The earliest Mahayana literature was concerned above all with the **perfection of wisdom** (prajnaparamita), part of the bodhisattva path towards full Buddhahood. Of the various sutras that were written, **the Heart Sutra**, originally composed in Chinese, is most important. Like all perfection of wisdom literature, it deals with the process of perfecting knowledge of the empty nature of all dharmas. It suggests that there are different levels of wisdom, and as one's understanding grows, it gradually nears perfection. Wisdom in this sutra is personified as a goddess. It also features Avalokitesvara, who says that, like all dharmas, even the five khandhas (the various psycho-physical events that make up human beings) are in reality empty (sunyata). A belief in emptiness is vital for the development of bodhicitta. It is only because the bodhisattva views all dharmas as empty that they see no difference between themselves and others. This insight inspires them to act selflessly and compassionately for the benefit of all sentient beings.

The Heart Sutra

For a fuller understanding of the implications of the Heart Sutra's teaching on emptiness, see page 118 on nirvana and samsara.

Buddhist ethics

Buddhist ethics is largely concerned with how to live in order to attain enlightenment for oneself or others. The ethical behaviour required to achieve that aim differs across the various schools of Buddhism, but is typically inspired by the **three refuges**:

Read pages 132–133 of the *OCR AS Guide* for more information.

- **The Buddha**. The Buddha's own life is seen as exemplary: he renounced his wealth and status, discovered the truth about reality and then generously set out to share his wisdom with others.
- **The dharma**. The vast body of teaching in the Buddhist scriptures; much of it is to do with how one should behave.
- **The sangha**. This may serve as an example of correct Buddhist practice to the lay community, and the advice of monks may be sought on a variety of ethical issues.

Route L: Religious ethics with Buddhism. Compare the foundations of Buddhist ethics and Christian ethics, for example natural law and agape. Read pages 21–22 of the *OCR AS Guide*.

Other distinctive features of Buddhist ethics include:

- The interdependence of **right understanding** and **right action**. Correct ethical behaviour is not possible without wisdom and mindfulness, a fact that highlights the close association of all aspects of the Noble Eightfold Path.

Further reading

Read *pages 40–42 of An Introduction to Buddhist Ethics* by Peter Harvey (CUP 2000) for a very clear explanation of the place of ethics on the path.

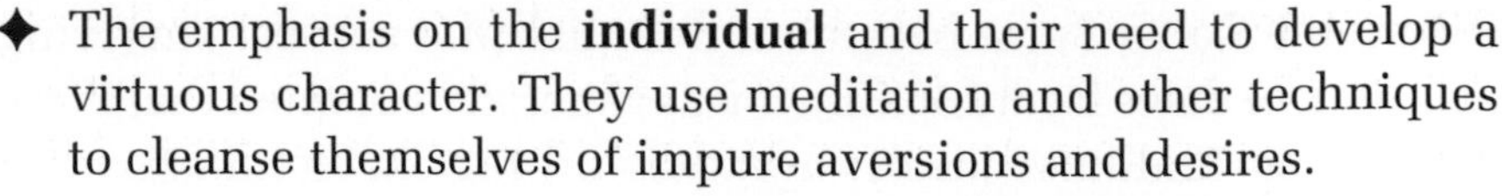

- The emphasis on the **individual** and their need to develop a virtuous character. They use meditation and other techniques to cleanse themselves of impure aversions and desires.
- This allows them to act naturally act out of **compassion** towards others. This is emphasised both because it is karmicly fruitful and because, for a bodhisattva in particular, one person's suffering is the concern of all.
- A belief in the importance of **intention.** Although Buddhist ethics aims towards a goal (enlightenment), it is not consequentialist in that the morality of an action is not defined by its effects. Rather, the intention of the agent is key. An arhat, for example, will generate no karma (and therefore will not be reborn) because, being enlightened, they are entirely detached from their actions. Critically, they experience no craving, which is what generates karma in the first place.

Route L: Religious ethics with Buddhism. Consider whether Buddhist ethics are teleological or deontological.

The Five Precepts

Further discussion

Consider the following. Given that the first precept is concerned with right action, how do you think the other precepts are linked to aspects of the Noble Eightfold Path?

These are the five core rules that are respected across the Buddhist world. While those in the Sangha will tend to observe more specific and detailed ethical guidelines, the five precepts embody the main principles of Buddhist ethics. They also help the development of the five corresponding **virtues**. Although regarded as ideals, there is considerable diversity of opinion as to how they ought to be interpreted.

Non-injury (ahimsa). One must not harm other living beings intentionally. In particular, killing is forbidden – this includes not just humans but all living beings who have the capacity to feel pain. This opposition to killing stems from a deep concern for the welfare of all sentient beings: it demonstrates the key virtue of **compassion**. The belief in ahimsa is also underpinned by the belief in countless rebirths – this would imply that any being we encounter in this life may have been a close relative in a past life.

No stealing. One must not take the property of others without their consent. This precept covers not only stealing but also various forms of associated behaviour such as cheating and exploitative business practices. It can also include gambling. Ensuring that one does not steal helps to cultivate the virtue of **generosity**, since it discourages attachment to worldly goods.

No sexual immorality. One must avoid sexual misconduct at all times. In fact, celibacy is seen as the ideal (as observed by the monks of the Sangha), but for those unable to remain celibate, the key priority is that one does not cause suffering to another through sexual impropriety. The precept was traditionally understood to mean that no man should commit adultery with the wife of another, since that is a sign of craving and lack of satisfaction with one's own situation. Today, it refers more broadly to not having sexual relations with someone who is in a relationship with another; it also suggests that various obsessive and deviant forms of sexual behaviour are immoral. It helps to develop the virtue of **contentment**.

No lying. One must refrain from dishonest, deceptive and false speech: exaggeration and other mild forms of deceit are also discouraged. Observing this precept helps to cultivate **truthfulness** towards others. The Buddha himself sought to lead people away

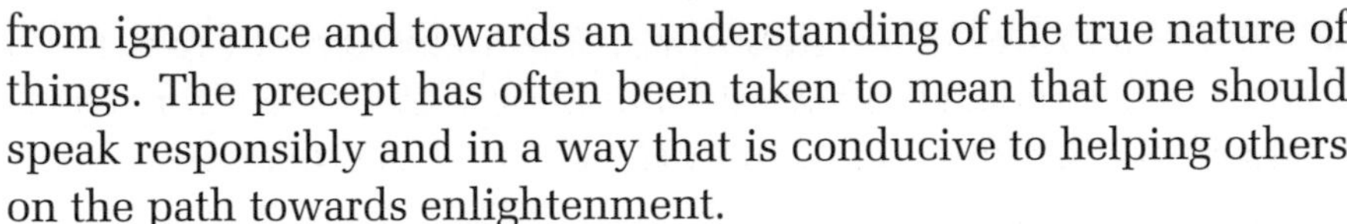

from ignorance and towards an understanding of the true nature of things. The precept has often been taken to mean that one should speak responsibly and in a way that is conducive to helping others on the path towards enlightenment.

No intoxicants. One must avoid intoxicating drugs and liquors. This precept is necessary for right **mindfulness** because it ensures that the mind stays clear, focused on observing the dharma. Alcohol consumption is not unheard of in Buddhist countries, however, which suggests that it is not viewed as intrinsically wrong. Rather, it is condemned because of the potentially harmful side effects of impure thoughts and irresponsible actions.

Route L: Religious ethics with Buddhism. What is the purpose of observing the precepts? Consider: (a) how they help cultivate virtues and (b) the similarities and differences between Buddhist ethics and virtue ethics. Read chapter 9 on virtue ethics in Peter Vardy and Paul Grosch's *The Puzzle of Ethics* (Fount HarperCollins 1999). For a more detailed study of the Five Precepts and their application, see pages 66–79 of *An Introduction to Buddhist Ethics.*

Monastic ethics

It is important to remember that the Buddha and his first converts were themselves monks. It is therefore not surprising that the monastic lifestyle is viewed as the pre-eminent Buddhist lifestyle by Theravada Buddhists. For those unable to commit to life in a Sangha, the lay life is a helpful stepping stone: the hope for many lay Buddhists is that they may generate enough good karma to be reborn as a monk in the next life. Monastic ethics draws on the Five Precepts, but monks abide by a different set of rules from those living outside. These rules are contained in the *Vinaya*, one of the parts of the Pali Canon.

Further discussion

What attachments are likely to develop while living an ordinary life in a household?

See the section on Pali Canon on page 124 for more on the Vinaya.

The importance of the Sangha in Buddhism illustrates the significance of **renunciation** within the tradition. A Buddhist monk will literally renounce attachment to the world and the various diversions that it offers, such as popular entertainment, drink and sexual relations. In particular, the commitment to celibacy is what defines the monastic lifestyle and distinguishes it from that of the lay Buddhist. Furthermore, the monastic codes are quite strict about what behaviour is and is not appropriate for a monk. The latter includes things permissible for a lay person, such as eating after noon, sleeping in a comfortable bed, and dealing with money.

Route L: Religious ethics and deontological ethical systems. Consider whether monastic ethics are fundamentally deontological.

Mahayana ethics

Monasticism is less important in the Mahayana tradition. This is partly because the bodhisattva skilfully helps lay people to achieve enlightenment, which may involve living alongside them. Thus the Sangha does not play such an important role in Mahayana Buddhism in terms of defining ideal ethical practice: it is perfectly possible to live a Buddhist life in normal society. In the Zen tradition, too, it is not as important to obey a set of strict ethical guidelines as it is to realise one's Buddha-nature through living in the everyday world; living according to this inner nature is to live a life of altruistic loving-kindness towards others. In the Pure Land tradition, the emphasis is on being saved through devotion to Amitabha: ethics ultimately takes second place to faith.

Route L: Religious ethics with Buddhism. Consider the similarities between the ethics of the bodhisattva and Situation Ethics. Read chapter 13 of *Ethical Theory* by Mel Thompson (Hodder and Stoughton 1999).

The ethics of the bodhisattva

The bodhisattva path is fundamentally ethical insofar as it is concerned with the welfare of others. It is motivated by a deep compassion for all sentient beings that is developed at the bodhicitta stage. While compassion is an important feature of Buddhist ethics in general, for bodhisattvas it is the dominating concern of life. Life is lived altruistically – for the benefit of others – which means that the bodhisattva path is in many ways more demanding than other Buddhist paths. As part of the development of the perfections, for example, they will transfer the karmic merit

Route L: Religious ethics with Buddhism. Consider whether the bodhisattva's transfer of karmic merit undermines individual freedom and autonomy. Read pages 37–40 of *Buddhism* by Damien Keown.

generated by their own good deeds to others for their sake. Knowing that they possess no self and that karma is empty anyway, they have no hesitation in letting other beings reap the karmic rewards of their own good deeds. This merit aids their journey on the path to nirvana.

Skilful means and the Five Precepts

The bodhisattvas usually follow the Five Precepts; they also have some of their own. Anything not conducive to realising the bodhisattva ideal, such as being impatient with others, is regarded as immoral. However, the absolute commitment to compassion allows the bodhisattva to be more flexible in their application of the Five Precepts. It is said of the true bodhisattva that while their mother is the perfection of wisdom (prajnaparamita) their father is skilfulness in means (upayakausala). Thus, using skilful means, the bodhisattva takes a situational approach and assesses whether, in any particular situation, it is appropriate to uphold or break the precepts. There is a story, for example, of a bodhisattva feigning illness in order that people might visit him, which would allow him to teach the dharma to them. Furthermore, there is a clause in the *Upaya-Kausalya Sutra* that actually condones the taking of a human life when it develops from a 'virtuous thought' – this might include the killing of one individual in order to save the lives of many. Other instances of leniency include permitting male bodhisattvas to give in to the advances of a lay unmarried women in order that she does not store up bad karma for herself through resentment towards him.

Route L: Religious ethics with Buddhism. Consider the ways in which the ethics of the bodhisattva are: (a) relative, (b) consequentialist. Compare with utilitarianism and rule-utilitarianism.

Further discussion

Consider the advantages and disadvantages of such a flexible approach to the Five Precepts.

Although the precepts are important to Mahayana Buddhists, the doctrine of skilful means makes them less binding than in the Theravada tradition. This illustrates the supreme importance of intention in Buddhist ethics, since almost anything is permitted for a bodhisattva as long as it is grounded in compassion. Furthermore, the bodhisattva is not particularly concerned about generating bad karma for themselves: at worst this will bring about future rebirths that will simply allow them to continue their mission.

Practical ethics

Buddhist views on practical ethical issues draw on the Five Precepts and the dharma as a whole. Below is a summary of views on some of the key topics.

Route L: Religious ethics with Buddhism. The approach of Buddhist ethics to these practical issues may to be considered alongside those of Christian ethics and secular ethical systems. See pages 115–128 of *Buddhism* by Clive Erricker; read the chapter on ethics in this guide, pages 31–51.

Environment. According to the *Buddhist Declaration on Nature*, 'the fact that (animals) may be incapable of communicating their feelings is no more an indication of apathy or insensibility to suffering than in the case of a person whose faculty of speech is impaired'. Buddhists see themselves as part of the samsaric process of dependent origination. They aim not to subdue and control nature, but to live in harmony with it. They emphasise an ethical responsibility not just to human beings but to all sentient beings precisely because all beings are part of the same flux of existence. It is conceivable, then, that one might be reborn as an animal, or that any animal might have been a close relation in a previous life. So there are definitely resources in Buddhism for an eco-friendly ethic.

Further study

Try to develop an eco-friendly ethic based on Buddhist teaching. Chapter 4 in *An Introduction to Buddhist Ethics* by Peter Harvey will give you some ideas.

Sex and relationships. While sexual relationships are not allowed in the Sangha, they are obviously appropriate for lay Buddhists. Homosexuality in Sanghas is generally condemned, although it is

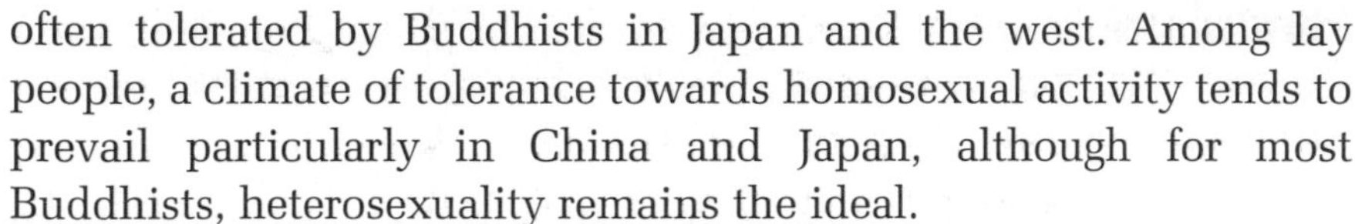

often tolerated by Buddhists in Japan and the west. Among lay people, a climate of tolerance towards homosexual activity tends to prevail particularly in China and Japan, although for most Buddhists, heterosexuality remains the ideal.

Route L: Religious Ethics with Buddhism. Read *Sex and Relationships*, by Michael Wilcockson (Hodder 2000) and the chapter on ethics in this guide, pages 31–51.

Abortion. The classical texts of Buddhism consistently oppose abortion, on the grounds that life begins at conception: it is thus a clear breach of the first precept. Furthermore, each reincarnation is precious because it is an opportunity to attain Buddhahood. Indeed, in countries where Theravada Buddhism is dominant, such as Sri Lanka and Thailand, abortion is illegal unless the mother's life is in severe danger. In Mahayana countries, though, such as Japan and Korea, however, abortion is more prevalent.

Route L: Religious Ethics with Buddhism. Consider the following: most Buddhists and Christians are united in their opposition to abortion, but for differing reasons; explain what these differences are. Read chapter 3 of *Issues of Life and Death* by Michael Wilcockson (Hodder 1999).

Euthanasia. This is generally frowned upon by Buddhists because, like abortion, it breaks the first precept. Also, because it is likely that the patient will be reborn anyway, euthanasia does not bring an end to suffering, but postpones it to the next life. The key issue, as always, is intention. Is the doctor's decision to comply with the patient's wishes a sign of unethical motivations such as aversion (to the suffering of the patient)? Certainly the patient is demonstrating aversion to suffering. Compassion for the patient may be the intention, but Buddhists might question whether this compassion is grounded in ignorance or wisdom. A truly wise person would know that suffering is a natural consequence of the impermanence (dukkha) of life, and rather than trying to resist it, would probably prefer to let nature take its course.

War and peace. Engaging in war is forbidden in the first precept, but that is not to say that Buddhists have never involved themselves in violence or military activity. The Buddha saw patience and forgiveness as the only appropriate attitude towards provocation, since anger is only a product of a deluded attempt to protect the interests of the (non-existent) ego. Anger may be regarded as the first step towards violence: if anger is eliminated through right understanding, then the need for violent activity would not arise. War would also conflict with the principle of compassion, and the commitment to a right livelihood would preclude those professions that contribute to the harming of others. Many Buddhist leaders today, such as the Dalai Lama, are in fact peace activists, who have been active in promoting peace in various trouble spots in the Buddhist world. The fact that there have been social and political conflicts, however, confirms that their peaceful ideals are not always shared by ordinary people in Buddhist countries.

As Peter Harvey has commented, 'it is difficult to find any plausible Buddhist rationales for violence, and Buddhism has some particularly rich resources for dissolving conflict'. *An Introduction to Buddhist Ethics*, page 239. In theory, at least, Buddhism is a peaceful religion.

Route L: Religious ethics with Buddhism. Compare Buddhist with (a) Kantian, (b) Christian, (c) utilitarian approaches to war and peace. See chapter 6 of *Issues of Life and Death*, by Michael Wilcockson.

Test yourself

1. 'Pure Land Buddhism is so different from the teachings of the Buddha that it cannot really be considered Buddhism.' Discuss.
2. To what extent is meditation important for all the different Buddhist schools?
3. Assess the importance of the Pali Canon in Buddhism.
4. 'Buddhism forbids all forms of killing.' Discuss.

Hinduism

Samkhya system

Samkyha is most accurately described as a philosophical rather than a theological system. Note that although there is no mention of God, it is still considered to be a tradition within Hinduism.

This is an atheistic philosophy, meaning 'enumeration'. The classical Samkhya text is the *Samkhya Karika* (Verses on Samkhya) by Isvarakrishna around the 3rd century CE. It identifies two principles that make up the world and everything in it. **Prakrti** refers to matter or nature, but also to the realm of mind. **Purusha** refers to the true self or spirit: it is pure consciousness.

Further discussion

Let us take the statement: 'I am James, a 17-year-old student of religious studies' as an example. Adherents of the Samkyha system would argue that James' outward characteristics (including his name) are not really *him*, because they belong to the realm of prakrti. His true inner self, purusha, is different.

Further reading

Read pages 67–70 of *Hinduism* by R. C. Zaehner (OUP 1966), for a more detailed explanation of the Samkhya system.

Within prakrti there are 24 kinds of being, known as **tattvas** or principles. Buddhi (intellect), also known as mahat (the great one), is the most important category. It is from this that the sense of ego (ahamkara) develops, from which the other tattvas arise. Another faculty is mind (manas), which interprets and orders the information gathered by the five senses. There are also five organs of action. Five subtle elements are experienced by the five senses: sound, taste, form, touch and smell. Five gross elements arise from the five subtle elements, including air, fire and water.

According to the Samkyha philosophy, prakrti is active and constantly changing. This process of change is marshalled by the **three gunas** (principles of all material beings): sattva (being), rajas (energy) and tamas (darkness). Sattva is the quality of goodness, purity and tranquillity; rajas is a dynamic quality that makes the generation of karma possible; tamas dulls the senses and the mind.

Liberation

Being able to distinguish between purusha and prakriti is necessary for attaining **kaivalya** (liberation). It is an arduous path, particularly because there is no god to supervise and guide the aspirant. Liberation is finally achieved when one uncovers the true self and experiences pure consciousness.

Route E: Philosophy of religion with Hinduism. How does the distinction between purusa and prakrti in Samkhya differ from western dualist views of the nature of the person? See pages 234–235 of *An Introduction to Hinduism* by Gavin Flood (Cambridge 1996) and compare with pages 77–80 of Peter Cole's *Philosophy of Religion* (Hodder and Stoughton 1999).

Yoga

Yoga is a broad and ancient concept. The origins of the term lie in the Sanksrit word yuj meaning to unite, control or bind, and all types of yoga involve self-discipline and control of the mind. An aspirant may seek divine guidance along the way, but often it is an individual pursuit: an attempt to gain mastery and knowledge of the self through detachment from the everyday world. In doing so, it is possible to relieve the suffering caused by ignorance.

The Yoga Sutras of Patanjali

All quotations from the Yoga Sutras are from Alistair Shearer's translation *The Yoga Sutras of Patanjali* (Rider 2002).

The Yoga Sutras describe the methods of classical yoga, also known as **Raja-Yoga** (Royal Yoga). They are divided into four chapters. The 196 sutras (verses) are attributed to Patanjali (2nd century BCE), but it is unlikely that he wrote them. They probably evolved over a period of about six centuries, between 100 BCE and 500 CE. This form of yoga has many similarities with Samkhya.

Route E: Philosophy of religion with Hinduism. Consider how the yogi attains the goal of self-realisation and compare this process with the different ways in which truth is discovered in the Christian tradition. See pages 69–70 of *OCR AS Guide*.

Chapter 1 discusses the types of mental activity that are quelled by correct yogic practice. It presents them as the root cause of suffering and yoga as the solution to it. The different stages of stilling the mind are also introduced.

Chapter 2 begins with a further exposition of why suffering occurs: attachment to one's actions generates karma and future rebirths. It then sets out how it is possible to escape through mastery of yoga.

Chapter 3 deals with the process of self-realisation; the powers that the advanced yogi can acquire are also described. These vary from mastery over the physical body to tremendous intellectual insight.

Chapter 4 concentrates on the goal of yoga (self-realisation), and how tendencies in this life are the product of past actions.

The yogic path, as set out in the Yoga Sutras, involves eight 'limbs': **yama** or 'The Laws of Life' involve non-violence, honesty, not stealing, celibacy and not being avaricious. **Niyama** are the five rules for living a disciplined existence. They suggest that the life of a yogi must be simple, they must be content with their lot, prepared to undergo physical hardship, study the scripture frequently, and be devoted to the Lord.

The third limb is regular practice of the physical postures or **asana**. Control of the body is necessary for observance of the fourth limb, **pranayama**, which represents the exercises designed to regulate and steady the breathing. The fifth limb is called **pratyahara**, which is when the senses are withdrawn, and one is no longer aware of or distracted by the immediate physical environment. The sixth limb is known as **dharana**, which means concentration: this helps to focus the mind. Meditation, **dhyana**, is the seventh limb: it allows the mind to become one-pointed. Finally, **samadhi** is a state of deep, inward concentration, experienced on four levels. It is achieved when the mind becomes fixed on one point ('ekragata'). The Yoga Sutras 4.29–30 state that those who have attained samadhi have made the vital distinction between the 'subtlest level of mind' (which is still prakrti) and the true self (which is purusha). This awareness of the self is called the highest knowledge.

Stilling the mind. The second sutra gives a useful definition of the chief purpose of yoga: '...the settling of the mind into silence' (1.2). There are five types of mental activity: understanding, misunderstanding, imagination, sleep and memory. Yoga is practised so that the mind may become perfectly still: isolated from the world and no longer occupied by ordinary mental activity. It requires substantial and careful effort over a long period of time.

Relieving suffering. The sutras recognise that there are obstacles on the path to liberation, such as illness, tiredness, doubt, carelessness, laziness, attachment and ignorance. All such distractions lead to suffering, but they can be avoided through correct practice of yoga. The sutras suggest that there are five specific causes of suffering, which are universal conditions of human existence. These are **avidya** (ignorance), **asmita** (selfishness), **raga** (passion), **dvesa** (hatred) and **abhinivesa** (attachment to life). Of these the most damaging is avidya, since it is from this that the other four arise. The sutras define the concept as confusing that which is temporary with that which is permanent.

Achieving liberation. Kaivalya or aloneness is the ultimate yogic goal – one who has attained it is genuinely a liberated soul. It is achieved when one realises that one's true identity (purusha) is different from all that is prakrti. As a result, one is no longer is attached to the prakritic self, or concerned by the (prakritic) world. Having completed the journey of self-discovery, the aspirant is

Connections Route E: Philosophy of Religion with Hinduism. Does the concept of reincarnation provides an explanation for suffering? Read chapter 16 of *Death and Eternal Life* by John Hick (John Knox 1994) for a study of reincarnation and the problem of evil.

The yogic path

Read sutras 2.29–3.8

Further reading

See the helpful account on page 97 of *An Introduction to Hinduism*.

Route L: Religious ethics with Hinduism. Read Yoga Sutra 4.9–11 and consider whether the law of karma and rebirth is wholly deterministic. See also *OCR AS Guide* pages 147–148 and Zaehner's *Hindus* pages 59–61. Compare these views with western accounts of determinism: see pages 31–33.

It is important to note that prakriti is not illusory. Ignorance stems from not being able to distinguish between the self (purusha), which is eternal and pure, and the non-self (prakrti), which, though also eternal, is constantly changing and impure.

Aims of Yoga

Read *Yoga Sutras* 1.6–7.

Read *Yoga Sutras* 1.30.

Route E: Philosophy of religion with Hinduism. Consider the effectiveness of yoga as a response to the problem of suffering.

Unlike Samkhya, the Yoga Sutras do mention God. However, as Zaehner points out (*Hinduism*, page 71) the role of God in Patanjali's system is not as central as it is in the *Upanishads*. Liberation is not the soul's union with Brahman, but its isolation from all other souls, including God. One has become like God (who himself enjoys this state of isolation) but not at one with God.

freed from attachment to thoughts or actions, and no longer experiences suffering. The closing lines of the Yoga Sutras put it thus: 'pure unbounded consciousness remains, forever established in its own absolute nature. This is Enlightenment.' (4.34)

Other forms of yoga: aims and practices

Further reading

Read Patrick Olivelle's translation of the *Upanishads* (OUP 1996), and *An Introduction to Hinduism*, pages 94–96 for a fuller discussion of yoga in the Vedic and Upanishadic traditions.

Although the classical presentation of yoga is found in the sutras of Patanjali, there are other forms. Yoga is discussed quite frequently in the **Upanishads**, many of which predate Patanjali's Sutras. The earliest mention of the term is in the *Katha Upanishad*; the meditative path of a yogi is also presented in the *Svetasvara Upanishad*. The various *Yoga Upanishads*, which date from between 100 BCE to 300 CE, supply further guidance on the practice of yoga. According to the *Maitri Upanishad*, yoga involves six disciplines, including control of breathing, restraint of the senses, meditation and concentration.

See pages 146–147 of the *OCR AS Guide* for more on the *Bhagavad Gita* and the three types of yoga.

The concept of yoga has a high profile in the **Bhagavad Gita**, although its meaning here is broader than in the Yoga Sutras. Rather than yoga meaning a particular path to liberation, the Gita identifies three paths by which the individual may be released from bondage to samsara and experience union with the Lord. **Jnana-yoga** (the path of knowledge, similar to that presented in Samkhya and the Yoga Sutras), **karma-yoga** (the path of action) and bhakti-yoga (the path of loving devotion to the Lord) are presented as alternative yet complementary paths. **Hatha-yoga** differs from Patanjali's system in that it focuses more on the physical dimension of yoga. Other types of yoga, still practised today, include **Kundalini yoga** and the yoga of inner sound.

Further study

The closest Sanksrit equivalent to the term 'ethics' is dharma. Dharma is notoriously difficult to define, but may be variously translated as teaching, belief, religion, law, duty, virtue, correct behaviour and so on. It often refers to the cosmic order (the way that the world is): it is eternal and cannot be changed. Research the origins and usage of the term dharma. Refer to the books suggested in this chapter.

Hindu ethics

There is no universal ethical code for Hindus, which is not surprising given the diversity of the religion. This is partly due to the fact that no religious text or creed is regarded as absolutely binding by all. This allows for a variety of ethical practices within Hinduism, inspired by different textual traditions. For example, while Hindus often emphasise one's responsibility to family and society, there are-well established traditions of renunciation.

Varnashramadharma

For the majority of Hindus, salvation is attained by fulfilling duties (dharma) according to caste (varna) and stage of life (ashrama). Both factors help to determine correct ethical behaviour.

See pages 130–132 on yoga, and pages 138–139 on the Ramakrishna Mission, for examples of ascetic practice in Hinduism.

Hindu society has traditionally been divided into four main varnas: priestly (brahmin), warrior (kshatriya), merchant (vaishya) and the lowly servant (sudra) castes. As it is believed that the caste hierarchy is natural and sacred, it is not possible to change one's caste. Consequently, although the caste system has religious origins, it has important social implications too.

'And do thy duty, even if it be humble, rather than another's, even if it be great. To die in one's duty is life, to live in another's is death.' *Bhagavad Gita* 3: 35, translated by Juan Mascaro (Penguin 1962).

Stories about **avataras** (descent forms of the deity) that are recorded in a variety of Hindu scriptures, such as the *Bhagavad Gita* and the *Ramayana,* reinforce the importance of caste duty. In the *Bhagavad Gita*, for example, Krishna makes it clear that it is Arjuna's dharma (duty) as a kshatriya to fight.

The notion of life-stages (ashramas) arose during the 5th century BCE and initially referred to the lifestyle of the brahmins who lived together in hermitages. The Vedic tradition suggests that all high-caste Hindu males ought to follow ashrama-dharma, a four-stage process of ideal living:

The Four Life-Stages

1. Once initiated into his second birth by a Brahmin (thus qualifying him for study of the Vedas), the young man leaves his parents and goes to live with his teacher in a **brahmacarya** – this is the first of his life stages. He may reside with him for a year or longer. Throughout this time he is engaged in the study of the Vedas and will perform austerities (tapas) and live a celibate, almost ascetic lifestyle. He is known as a *brahmacarin*, 'one who moves with or applies himself to Brahman'.
2. The householder stage is next, known as **garhasthya**. The man is to get married and have children, and sustain religious devotion within the home by keeping sacred fires in honour of the devas (gods).
3. Once his children have grown up and become householders, a man should retire from his householder's duties and become a hermit or forest-dweller. This stage is called **vanaprastha** (life in forest). He lives increasingly simply: having given up most worldly comforts and possessions, he is reliant on begging for food. He may take his wife with him.
4. **Samnyasa** (renunciation or homelessness) involves leaving behind all worldly duties (including tending the sacred fire) and complete detachment from personal relationships too. Although this path may be the ideal, the tradition recognises that it is not for everyone. It is conceivable that a man will stay in his house all his life, living off his sons.

Further reading

This is set out in the Laws of Manu. Read pages 92–97 of *Hindus* by Julius Lipner (Routledge 1994) for more information.

Route L: Religious Ethics and Hinduism. Consider whether the emphasis on the individual's caste and life-stage makes it a relativist form of ethics. Read pages 79–80 of the *OCR AS Guide* and compare with other ethical systems. Read chapter 3 of Lipner's *Hindus* for a full discussion of the origins, meaning and relevance of varnashramadharma.

Four Purushartas

The **purushartas** refer to the key ethical goals of life:

Trivarga (group of three). The earlier references to purushartas focus on three aims. One is **dharma**: this stresses the importance of noble and correct behaviour in accordance with the eternal laws of the universe; it may also refer to correct ritual practice such as keeping sacred fires appropriately. Another aim is **artha**: this refers to worldly success, wealth and prosperity. The third aim is **kama**, meaning love, passion or desire. These three purushartas are known as trivarga. The trivarga are worldly aims, concerned with obligations to family and society. There is no consensus as to which of the three aims is most important. Some texts see artha as fundamental because prosperity allows dharma to be practised and kama to be experienced, but more common is the belief that dharma is central. Yet other sources suggest that all four goals are equally important and interdependent.

Caturvarga (group of four). According to Vedanta, which has been the dominant tradition of Hindu philosophical theology for the past 12 centuries, **moksha** is the ultimate artha (purpose) in life. Thus the trivarga is replaced by the caturvarga. Even for those who pursue the other purushartas during life, moksha usually remains the highest goal. Moksha means liberation from samsara, the cycle

Further reading

See Gavin Flood's essay 'The Meaning and Context of the Four Purushartas' in Julius Lipner (ed.) *The Fruits of Our Desiring: An Enquiry into the Ethics of the Bhagavadgita for our times* (Bayeux Arts 1997) for a fuller discussion of the significance of the four purushartas.

Route L: Religious ethics with Hinduism. Do the four purushartas represent a teleological strand within Hindu ethical thinking? Compare with different western ethical theories such as utilitarianism. Read pages 106–111 of *Ethics* by Louis P. Pojman (Wadsworth 2002).

Further reading

For more on Vedanta, see pages 141–2 of the *OCR AS Guide*.

Further discussion

Do you think there is a tension between the goal of moksha and the other three purushartas? For a further discussion of karma, moksha and samsara, see pages 147–148. Refer also to the Chandogya Upanishad. 5.10.7.

Route L: Religious ethics with Hinduism. What are the implications of ahimsa for debates about war and peace? For more on the application of ahimsa, see sections on practical ethics, pages 134–135, and on Gandhi, pages 139–140.

Further reading

Julius Lipner *Hindus*, pages 223–226, discusses the tension between ahimsa and dharma.

of rebirth. One who seeks moksha will typically undertake a life of asceticism and renunciation of worldly comforts (as practised during the forest-dweller ashrama). While the trivarga emphasises worldly ideals – correct behaviour, love and prosperity – moksha may demand a rejection of these ideals in favour of a life of detachment from the world.

Ahimsa (non-killing or non-injury) is regarded as an ethical ideal by most if not all Hindus. It applies to non-human beings too. According to the **Law Codes of Manu**, ahimsa is grouped alongside truthfulness, purity, not stealing and power over the senses as dharma to be observed by all four castes. It is also one of the **five virtues** (yamas), alongside truthfulness, honesty, non-covetousness and continence. **Gandhi** gave pre-eminent significance to it, both in his life and in his teachings, as did his followers. One exception to the rule is killing for a sacrifice, which is not strictly considered to be an act of violence (himsa). Another is killing in the line of duty in order to uphold varnashramadharma.

Sarvepalli Radhakrishnan (1888–1975) was president of India 1962–7. He was also an influential scholar of Hinduism.

Sanatanadharma. This means the eternal dharma of Hinduism. It is best understood as a set of guidelines with ancient Vedic authority. The modernisers of Hinduism in the 19th century often saw themselves as followers of sanatanadharma, and the term is still common among modern Hindus today. For some, sanatanadharma is a way of describing Hinduism itself. The belief that there is only one eternal dharma of Hinduism can imply that it ought properly to be observed by all humanity, although not all Hindus would share this view. **Radhakrishnan** contrasted the universal, objective sanatanadharma with *svadharma*, one's own interpretation of it. He suggested that although the values of sanatanadharma are absolute, the individual plays an important role in interpreting them. Gandhi, among others, recognised that although sanatanadharma is of vital importance to Hindus, and many have called themselves *sanatanists* (followers of the eternal dharma), there is no universal agreement over its specific content.

Practical ethics in Hinduism

Further reading

Read *Moral Issues in the Hindu Tradition* by Robert Jackson and Dermot Killingley (Trentham Books 1991) for a helpful account of the key issues.

Route L: Religious ethics and Hinduism. Consider the similarities between traditional Hindu and Christian attitudes towards sexual ethics and gender roles. Read pages 167–170 of *Hinduism* (Teach Yourself 2003), and pages 10–14 of Sex and Relationships by Michael Wilcockson (Hodder and Stoughton 2000).

Sexual ethics. In general, Hindus believe that sex must take place within marriage, not outside it. Furthermore, its main purpose is for procreation. Divorces are very rare and are generally frowned upon. Remarriage is possible, but it will generally fall to the mother to look after the children: traditional gender roles still hold sway in most Hindu families. Celibacy has a long tradition in Hinduism, but is not necessary for attaining moksha.

Medical ethics. The Hindu tradition has tended to regard abortion as immoral, largely because it contradicts ahimsa. A widespread belief is that ensoulment takes place at conception, which means that the embryo is a person right from the start of the pregnancy. Another view is that abortion frustrates karmic destiny. An embryo in the womb is the product of its previous lives, and so to interrupt a life-cycle would interfere with the natural process of karma and rebirth. By contrast, birth control is quite common in Hindu societies and the practice does not usually draw the kind of stinging attacks that it receives from many Christians in the west. Euthanasia has received little or no treatment in the Hindu scriptures; as a rule it is not morally acceptable although suicide is not generally considered to be wrong.

Reverence for life. The principle of ahimsa is often applied to the animal world too. In particular, the cow is believed to be a sacred creature, revered as a mother and a source of life. It is generally considered immoral to eat it. Underlying this practice is a conviction that the Supreme Being manifests himself in a variety of ways, and that animals also possess an atman. Indeed, many Hindus believe that it is possible to be reborn as an animal in the next life and that one may have been an animal in one's previous life.

Route L: Religious ethics with Hinduism. Hinduism tends to regard the individual atman (self) as an intrinsically valuable manifestation of the divine. Compare the traditional Hindu position on abortion with western religious and secular views. Read page 170 of *Hinduism*. See also pages 82–84 of the *OCR AS Guide*.

Environmental ethics. One reason that the lifestyle of the sannyasi is considered virtuous is that he takes from the environment what he needs to survive, but does not interfere with nature by farming or killing animals. This behaviour expresses the idea that the created world is sacred, even a manifestation of god. This belief has been popular among Hindus for many centuries, encouraging them to treat the environment with respect. Yet as the *Bhagavad Gita* urges, one must continue to act in the world: agriculture, although sometimes harmful to nature, is necessary.

Further reading

Read pages 114–117 of *Hinduism: A Very Short Introduction* by Kim Knott (Oxford 1998) for more on the significance of the cow in Hinduism.

See *Bhagavad Gita* 11.7.

Further reading

Look up the *Mahabarata* 3, 199, 1–2. This features the story of the Brahmin who encounters a hunter, who defends his violent trade. Read page 41 *Moral Issues in the Hindu Tradition*, by D. Killingley and R. Jackson for an insightful discussion of this passage.

Reforming movements in Hinduism

Despite its enduring traditions, aspects of Hinduism have changed quite significantly over the last two centuries and are continuing to do so. A number of movements have played an important role in helping to redefine what it means to be a Hindu. Many of the ideas used by reformers were in fact borrowed from the west, so that much of the social and ideological reform that has taken place would almost certainly not have happened had it not been for the strong British presence and influence in India.

Brahmo Samaj

As a force for social reform, for modernisation, for the spread of Christianity and its reconciliation with Hinduism, the Brahmo Samaj (Society of the Worshippers of God), is very important. The movement grew out of an anglicised, high-caste group of Bengalis called the **bhadralok**; its centre was Calcutta, the capital of Bengal and capital of India at that time.

Further reading

For a detailed study of the history and impact of the Brahmo Samaj, see *The Brahmo Samaj and the Shaping of the Modern Indian Mind* by David Kopf (Princeton 1978).

Although an Indian organisation which drew extensively on the Hindu tradition, the structure and philosophy of the Brahmo Samaj was in many ways quite western. It was inspired in part by the Christian reform tradition, and was influenced by **Unitarianism**. The various leaders of the movement were also attracted to European enlightenment thinking: a belief in the power of reason and in ideas of scientific progress. Thus the religion practised and preached by the Brahmo Samaj, Brahmoism, was a distinctively modern form of Hinduism. Idol-worship, for example, was generally considered sinful: Hinduism needed to progress. Members of the Brahmo Samaj were also quite open to Christianity and other religions: they tended to stress what they had in common, rather than what separated them. The Brahmos were ethical monotheists, who sought to achieve social reform in the name of their faith.

Unitarianism is a Christian theology that teaches essential human goodness, minimises the role of tradition and ritual in church practice, emphasises monotheism and tends to regard Jesus' role as exemplary.

Ram Mohan Roy (1772–1833)

The history of the Brahmo Samaj can be traced back to 1828, when Ram Mohan Roy, a Bengali Brahman, established the Brahmo Sabha (Assembly of Brahman). Only later did the movement become commonly known as the Brahmo Samaj. Roy was a strict monotheist, seeing Jesus Christ not as the son of God but as the

Further reading

Read pages 63–6 and 118–119 of Lipner's *Hindus* for more on Ram Mohan Roy.

ideal human being: the exemplar of the perfect way of living before God. As a **rationalist**, he also believed that God's moral laws could be discerned through the application of reason and the study of nature. His confidence in human reason helps to explain his view of reforming Hinduism: he believes that his 19th-century 'enlightened' perspective enabled him to discriminate between what was worth keeping and what was not. He was not only opposed to the veneration of idols but also sought to rid Indian society of the popular rituals and practices that he considered immoral and superfluous to a correct approach to God. He campaigned, too, for the abolition of **sati** (widow-burning). In this way, he hoped to make Hinduism more ethical, in keeping with the core values of the *Upanishads* and other great religious texts.

Debendranath Tagore (1817–1905)

Debendranath was the father of the famous poet and writer Rabindranath Tagore (1861–1941), who was also leader for a period.

Debendranath was the next significant leader of the Brahmo Samaj when he joined in 1842, nine years after the death of Ram Mohan. Under Debendranath, the Brahmo Samaj became more overtly Hindu – he was less attracted to Christianity than his predecessor, and believed that the *Upanishads*, not the Bible, were the ultimate vehicle to salvation. He established a journal called *Tattvabondhi Patrika* to help disseminate Brahmo philosophy to the masses. *Patrika* also raised the profile of the Brahmo campaigns for female education, widow remarriage and monogamy.

Keshab Chandra Sen (1838–1884)

While Debendranath represented the more orthodox wing of the Brahmo Samaj – he still wanted to retain elements of the caste system, for example – Keshab Chandra Sen was more 'Christianised'. He joined the society in 1857 and made an almost instant impact. Following a dispute over whether or not a certain traditional religious ceremony involved idolatry, a schism emerged between the conservatives and the progressives. The conservatives rallied round Debendranath, whom they perceived as being more loyal to age-old Hindu rituals, to form the *Adi* (original) *Brahmo Samaj*. The majority, though, turned to the young, dynamic, westernised Keshab, who established the *Naba Bidhan Samaj* or Church of the New Dispensation.

Further reading

See page 153 of Zaehner's *Hinduism*, for more on this decisive event in the history of the Brahmo Samaj.

Keshab's own religious identity was subject to change, much like that of the Brahmo Samaj itself. At times he appeared to shun Hinduism, but on other occasions he turned to it for inspiration. Although Brahmo religious services under his leadership often featured more readings from the Bible than the *Upanishads*, he sought to integrate Caitanya devotionalism into services too. He had a pluralistic outlook towards other religions, and saw many of the great religious figures from other traditions as appropriate objects of devotion. He believed that his Church of the New Dispensation was an ideal forum for bringing these various traditions together, in the hope of attaining common ethical and religious aims.

Caitanya – literally 'consciousness' – (1486–1553), was a devotee of Krishna, whose many followers believed was an avatara of both Krishna and Radha.

The extent to which the Brahmo Samaj should observe traditional Hindu practice continued to be a controversial issue during Keshab's leadership. The marriage of Keshab's daughter according to ancient ceremonial laws enraged many members who were opposed to such practice on the grounds that it was outdated. This led to a further secession: the *Sadharan* (common or universal) *Brahmo Samaj* was formed in 1874, led by Pandit Shivanath Shastri.

The Brahmo Samaj might have been more influential had it not been so prone to internal divisions, but it has nonetheless made a considerable contribution to helping India become the nation it is today. The most important legacy of the 19th-century leaders was in helping to construct a modern Indian identity. The work of the Brahmo Samaj encouraged Indians to think about what it was to be a Hindu living under British rule. It fostered the idea that 'Hinduism' was a distinct religion, existing alongside others, rather than simply a term to describe the religious activity of the people of India. Furthermore, it heightened awareness of the presence of the British and of Christianity within India. As the history of the Brahmo Samaj suggests, the question of whether Indian Hindus should embrace 'British' Christian ideas and practices, or retain their own ancestral traditions, was of national and political, as well as religious, significance. It was also quite divisive.

The Brahmo Samaj retains a nationwide presence in India today. Its most recent conference was in 2003: the 113th conference of the Brahmo Samaj held in Patna, Bihar, north India. More information on the Brahmo Samaj can be found on the Internet.

Christianity in fact has an ancient history in India which predates its arrival in Britain. Nevertheless, extensive European missionary activity in India meant that it was closely associated with British and other European colonisers.

Arya Samaj

Founded in 1875 by Dayananda Sarasvati (1824–1883), the Arya Samaj advocates an aggressive Hindu nationalism and a 'return' to Vedic teaching and the **sanatanadharma** of Hinduism. It is most active in the Punjab, northwest India, and in the northern part of India as a whole. Unlike the Brahmo Samaj, the Arya Samaj continues to be a potent political force in India today.

See page 134 for more on sanatanadharma. The word Arya means 'noble', and refers to the tribes who entered northwest India, probably from the Middle East, approximately 3,000 years ago. Their sacred scriptures were the Vedas. The use of the term to describe this movement is therefore significant: they want to return to the Vedic Hinduism practised by the Aryans. Read pages 49–50 of the *OCR AS Guide*.

The Arya Samaj has also campaigned vigorously for a variety of social reforms, including the advancement of women. Many of these have been in the field of education: the organisation has established numerous **gurukalas** across India. These are schools set up to teach Hindu children – boys *and* girls – how to become true followers of the sanatadharma contained in the Vedas. Sanskrit is also studied, since it is the language of the Vedas. The schools have helped to promote Hindu unity, but at the exclusion of non-Hindu Indians and the many Hindus who do not identify with the ideals of the movement. Similarly, their advocation of Hindi as the national language of India, while uniting Indians across linguistic boundaries, in practice can exclude non-Hindi speakers. In the spirit of modernity, Dayananda argued for the autonomy of individuals to choose their own marriage partners, as opposed to the traditional custom of arranged marriages. And in his reconception of the caste system, he insisted that varna refers not to station in society, but rather to one's character and achievements.

Further reading

Read pages 156–159 of Zaehner's *Hinduism* on the Arya Samaj.

Sarasvati was an ardent reformer who wanted to transform Hinduism. This would come about by purging the religion of impure, corrupting influences, and returning it to its original, pure form. He promoted belief in an all-powerful, impersonal God as represented in the Vedas; he was deeply sceptical of certain elements of popular religion, such as idol-worship and pilgrimage. He regarded the great religious epics (such as the *Mahabharata* and the *Ramayana*) and the *Puranas* as unhelpful: they lacked the divine authority of the Vedas and, in their propagation of false teachings such as the doctrine of *avatara*, often conflicted with Vedic revelation.

The Arya Samaj believed their version of the sanatadharma to be superior not only to other forms of Hinduism, but to all religion. Their view of the religion was monolithic – namely, there is one legitimate type of Hinduism, and other expressions, such as those

Further discussion

Consider whether or not the Arya Samaj is more Hindu than the Brahmo Samaj.

Further reading

Read Zaehner's analysis of the Arya Samaj on pages 156–159 of *Hinduism*. Do you agree with his conclusions?

present in much folk religion in India, are not valid. Unlike the Brahmo Samaj, the Arya Samaj has historically seen Islam and Christianity as threats to Hinduism. Rejecting the principle of **ahimsa**, it has at times supported the use of violence as a way of defending the Hindu tradition and ensuring its dominance in India. A fiercely nationalistic organisation, the Arya Samaj has tended to regard the Brahmo Samaj as too westernised to be a genuine Hindu movement.

The achievements of the Arya Samaj, particularly in terms of social reform and the boost to women, are substantial. The movement has also championed the cause of Hindu nationalism and has played an important role in developing a more self-confident, at times aggressive, Hindu identity. Whether this has been a good thing, though, is open to question. Its association with Hindu militancy is one of the more unfortunate features of the movement's history.

The Ramakrishna Mission

The Ramakrishna Mission is a movement inspired by the vision of Sri Ramakrishna, a brahmin mystic from Calcutta. Eleven years after his death in 1886, a monastery or **math** was formally established in his name by one of his devotees, Swami Vivekananda, at Baranagore near Calcutta. In 1899 the math moved its headquarters to Belur, which remains the centre of the monastic order today. Its aims are ideological as well as social. Spreading Ramakrishna's message of religious tolerance and promoting the view of Hinduism developed by Vivekananda, the Ramakrishna monks have worked extensively in education, running schools across India and publishing widely. They have also supported the advancement of women and helped to care for the sick and marginalised in society. Underlying the mission's commitment to social welfare is a belief in the importance of karma-yoga: it is through active service to others that self-realisation is possible. Its achievements were recognised in 1999 with the awarding of the Gandhi Peace Prize.

The Ramakrishna Mission has spread itself across India. There are now 84 maths there and 31 in other parts of the world, including the United Kingdom.

Ramakrishna Paramahamsa (1834–1886) was a deeply pious man who spent most of his life in a Kali temple just outside the city. Such was his devotion to Kali, he even worshipped his wife as an avatara of the goddess. He had a significant following and drew many devotees from the **Brahmo Samaj**. A saint-like figure, he helped Keshab Chandra Sen and others to see Hinduism in a more positive light. His attitude towards other religions is markedly different from that of the Arya Samaj: exceptionally open-minded, he believed that God takes on a variety of different forms and his reality is not confined to the revelation found in the Vedas. Not only did he worship various Hindu expressions of the divine, he also practised Islam and Christianity during his lifetime. He did not think that any particular way of referring to God – as Brahman, Allah, Krishna or Trinity – was any 'truer' than another. Thus he believed all religions are equally valid paths to salvation: he urged his followers to remember that the most important task in life is to seek God, the one eternal reality.

Advaita means 'non-duality'. Advaita Vedantins believe that only one reality exists, and that is Brahman. See page 41 of the *OCR AS Guide* on Shankara for more on Advaita Vedanta.

Swami Vivekananda (1863–1902), born Narendra Nath Dutt, was a disciple of Ramakrishna. He developed the insights of his guru and produced an all-embracing Advaita Vedantic philosophy which had wide appeal. He made great inroads in the west, to the

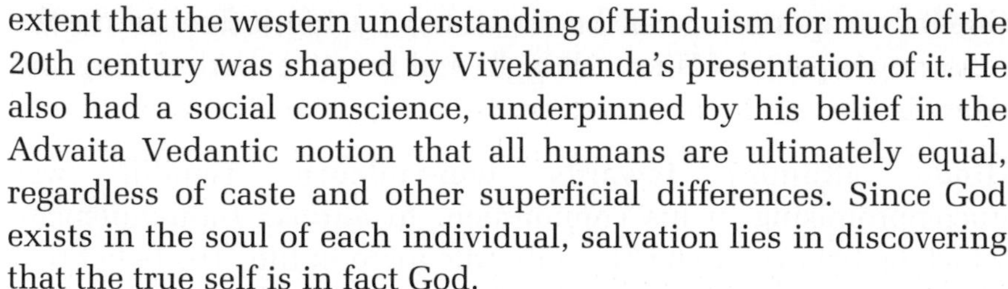

extent that the western understanding of Hinduism for much of the 20th century was shaped by Vivekananda's presentation of it. He also had a social conscience, underpinned by his belief in the Advaita Vedantic notion that all humans are ultimately equal, regardless of caste and other superficial differences. Since God exists in the soul of each individual, salvation lies in discovering that the true self is in fact God.

Route L: Religious ethics with Hinduism. Consider how the nature of the self is expressed in Advaitic philosophy; read Zaehner *Hindus*, pages 75–78. Compare this view with western dualism; read pages 194–198 of *Philosophy of Religion for A Level* by Jordan, Lockyer and Tate (Nelson Thornes 2002).

At the **World Council of Religions in Chicago** in 1893, Vivekananda preached what seemed like a radical message: all religions are equal, even in their great diversity, which makes religious conversions unnecessary. He therefore asked western religious leaders for a change in their attitude towards India. Rather than spreading the Gospel in the hope of drawing Indians towards Christianity, westerners ought to support India with financial aid to raise living standards. In this respect, he was a true pioneer.

It is significant, though, that the authority for his teachings lay in the *Upanishads*, which he gave pre-eminent status amongst the holy scriptures of the world.

It is through the work of the Ramakrishna Mission, which Vivekananda founded, that his Advaitic message reached the people of India and the world beyond. In the west, the Mission portrayed Hinduism as worthy of respect as a world religion. It was presented as rational and up-to-date, but with ancient roots and an eternal and universal message of belief in the one true God. On Indian soil, the movement promoted an egalitarian, inclusive religion that many sectors of Indian society, especially the middle classes, were proud to identify with. While allowing for the existence of diversity within the religion, the overall message was of a fundamental unity, grounded in the belief that God dwells in every human being. It is a testimony to the impact of the movement that its view of Hinduism continues to be so popular today.

Gandhi was born in 1869 in a part of northwest India that now belongs to the state of Gujurat. After marrying at the age of 13, he left for London in 1888 to train as a lawyer before returning to India in 1891. In 1893, he moved to South Africa where he remained for over two decades. His time in South Africa helped to shape the young Gandhi into the political leader that he eventually became: in particular, his experiences of racism instilled in him a determination to stamp out injustice whenever he encountered it.

Gandhi

His full name was Mohandas Karamchand Gandhi, although he is often referred to as 'Mahatma', which means 'Great One'.

He returned to India in 1913, and soon became deeply involved in the struggle for independence from British colonial rule. His values were instilled in his co-workers at the ashram he set up in north India. For Gandhi, 'ahimsa and truth are… like two sides of the same coin'. This conviction inspired his movement for change, known as **satyagraha**, which he saw as 'the force which is born of truth and love or non-violence'. The satyagraha movement, a non-violent form of resistance to oppression, helped Gandhi to translate his philosophy into action. Gandhi was an able and charismatic politician, who used his iconic status effectively to help achieve his political aims. In particular, he launched various campaigns for social reform, such as the non-cooperation movement in 1920, and the Constructive Programme. He became President of the Congress in 1924, and remained a prominent public figure and a close ally of Nehru right up until his death in 1948, just months after independence had been granted.

Quoted in *Gandhi: In My Own Words* (ed) Richard Attenborough (Hodder and Stoughton 1982).

Gandhi's importance can be measured by his influence on the following aspects of Hindu thought and practice, both during and after his life:

Gandhi on Non-Violence ed. Thomas Merton (New Directions Books 1965), page 25.

Hindu attitudes towards non-violence. Gandhi was uncompromising in his commitment to **ahimsa** (non-violence), which he believed to be 'the only true force in life'. His belief that violence was not only immoral but also unproductive won him many followers who joined his numerous satyagrahas (peaceful campaigns). In fact, his non-violent stance was in part due to exposure to non-Hindu traditions such as Jainism and Christianity; but this did not prevent him from acting as an inspiration to many Hindus who saw him as embodying a sacred and ancient Hindu principle. As such, he raised the profile of non-violence and encouraged Hindus to see it as *the* authentic Hindu response to difficult situations, consistent with sanatanadharma. He thus transformed ahimsa from an ideal into a real ethical possibility, helping to promote the idea that Hinduism is a peaceful religion.

Route L: Religious Ethics with Hinduism. Consider Hindu and Christian attitudes towards non-violence. In particular, compare Gandhi's approach with the New Testament, bearing in mind that he was deeply inspired by the Sermon on the Mount (Matt 5–7). Read chapter 6 of *Gandhi: A Very Short Introduction* by Bhikhu Parekh (OUP 1997), which presents Gandhi's vision of a non-violent and just society; see also chapter 14 of *The Puzzle of Ethics* by Peter Vardy, which outlines Christian views. Remember that Hinduism is far from being entirely pacifist; in the *Bhagavad Gita*, it is Arjuna's varnashramadharma to fight. See page 132 on varnashramadharma; see also page 146 of the *OCR AS Guide*.

Hindu views of other religions. Gandhi once said that 'the Bible is as much a book of religion with me as the Gita and the Koran'. Measuring religious value largely in terms of ethical truth, he saw the great religious traditions of the world primarily as sources of guidance as to how one should live. He was more concerned with orthopraxy (right practice) than orthodoxy (right belief): for him, belief was useless unless it led to action and so the test of any particular idea was whether it was worth living by. Like Ramakrishna and Vivekananda, he helped to promote the idea that 'religions are different roads converging upon the same point' and that it does not 'matter that we take different roads so long as we reach the same goal'. His positive attitude towards Islam was exemplified by his political aims. Gandhi was an Indian nationalist, but not a Hindu nationalist – he did not believe the state should be exclusively Hindu. While he lost the battle to prevent partition, his martyr's death at the hands of a Hindu fanatic ensured that Gandhi became an emblem of religious tolerance. This helped, temporarily at least, to dampen the nationalist zeal of Hindus across India.

Quoted in *Gandhi: In My Own Words*, pages 70–71.

Hindu society. Gandhi's other major concern was, as Parekh has argued, the 'moral regeneration' of India, which would be achieved through satyagrahas and his programmes for social reform. Most famously, he campaigned for the integration of untouchables, whom he called harijans (children of God), into Hindu society. While he saw it as necessary to uphold the caste system, because it is consistent with Hindu sanatanadharma, he was firmly opposed to the practice of untouchability. Although often criticised by untouchable leaders, he certainly helped to shape modern Hindu attitudes by challenging age-old prejudices of caste Hindus. He also sought to improve the status of women in India.

See page 13 of *Gandhi: A Very Short Introduction*.

Further reading

Read more on untouchability in India on pages 114–118 of *Hindus* by Julius Lipner.

Hindu religious practice. Gandhi had great respect for many of the ancient rituals and customs of Hinduism. According to Zaehner, 'he saw that the Hindu rites in home and temple, performed in the presence of images representing some aspect of the divine, were the very cement that held Hinduism together. Do away with these, and you do away with Hinduism.' Though primarily a reformer, his endorsement of traditional religious practice helped to ensure that it remained part of the fabric of the religion during times of tremendous social and political change.

R. C. Zaehner, in *Hinduism*, page 184.

Test yourself

1. Assess the main aims of yoga.
2. Discuss the relevance of varnashramadharma for Hindu ethics.
3. 'The four purushartas are contradictory.' Discuss.
4. How Hindu is the teaching of the Brahmo Samaj?

Connections

Philosophy of Religion with Eastern Religions (Route E)

Your answers should be on **either** Buddhism **or** Hinduism.

Existence of evil and suffering. Consider whether the doctrine of karma and rebirth in **Buddhism** or **Hinduism** provides a satisfactory explanation for the existence of evil and suffering. Read pages 230–241 of Julius Lipner's *Hindus* for a discussion of karma and rebirth in **Hinduism**. Another question is whether the existence of 'evil' undermines **Buddhism** in the same way that it undermines theism. Read chapter 3 of Walpola Rahula's *What the Buddha Taught* for an illuminative development of the idea that dukkha is not just a part of life, but life itself. Compare with western views about evil; consider the philosophical presentation of the problem as it exists for theists and the various possible responses to it. Read chapter 6 of *Reason and Religious Belief* (Oxford 1991) by Peterson et al. for a lucid summary of the main arguments.

Concepts of life after death. Consider the **Buddhist** view of nirvana. Walpola Rahula's *What The Buddha Taught* is again worth reading: see chapter 4. Be aware, though, that nirvana may be attained during this life as well as after it. The Mahayana belief in heavens should also be considered – Pure Land Buddhism is particularly noteworthy here. Consider **Hindu** views about moksha and karmic heavens and hells. Read the presentation on page 148 of the *OCR AS Guide*, plus chapter 3 in Zaehner's *Hinduism* gives a broad treatment. See also chapter 9 of *Hindus* by Lipner. Beliefs about reincarnation should also be studied. Consider western perspectives on life after death, including resurrection and beliefs about heaven and hell; chapters 10 and 15 in John Hick's *Death and Eternal Life* are very helpful.

Persons, souls and atman. Consider the **Buddhist** view of what it means to be a person, especially the teaching on anatta (no-self). The classic text is *The Questions of King Milinda*, which compares the self to a chariot: read pages 133–134 of the *OCR AS Guide* and pages 65–67 of *Buddhism* by Denise Cush. **Hinduism**, like Christianity, talks of a true, eternal self that continues to be reborn until moksha is finally attained. There is a distinction made between purusha (spirit) and prakrti (matter): see pages 130–132 on samkyha and yoga. Also read page 148 of the *OCR AS Guide* for a discussion of Upanishadic treatment of the self. The *Bhagavad Gita* is another important source of teaching on the self. For an illuminating discussion of the self in Hinduism consult pages 241–247 of *Hindus* by Lipner. Compare with western views: see pages 13–16. Read chapter 2 of Hick's *Death and Eternal Life* for an excellent overview.

Ultimate truths. Consider the **Buddhist** views on how religious truths are discovered. See pages 172–175 of Williams' *Buddhist Thought* (Routledge 2000) for a discussion of Mahayana belief in *dharmakaya*: the doctrine that the Buddha continued to reveal truths after his death. Consider how meditation helps to develop wisdom and understanding of fundamental truths such as dependent origination and anatta. Read chapter 11 in *An Introduction to Buddhism* by Peter Harvey. Consider yoga and samkhya in the **Hindu** tradition. Contrasts can be made with the discovery of ultimate truths through religious experience, miracle and revelation in the Christian tradition. Read pages 17–18 and 69–70 of the *OCR AS Guide*.

Scriptures as sacred texts. Consider the **Buddhist** view of the Pali Canon, Lotus Sutra and Heart Sutra. Consider the **Hindu** view of the *Bhagavad Gita*, and the distinction between sruti and smrti revelation. See chapter 4 in *Hindus* by Lipner. Consider revelation as understood in the western context: read pages 24–25.

Existence of God. The Buddhist view of samsara as a continuous process with no first cause differs markedly from the theistic view of God as first cause. Contrast the **Buddhist** theory of dependent origination (page 135 in the *OCR AS Guide*) with the cosmological argument (*OCR AS Guide* pages 64–66). Unlike Christians, **Hindus** do not typically present a causal argument for God on the basis of the existence of the universe. As Zaehner notes (*Hinduism*, page 61) since Upanishadic times they have tended to see creation as a cyclical process, believing that the universe has always existed. Read page 230 of *An Introduction to Hinduism* by Flood for a presentation of Hindu thought about causation; see pages 48–49 for the Vedic creation myth.

Test yourself

1. To what extent would **either** Hindus **or** Buddhists agree with the view that suffering is an important part of developing spiritual understanding?
2. With reference to **either** Hinduism **or** Buddhism, assess critically the claim that people have no eternal souls.
3. 'Eastern religions consider all arguments for the existence of God to be meaningless.' Discuss with reference to **either** Hinduism **or** Buddhism.

Religious Ethics with Eastern Religions (Route L)

Karma and free will and determinism. Consider the **Buddhist** (pages 134–135 of the *OCR AS Guide) and* **Hindu** (pages 147–148 of the *OCR AS Guide*) views of karma and rebirth. For Hinduism, see Lipner's discussion in *Hindus*, pages 229–241. For Buddhism, see pages 23–28 of Harvey's *An Introduction to Buddhist Ethics*. Compare these perspectives with western views about freewill and determinism. Read pages 31–36. See also chapter 5 of Palmer's *Moral Problems* (Lutterworth Press 1991).

Practical ethics. Consider how **Buddhism** or **Hinduism** has traditionally approached issues of war and peace, justice, the environment, sex and relationships, and the ethics of life and death. Consider too the practical ethical implications of Buddhist belief in the Five Precepts and the Hindu belief in ahimsa. Compare with western religious and secular approaches to these contemporary moral issues. Part two of *The Puzzle of Ethics* by Peter Vardy (Faut 1999) is also a useful resource.

Absolutism, relativism and purpose in morality. Consider whether **Buddhist** morality is relativist; distinguish between the different schools of Buddhism. Compare Buddhist ethics with western ethical systems such as utilitarianism and Kantianism – Harvey's *An Introduction to Buddhist Ethics*, pages 49–51 has a helpful summary. Consider the nature and purpose of **Hindu** ethics (dharma), with reference to important ethical traditions such as varnashramadharma. Consider the extent to which Hindu or Buddhist ethical systems are motivated by concerns about karma and rebirth, and aspirations to achieve moksha (Hinduism) or nirvana (Buddhism). Does this makes them teleological? Compare with the purpose of Christian ethics and western non-religious ethical systems – read pages 75–81 of the *OCR AS Guide*.

Test yourself

1. 'Eastern religions have no moral absolutes.' Discuss with reference to **either** Hinduism **or** Buddhism.
2. To what extent do **either** Hinduism **or** Buddhism take a utilitarian view of euthanasia?
3. 'A belief in karma must mean you believe in hard determinism.' Discuss with reference to **either** Hinduism **or** Buddhism.

Islam

Beliefs about God

Further reading

Make sure you look up all references to the Qur'an. Make and learn a list of appropriate quotations. The translation used here is *The Koran* by N. J. Dawood (Penguin 1997).

Tawhid

Absolutely central to Islamic theology is the concept of the 'oneness' of God. God is utterly transcendent (beyond the world of matter), the only author of creation and the controller of destiny. This is called tawhid and can be summarised simply as 'there is no god but Allah'. The whole of surah 112 summarises the concept: 'God is One, the Eternal God. He begot none, nor was he begotten. None are equal to Him.' But God is not a remote deity. He knows all human thoughts and is immanent (inherent) in his creation. According to the Qur'an, he is 'closer to him [man] than his jugular vein' (50: 16).

Shirk

Everything that compromises or distorts tawhid is the sin of **shirk**. Shirk means 'association' and refers to the sin of undermining God's unity by associating him with the human level, through art or sculpture, or by making human attributes aspects of God's nature. Shirk can be caused by pride, ignorance and foolishness – anything that fails to consider God as the ultimate reality. A **kafir** (unbeliever) is anyone who distorts tawhid, intentionally or not.

God as creator

'God is the Creator of all things. He is the one who conquers all' (13: 16). The Qur'an is absolute in its monotheism and its rejection of the idea that any aspect of the creation could be the result of any other power, or just chance – everything has its allotted place in the creation (29: 61). God is constantly involved with his creation as provider. The Qur'an unpacks God's nature through his **beautiful names** (7: 180). He is **al-Khalik**, 'the Creator, the Originator, the Modeller. His most gracious names' (59: 24). The creation has to be understood in terms of the Last Judgement, when as the First (al-Awwal) and the Last (al-Akhir) God, he as just judge will bring this world to its conclusion (57: 3). As the giver of life, God will also resurrect the dead on the last day (41: 39).

'Countless are the beasts that cannot fend for themselves, God provides for them, as He provides for you' (29: 60).

Traditionally God has 99 'beautiful names'.

Beautiful names

There was considerable debate among the early Muslim scholars about just how literally the beautiful names should be treated. Al-Khayyat argued that the names are metaphors for God's divine qualities (sifat), and that the Qur'an's references to God's face, throne or hands were to be interpreted as aspects of God's essence. This established an important principle of interpreting the Qur'an and maintaining tawhid. Muhammad never addressed God as 'father'. As Maqsood has said: 'This cannot have been an accident. The word 'Father' has human and sexual connotations, and, although Muslims are aware of God in an intimate and personal way, they think of Him as Creator rather than Father. To a Muslim, the concept of 'father' has dangerous implications that can lead to *shirk* (the division of the unity of God).'

Route Q: Developments in Christian Thought with Islam. *Islam* by Ruqauyyah Maqsood (Hodder and Stoughton 2003), page 37. Consider the implications of her quotation for Islam and feminism.

The environment

The concept of God as creator has important implications for Muslim environmental ethics. The Qur'an is clear that humans are **khalifas** or guardians (6: 165) of the earth, which God has given them to maintain until Judgement Day, when each person will be

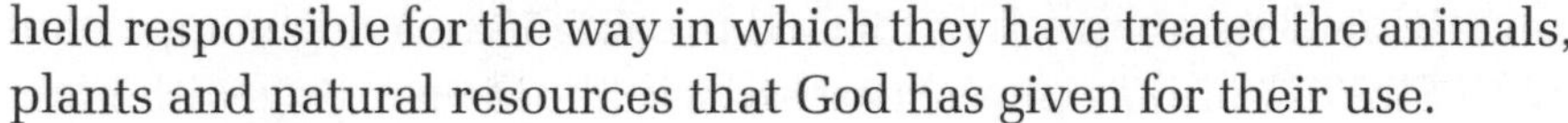

held responsible for the way in which they have treated the animals, plants and natural resources that God has given for their use.

Route M: Religious ethics with Islam. Consider these ideas along with the important idea in the Qur'an of God's 'balance', which humans must not transgress (55: 7–9). Read chapter 23 of *Islam* by Ruqauyyah Maqsood for more on this.

God as judge

As judge, God is the controller of destiny. Every creature comes under his power. God's justice is different from human justice insofar as God knows everything. This means that no one would escape punishment, were it not for God's mercy and compassion: 'If God punished men for their sins, not one creature would be left alive. He reprieves them till a time ordained' (16: 61). However, among the early Muslim scholars the issue of God's justice was hotly debated. The **Mu'tazila** argued that for God to be truly just, humans must have freedom to choose good or evil without God determining the outcome. One aspect of their argument was that freedom in creation could result in innocent suffering. This is one consequence of God's justice.

The Mu'tazila was founded by a group of Muslim scholars in the 8th century CE but its influence continued for another five centuries.

Further reading

See page 75 of *Muslims: Their Religious Beliefs and Practices* by Andrew Rippin (Routledge 2001).

God as guide

The Qur'an frequently makes reference to God as guide. Although God created man perfectly, he allowed him the freedom to choose to worship God or to pursue his own interests. When Adam chose to eat from the tree of immortality against God's wishes, God's punishment was to reject him from Paradise. However, out of mercy and forgiveness for his creatures, God has guided humans to truth through his revelations, messengers and prophets. The ultimate book of guidance is the Qur'an.

'God's guidance is the only guidance. We are commanded to submit to the Lord of the Universe, to pray, and to fear Him.'

See page 149 on the story of Noah.

Articles of belief

Iman means faith. When Muhammad was asked to define faith, he said it was belief in God, his angels, his books, his prophets, the Last Day, and the decreeing of both good and evil. Because the Qur'an often alternates between two words, iman and islam (submission), theologians have applied different criteria as to what constitutes a true believer. A tradition from Muhammad states that whoever has in his heart the weight of a grain of faith (iman) will escape hell. There has been much dispute as to what iman means here. Some say it means believing in the mind; others add witnessing through words; some others add good deeds. Traditional Islam states that all three will ensure a place in Paradise. However, some theologians argue that a single unrepented sin at death would make islam impossible, and place the person in hell – even if they had lived a righteous life according to iman. Others argue that the 'fire' of hell is purgatory and cleanses sin, making the person ready to enter Paradise.

'The works of the unbelievers are like ashes which the wind scatters on a stormy day... as for those who have faith and do good works, they shall be admitted to gardens watered by running streams.' (Qur'an 14: 18 and 23.)

Allah

Without belief and awareness that God is the one who has caused the universe and is the source of morality, a person cannot enter paradise, the reward of faith. The Qur'an makes this point frequently: 'Believers, Jews, Christians, and Sabaeans – whoever believes in God and the Last Day and does what is right – shall be rewarded by their Lord; they have nothing to fear or to regret' (2: 62). God is often depicted as light or **nur** – a symbol of his mercy and forgiveness as well as a depiction of the life of purity, truth and

Nur

'He will bestow on you a light to walk in, and He will forgive you: God is forgiving and merciful.' (Qur'an 57: 28.)

See www.muslimphilosophy.com/sina/default.htm

revelation. The nur doctrine of God became increasingly important with Muslim philosophers, particularly those engaging with Plato (where the Good is depicted as the Sun) and Aristotle (where the Unmoved Mover is described in terms of light). Ibn Sina (980–1037 CE) argued that God's light is the link between body and soul.

As we have seen, God is the sole creator of the universe. As such – although he may be involved immanently with it – he is not to be equated with it. He is of himself self-subsisting, eternal, omnipotent (all-powerful) and omniscient (all-knowing): 'He has knowledge of all that land and sea contain: every leaf that falls is known to Him' (Qur'an 6: 59).

Philosophical arguments

For a reminder of a priori and a posteriori, design and first cause arguments, see pages 63–70 of the *OCR AS Guide*.

Route F: Philosophy of Religion with Islam. Muslim kalam arguments should be compared to Aquinas and other non-Muslim scholars. Read *Religion and Religious Belief* by Michael Peterson and others (OUP 1991), pages 74–80.

For traditional Muslims, the arguments for the existence of God are to be found in the revelations of God contained in the Qur'an. This is the a priori of faith. The Qur'an also suggests a form of the design argument, that the world is balanced and ordered by God. But early Muslim scholars developed a form of first cause argument, using a form of dialectic proof called **kalam**. Al-Kindi (c. 870 CE) and the Sufi scholar al-Ghazali (1058–1111 CE) argued, using a combination of a priori and a posteriori statements, that:

(a) everything that exists has a cause to its existence

(b) the universe began to exist (as suggested by the Qur'an)

(c) therefore the universe has a cause to its existence, which is God.

Angels

Jinns

Besides visible creations, Islam teaches that there are other invisible forces in the universe that affect human behaviour. The Qur'an distinguishes between **jinns** and **angels**. Jinns are elemental forces of nature made from fire (15: 27), which are, in themselves, neither good nor bad. Sometimes they can hinder human actions. Jinns have free will and according to Surah 72 ('The Jinn'), some have converted to Islam while others have not, choosing other paths: 'Some of us are Muslim and some are wrong doers. Those that embrace Islam pursue the right path; but those that do wrong shall become the fuel of Hell' (72: 14–15).

Angels

As God is light (nur), their relationship to him is different from the jinns, who are made of fire (nar).

Unlike Jinns, angels or **mala'ika** ('messengers') do not have free-will. Their role is to carry out God's will (ibada) and convey his messages to humans. According to tradition, angels are made of light. The presence of angels can therefore be felt in prayer or contemplation of God as peace, love and worship. Generally they cannot be seen, except by very special people or at times of crisis. Angels can take on various forms. The angel Jibril (Gabriel) was seen in human form by Abraham and Mary. But according to the hadith, Muhammad saw Jibril as an enormous creature with thousands of wings.

The Qur'an also states that God records everything.

Angels are there to record all individual deeds. According to the Qur'an, each person has two angels who write down everything that person says (50: 17–18) in the Record, and who act as guardian angels, offering guidance in preparation for Last Judgement: 'Yet you deny the Last Judgement. Surely there are guardians watching over you, noble recorders who know all your actions' (82: 9).

Besides Jibril (whose role, as head of the hierarchy of angels, was to deliver God's revelations) the other named angels in the Qur'an are: Azra'il (who receives the souls of the dead), Mika'il (who protects the faithful and places of worship), and Iblis (the devil, or Shaytan/Satan). Munker and Nakir (who question souls at Judgement) and Israfil (who calls the souls of the dead at the Last Judgement) are popular in tradition but not actually mentioned in the Qur'an. There is also a whole class of angels (the mukarrabun) who praise God continually (21: 20).

Named angels

The Qur'an makes frequent reference to the devil, Iblis. Angels and jinns were created before humans. When God created Adam they were told to obey him, but Iblis alone refused (15: 28–40), and as a punishment became the enemy of humans and head of the jinn. Iblis means 'desperate', whereas as 'Shaytan' means 'rebellious'.

The devil

> **Further discussion**
> If Iblis was an angel, was he the only angel with free will to disobey God? Can angels sin?

Scriptures

God's revelation, or **nazala**, has been given at various times through his prophets and, according to tradition, by his angel Jibril. In each case the revelation has been lost, distorted, wrongly interpreted or mistranslated according to the beliefs and circumstances of those who edited them.

> **Route F: Philosophy of Religion with Islam**. The Qur'an's teaching on the Bible as revelation is linked with belief in the 'books' brought by the prophets prior to Muhammad. There is a great deal of debate about the correspondence of these books with the present Bible. See pages 24–25 of the philosophy of religion chapter.

- **Sahifa** are the scrolls given to Ibrahim, which are now lost.
- **Tawrah** is the revelation given to Musa, which in the Hebrew Bible comprises the Five Books of Moses (or Torah). Tawrah was given for legal guidance (5: 44–45). According to the Qur'an (6: 91) the Tawrah was distorted in two ways: firstly it was divided up falsely into 'separate' books or 'scraps of paper', and secondly some of it was suppressed and not written down.

It is possible that the Qur'an is referring to the Jewish tradition that Moses was given the Written Torah and Oral Torah. The Oral Torah has been revealed through the prophets and rabbis. The Qur'an appears to regard this process as distortion. See page 58 of the *OCR AS Guide*.

- **Zabur** are the psalms that God revealed to Dawud (4: 163). Surah 21: 105 quotes directly from Psalm 37: 29: 'My righteous amongst My servants shall inherit the earth.' It is not clear why the Qur'an should revere the psalms. Some later writers (Ibn Kutaiba, for example) considered that the psalms in the Hebrew Bible prophesised the coming of Muhammad, although others (such as Hakim Ibn Hazm) consider the biblical psalms to be forgeries of the original Zabur.
- **Injil** are the teachings given to Isa. Jesus' teachings in the Gospel 'in which there is guidance and light' (5: 46) were to confirm the Torah. There is much dispute as to whether the Christian Gospels are the same as the Injil referred to in the Qur'an. Surah 5: 46 conveys their function in limited terms as fulfilling the Torah, while the division into four very different kinds of gospel in the New Testament implies fragmentation and human interpretation.

The Qur'an clearly presents a wider picture of Jesus than merely a confirmer of the law. In the Qur'an, the hadiths and Muslim tradition, Jesus' role was as an ascetic and preparer for the Day of Judgement, as well as God's messenger.

In traditional Islam the Qur'an is the complete guidance and last revealed book. It is the **Umm-ul-Kitab** or 'Mother of Books'. It corrects all previous revelations in earlier scriptures (Qur'an 5: 48) and sets the standard by which to judge them (16: 44).

The Qur'an

Much more difficult is to ascertain how useful Torah and Injil are. The Qur'an's position is ambiguous. For example, in Surah 5: 68 it states: 'People of the Book, you will attain nothing until you observe

Revelation in other religions

Route Q: Developments in Christian Thought with Islam. Compare Islamic views with the Christian exclusive, inclusive and pluralist arguments. See pages 107–114.

the Torah and Gospel and that which has been revealed to you from the Lord.' This appears to suggest that Jewish and Christian scriptures are sufficient for salvation, providing that belief in the unity of God, the Last Day and ethical monotheism are adhered to (5: 69). But subsequent Islamic scholars disagreed. Are Torah and Gospel to be read selectively in the light of the Qur'an removing all errors (such as the resurrection of Jesus)? The ayah may be read inclusively or exclusively. Some, such as the modernist Islamic Indian politician and thinker **Abu'l-Kalam Azad** (1888–1958) have argued for a pluralist view of Islam, on the grounds that religion is universal and it is the duty of every religious person to submit authentically to their religious tradition and live a life of right action – this is what the Qur'an instructs. No religion has a monopoly over the other; when it thinks it does, this leads to agnosticism.

Further reading

Read pages 223–224 of *Muslims* by Andrew Rippin.

Revelation and interpretation

The Mu'tazila argued that as reason is God-given, it should form the basis of all Muslim teaching. They perfected the kalam means of argument, which argues by posing objections and answering them.

Tafsir refers to commentary on the Qur'an. In early Islam, the **Mu'tazila** argued that reason is prior to revelation, but that revelation as in the Qu'ran supplements, motivates and guides people. 'Abd al Jabbar argued that eating meat is against reason and Islamic principles, except that the Qur'an permits it, so reason cannot provide the whole basis for law. Revelation also provides the necessary motivation for people to understand the promise of after-life, reward and punishment.

They also argued that as the Qur'an was created in time and had not existed eternally, God could not have predestined the events of the universe. They interpreted much of it metaphorically. For example, God could not actually have spoken to people using human speech, because to do so would be to give God human attributes and reduce his transcendence.

Three approaches

Rippin suggests three modern approaches to tafsir:

- The **traditionalist** scholar is interested in the exact meanings of words, but does not doubt the objective reality that the Qur'an reveals concerning morality and the hereafter.
- The **Islamist** approach rejects western corruption of morality as Jahiliyya (ignorance) and considers that Islam is a total system. It avoids the traditionalist obsession with detail and looks at the larger picture painted by the Qur'an and the oneness (tawhid) of God's reality. This means seeing the emergent values of the Qur'an as a whole.
- For **modernists**, the Qur'an has to be understood in its historical setting, when it was dealing with specific issues that may no longer have any relevance today. Science provides one view of the world that can be accommodated by the wider view of reality that the Qur'an describes. Only in this way will Islam remain relevant in the modern world.

Sayyid Qutb's (1906–1966) tafsir *Fi Zilal al-Qur'an* is a good example of an Islamist approach.

Route Q: Development in Christian Thought with Islam. Read pages 37-40 of the *OCR AS Guide* . When discussing this topic you should note that there are no satisfactory terms which describe the differing interpretations of the Bible. The exam board uses 'fundamentalist', 'traditional' and 'liberal'. These correspond roughly to the three categories Rippin uses in Islam of 'traditional', 'Islamist' and 'modernist'. Read chapter 14 in *Muslims* by Rippin.

The most significant modernist thinker is Muhammad 'Abduh (1849–1905). See www.cis-ca.org/voices/a/abduh.htm.

Messengers

Risalah, or messengers, are the means of communication between God and humans. The Qur'an makes reference to 26 prophets who preceded Muhammad (though a hadith puts the number of prophets in history at 124,000). Many of the 26 are familiar to Jews and Christians, as they are to be found in the Hebrew Bible (Old

Testament) and the New Testament. Some are from Arab traditions outside the Bible. All are regarded as intermediaries of God who revealed his will to the world. The Qur'an also distinguishes those prophets who have a 'book' (rasul) from those who do not (nabi).

The prophets begin with Adam and conclude with Muhammad as the seal of the prophets. His revelation is pure, complete and final. However, as we have seen, one of the purposes of the Qur'an is to correct the distortions that have crept into the presentations of these prophets in the Bible through shirk. So, stories that may seem familiar to Jews and Christians often have unfamiliar detail.

> **Further reading**
>
> Read chapter two of *What is Islam?* by Chris Horrie and Peter Chippindale (Virgin 2003).

> **Further study**
>
> Read Qur'an 3: 84 and consider to what extent all the prophets share the same characteristics. Compare and contrast Muhammad with his predecessors.

Adam and his wife, the original couple, succumbed to Satan and failed to live up to God's covenant when they ate from the Tree of Immortality. Their punishment was to wander the world in discomfort, confusion and pain. As soon as they realised their foolishness, God forgave them, and according to tradition they were reunited with God on the plain of Arafat. This moment is remembered in Hajj when pilgrims gather at Mount Arafat to repent and ask forgiveness.

Adam

> Qur'an 2: 29–37; 20: 115–125.

Nuh (Noah) preached the oneness of God, the wrongness of idol worship and warned the people of God's judgement. They rejected him, and were drowned in the flood by God. Nuh, his family and animals were saved in the ark. Nuh prays: 'Forgive all faithful men and women, and hasten the destruction of the wrongdoers.'

Nuh

> Qur'an 7: 59–64; 23: 23–32 and 71: 1–28.

Known as the 'Friend of God' (al-Khalil), as a child Ibrahim (Abraham) was sent visions by God to show him the futility of polytheism. When he was older, he smashed the idols or gods in the temple except the supreme one. God saved him from the death threats of the elders and brought him to the Promised Land. Scholars have long pointed out that only in the Madinan surahs is Ibrahim presented as the **hanif muslim** who created the Ka'ba with Ismail (Qur'an 2: 124–27). In this way Ibrahim's early life is seen as a preparation for his life as a Muslim, and a model for Muhammad's cleansing of the Ka'ba.

Ibrahim

> Qur'an 6: 75–84; 14: 36–42; 21: 53–70.

> **Route Q: Developments in Christian Thought with Islam**. Muslim tradition interprets Ibrahim's near-sacrifice of his son as Ishma'il, whereas the Hebrew Bible states that it is Isaac (Genesis 22). Do both religions have a claim to God's covenant? Can this be resolved?

Musa (Moses) is the prophet with whom Muhammad has most associations: he predicts that Muhammad will be the prophet foretold in the Torah and Gospel (7: 157). Having killed an Egyptian for tormenting an Israelite slave (for which he repents and is forgiven) Musa escapes to the wilderness and tends the sheep, where he encounters God at night as a fire. After escaping from Pharaoh by performing nine miracles, he is given the tablets of the Law. So like Musa, Muhammad is one who has mystical experience of God and leads the people to a new place where he receives the law.

Musa

> Qur'an 7: 143–161; 14: 5–8; 28: 1–46.

For some modern theologians, Moses symbolises Islam's fight against injustice. This is a view also shared by Christian liberation theologians. See page 127 of the *OCR AS Guide*.

Isa (Jesus) is treated with enormous respect in Islam, as the prophet and messenger who preceded Muhammad. The whole of surah 19 is dedicated to his mother Maryam (Mary) and his miraculous birth. The Qur'an also records his miracles and teaching. The hadiths pay special attention to Isa's example (sunnah) as a man of prayer. According to one tradition regarding the Night Journey, Muhammad not only met Musa and Ibrahim, but also Isa. He asked Isa when the day of judgement would be. But the Qur'an makes one very important change to the Gospels' presentation of Jesus.

Isa

> Qur'an 3: 46 and 59; 5: 110–117.

Further reading

For information on Muhammad, read pages 55–57 of *OCR AS Guide* on the life of Muhammad, and chapter 13 of *Muslims* by Andrew Rippin on modern views of Muhammad.

According to surah 4: 157, Isa did not die on the cross, but only one who looked like Isa. It is an ambiguous ayah, but it seems to suggest that God took Isa into heaven before he died. Isa's death, therefore, is neither a sacrifice nor an atonement for sins.

The Last Day

Akhirah

Akhirah is the Arabic term used to refer to the Last Day, and includes notions of the after-life, judgement and the rewards of heaven and hell. Islam teaches that we only have one life and that this life is therefore a test of one's character to win a place in paradise.

Janna and Jahannam

God is concerned about the universe that he has created. On Judgement Day, he will reward and punish people in accordance with their good or evil ways. Every generation has been warned and Islamic preaching is often a call to repentance. As a matter of justice, akhirah enables those who have lived virtuous but as yet unrewarded lives to receive their due in **Janna**, or paradise. Each person is entirely responsible for their own sins, and so 'It is the Day when one soul shall be powerless to plead for another' (82: 19) and 'Your good actions will benefit only you, while evil harms only the person who does it' (41: 46). **Jahannam** (hell) is envisaged as a place of fire just below the earth's crust, and Janna is a paradise garden where all pleasures are provided for the faithful.

'In gardens of delight they shall enjoy honour and happiness facing each other on thrones: a cup will be passed to them from a clear-flowing fountain – delicious to drink and free from intoxication or headaches: and besides them will be innocent women, restraining their glances, with eyes wide with wonder and beauty' (37: 43–8).

Traditional and modernist approaches

Traditional Muslim eschatology has elaborated the teaching of the Qur'an. Whenever a person dies, the angel Azra'il takes the soul of the dead person to **barzakh** (the barrier): a state of limbo between death and resurrection. At some time there will be the signs of the end: **Dadjdjal** will lead people astray, then Isa or the Mahdi will descend and kill Dadjdjal and there will be a period of faithfulness. After this, Israfil will sound the last trumpet, all things will die and at the second trumpet blast, bodies will be resurrected and reunited. Then follows the Yawm al Din (Judgement Day) when each person is judged by God according to their Record. At the Yawm al Fasl (the Day of Dividing), people will pass along the Bridge to hell or paradise.

For modernist Muslims, the Qur'an and its tradition pose many problems because paradise and hell are presented in worldly terms, and in over-exotic and sexist ways (look at the paradise imagery). The extreme language is more a means to shock people into moral rectitude than a representation of reality. They thus argue that the language is metaphorical and that 'innocent women' is a mistranslation for 'priests' who administer all. The language is metaphorical because it is conveying the ineffable. Traditionalists consider that as the Qur'an is the word of God it is an accurate description of what is yet to come.

Route F: Philosophy of Religion with Islam. Read pages 231–232 of Rippin's *Muslims* and pages 16–19 of the philosophy of religion chapter in this guide.

The divine decree

Predestination

The divine decree is the final judgement that God makes on each person according to an individual's book of deeds and thoughts. In traditional thought, God's **sifat** (divine qualities such as omniscience) means that he knows what the outcome will be. **Al Qadr** – predestination – is based on the notion that as God controls everything (13: 42), he knows how we will complete our lives. It is a notion that has been much discussed by Muslim theologians.

The Qur'an teaches that 'The blessings God bestows on men none can withhold; and what He withholds none can bestow, apart from Him' (35: 2). God controls our destinies, as Joseph realises at the end of surah 12 – it is God who released him from prison and brought his parents to him: 'My Lord is gracious to whom He will. He alone is all-knowing and wise' (12: 100). But the Qur'an also states: 'When under your very eyes a man's soul is about to leave him...if he is favoured, his lot will be repose and plenty, and a garden of delight... but if he is an erring disbeliever, his welcome will be scalding water, and he will burn in Hell' (56: 83–94). If God is in control of everything, does this in turn mean that he wills evil and reduces human responsibility?

The doctrine of al Qadr was, however, disputed early. The **Qadariyya** argued that, although human bodies are controlled by the same laws of cause and effect as other material beings, souls enable the individual to choose freely between good or evil. In this way, individuals are equally responsible for their own actions, which God will judge on the Last Day. The Qur'an has to be reread against those passages that support free will. For example, surah 14: 27 says that God 'leads the wrongdoers astray': this simply means that God punishes the wrongdoers for the misdeeds they have *already* committed.

Free will

The Qadariyya were 8th-century Muslim scholars who gained their name from their views about al Qadr. They greatly influenced the rationalist Mu'tazila.

Al-Ashari (c. 874–935 CE) considered that, although God knows what we will do, we still have the freedom to choose, because God gives humans the power to act for the moment. People therefore 'acquire' the responsibility for their actions. Others have interpreted the Qur'anic phrase **insh Allah** – 'if God wills it' – more deterministically, arguing that we have very little free will and that God controls everything.

Further reading

Read pages 78–80 of Rippin's *Muslims*.

Muslim life

Qur'an, Sunnah and Shari'ah

The Muslim way of life is centred on following the Shari'ah. Although Shari'ah involves law, it is a much broader term referring to a complete code of Muslim conduct, including worship, morality, and criminal and civil law. God does not reveal himself, but instead his timeless Shari'ah: the 'straight clear path' for behaviour now and in preparation for the Last Day. In the early days, the role of the Caliphs was to interpret and apply the Shari'ah, but over a period of time a more formal system was needed. The legal scholars (or jurists) developed **fiqh**, the theory of law, which agreed that there should be four 'roots' (**usul**) when deciding on Shari'ah – the Qur'an, Sunnah, ijma and qiyas:

Shari'ah

Further reading

Read the very clear chapter on Shari'ah in *Islam: A Very Short Introduction* by Malise Ruthven (OUP 1997).

- As the **Quran** is the revealed word of God, it provides the bedrock of Shari'ah. However, only around 10 per cent of it applies specifically to law and conduct (mostly in the late Madinan surahs). This, and the problem of cancellation or abrogation (**naskh**) of certain ayahs, ensures the need for the Prophet's own example and words.

See pages 151–152 of the *OCR AS Guide*.

- **Sunnah** means example. In the early days, this included decisions and examples of the Caliphs. However, the **mahdabs** (Sunni law schools) established that the sunnah should be Muhammad's and his example at Madinah. This required the

The four Sunni mahdabs established in the 8th and 9th centuries are: Shafi'is, Hanafis, Malikis and Hanbalis. Their differences are essentially over custom (depending on geographical location), and this does not undermine their essential conformity. As Muhammad said: 'Difference of opinion in the community is a token of divine mercy.' Read chapter 6 in *Muslims* by Rippin.

establishment of reliable hadiths. Even so the hadiths often present contradictory sayings of Muhammad.

- **Ijma** means 'consensus' and refers to the practice of the community. In a Muslim society what is accepted by the people ultimately decides what constitutes Shari'ah. Muhammad said: 'My community will never agree upon an error.' So Shari'ah will vary from place to place according to custom.

Qiyas is therefore associated with ijtihad (see *below*) and a favourite hadith of Muhammad: when sending Mu'adh to Yemen, Muhammad asked him how he would make his judgements. 'In accordance with the Book of Allah,' replied Mu'adh. 'But what if you don't find it there?' inquired the Prophet. 'According to the Sunnah of the Apostle of Allah,' replied Mu'adh. 'But what if you don't find it there either?' asked the Prophet again. 'I will exert my own opinion', replied Mu'adh.

- **Qiyas** is the rational process by which a decision is made, drawing analogies from the Qur'an and sunnah when there is no specific ruling. Qiyas is also used, therefore, to decide between contradictory texts. For example, the Qur'an offers differing views about the use of alcohol but the common element (or **illa**) is the ban on intoxication. From this, some have argued for a total ban on all alcohol and drugs. The result of qiyas can only work providing it meets the approval of ijma. Once it does, it becomes the basis for further qiyas.

The jurist **Muhammad ibn Idis Al-Shafi'i** (767–820 CE) was pivotal in establishing 'usul al-fiqh' by establishing the centrality of the Sunnah of the Prophet and the reliability of Muhammad's hadiths. Al-Shafi'i's influence is fundamental to Sunni Islamic thinking and the establishment of the **mahdabs**.

Ijtihad

Ijtihad has the same root meaning as jihad: to struggle.

Ijtihad refers to 'personal effort' to uncover God's rulings on issues from the sources documented *above*. It is sometimes divided into **complete ijtihad** (the ability to arrive independently at God's rulings in all areas of fiqh) and **partial ijtihad** (the ability to do so only in certain areas of fiqh and established laws). A **mujtahid** is a person who exercises ijtihad. It is an ambiguous term and is much discussed today.

Ayatollah translates as 'the sign of God'.

Complete ijtihad was considered too demanding in the Sunni mahdabs, so the 'gates of ijtihad were shut' in the 6th century CE (although they probably continued to remain open until the 18th century). The preferred method was **taqlid**: decisions based on the authority of earlier mujtahid. But for Shia Muslims, the gates were left open for the chief jurist of the ulama (senior lawyers) – the **ayatollah** to act as mujtahid. The result has been that Shia Islam has been able to respond to new situations, while some feel that Sunni fiqh has become too removed from every day life.

Shari'ah and morality

Route M: Religious ethics with Islam. Read pages 20–24, 75–81 of the *OCR AS Guide*, and *Ethical Theory* by Mel Thompson (Hodder and Stoughton 1999).

The mahdabs rejected the Mu'tazila view that morality can be sharply divided into either good or bad. Fiqh recognises that human nature is based on a variety of intentions, which the law takes into account in five categories: that which is commanded, recommended, legally neutral, disapproved of and forbidden. The function of the law is to decide what is **haram**: explicitly forbidden. It is noted that the function of the **qadis** (local judge) when applying Shari'ah is far more to do with getting people to conform morally with God's law than administering punishment. How does Islamic morality compare to western ethics?

- Acts that are **fard** are obligatory. Duties that are **fard kifaya** are collective and categorical – such as attendance in jihad (holy war) or funeral prayers. Whereas in Kant the reason for acting is based on human will and reason alone, fard is in compliance with the will of God – who is the ultimate judge of all at the Last Day.

- Acts that are haram are prohibited and punishable in this world alone, according to the penalties set out in the Qur'an (so-called **hudud** offences). These include forms of theft, illicit sexual activities and wine-drinking. As revealed law, these are considered absolute, although there is an element of cultural relativism depending on how these are interpreted according to custom.
- Acts that are **mandub** are recommended but not required: they lead to reward in paradise, but choosing not to do them does not ensure punishment. These include charitable acts, extra prayers, fasts and so on. This highlights an essential element of Shari'ah – the development of a person's character as a Muslim. This closely corresponds to the notion of *arete* (excellence) in virtue ethics – especially in terms of establishing ummah, the worldwide Muslim community.
- Acts that are **makruh** are discouraged, but not punished. There is much debate here. One example is the male prerogative to divorce a wife – something of which Muhammad strongly disapproved. There might be some comparison here to utilitarian thinking, which considers the application of laws according to the degree of happiness they generate. In Benthamite terms, the rights of women in divorce procedures has been a significant issue.
- Acts that are **mubah** are permitted because they are morally neutral and evoke neither reward nor punishment.

Further reading

See pages 75–87 from the *OCR AS Guide* for more on virtue ethics. Read chapter 24 of *Islam* by Ruqaiyyah Maqsood for an outline of Muslim virtues.

Further discussion

To what extent do you think Muslim ethics would accept the consequential element of utilitarianism: that the ends justify the means?

Further discussion

Is Shari'ah too idealistic to be practical?

Origins and beliefs of Islamic sects

Muhammad's succession

When Muhammad died it was unclear whether he had nominated a successor or whether his role would pass in the normal eastern way to his eldest son. The implications of this were extremely important, as many of the new Muslim states had declared allegiance with Muhammad, not Islam. The senior theologians and lawyers at Madinah decided that the successor or **caliph** (khalifah means successor and guide) to Muhammad should be someone elected by the community, as a person of great personal integrity who would ensure that the Qur'an and the Sunnah of the Prophet were properly understood and interpreted. This is the basis of the Sunni branch of Islam. Sunnis consider that the first four caliphs were 'rightly guided' because they all knew Muhammad and were the first settlers in Madinah.

The caliphs

Abu Bakr (632–634 CE) expanded Islam by sending armies to conquer Arab tribes up to the borders of the Byzantine Empire. His view of Islam suggests that it is more than just a personal belief: it is also a political ideology. Ali, Muhammad's son-in-law, was rejected by the ulama, perhaps because he was away at the time or because he was not thought to be acceptable to both Madinan and Makkan tribes.

Umar (634–644 CE) continued Abu Bakr's work, capturing Jerusalem in 638 CE and north Africa in 641 CE. By the end of his reign the Islamic empire was as large as that of the Romans. Umar was assassinated by a Persian Christian slave.

Uthman (644–656 CE) accepted the Caliphate after Ali turned it down. He expanded the empire across north Africa and eastwards to the Chinese border and to India. His religious policies alienated him from many Muslims, and he was assassinated.

Ali (656–661 CE) was Muhammad's cousin and son-in-law, and in the eyes of many should have been the caliph to succeed the Prophet in the first place. Mu'awiya, Uthman's cousin and a general, refused to acknowledge Ali as caliph. However, Ali came to a compromise and Mu'awiya was appointed as a co-caliph. The move was disastrous. The Muslims of Oman declared a separate independent state, and Mu'awiya grabbed power and moved his capital from Madinah to Damascus. Those who still regarded Ali as the true caliph formed themselves in a separate party, the Party of Ali – in Arabic, the **Shi'at Ali**. Ali was assassinated in the mosque at Kufah in Iraq in 661 CE.

Shi'a Muslims believe that after his death, the authority of Ali passed to his son Hasan, who became their Second Imam. Mu'awiya's son Yazeed took over as Khalifah in 679 CE, but Husayn, Hasan's younger brother, refused to give him his allegiance. On the tenth day of Muharram, the battle of Karbala took place. Husayn's forces had no chance of victory against 4,000 of the enemy but he chose death rather than compromise. He begged for mercy for his son, but the baby was shot with an arrow. Husayn was beheaded but his other son, Ali Zain-ul-Abedin, who was ill at the time of the Karbala battle, survived.

Further reading

Read chapter 12 in *What is Islam?* by Horrie and Chippindale.

Sunni Islam

About 80 per cent of Muslims are Sunni. Sunni theology wasn't formalised until the 8th century CE, when Al-Shafi'i established the authority only of the Sunnah of the Prophet, and **al-Ashari** found the 'middle way' between the traditionalists and rationalists. The establishment of the four madhabs enables Sunni Islam to be far more uniform than Shi'a. The chief characteristics are:

- A Muslim leader/ruler need not prove descent from Muhammad, but he must be regarded as morally acceptable by the community (ummah).
- Once a ruler shows he can uphold the shari'ah, the community must follow him as the vicegerent of prophecy. He may choose one of the four madhab on which to base his law. The variations in Sunni Islam are therefore dependent on the geographical areas in which the four schools had influence.
- Sunnis believe that no person is free from sin, except Muhammad and the **Mahdi** who will guide Muslims and prepare them for the Last Day.
- There are very few sub-sects. Two recent ones have both been 'messianic' or Mahdist: the Ahmadiyah (Pakistan, west Africa and USA) and the 'Black Muslim Movement' in the USA, led by Elijah Muhammad, with whom Malcolm X famously fought for black rights.

Shi'a Islam

The historical origins of Shi'a Islam precede Sunni. Today, 20 per cent of Muslims are Shi'a, mostly in the Middle East. Unlike Sunni Islam, Shi'a Islam comprises many sub-sects. The major division is between the **Twelvers** (or ithna ashari – the majority) and the **Seveners** (or Isma'ilis). The Twelvers believe that the 12th imam mysteriously disappeared when he was four years old and is now 'hidden'. After the death of the sixth imam's eldest son (Isma'il), the Seveners refused to acknowledge the legitimacy of the younger son's succession and consider imams to be descended from Isma'il.

Further reading

Read Horrie and Chippindale *What is Islam?* chapter 13.

The majority of Muslims in Iran, Yemen and Azerbaijan are Shi'a; 50 per cent are in Iraq.

The imam

The imam must be a direct descendent of Ali and Fatima (Muhammad's daughter). In the absence of the imam, Shi'a ulamas choose a person of outstanding moral and religious character to be an earthly imam. Among the Twelvers, the imam (in some places called the ayatollah) is considered to be the embodiment of the hidden Imam and can therefore exercise ijtihad as a mujtahid. In Iran the ayatollah has special access to the sacred books given to the first 12 imams. The Isma'ilis believe that succession followed the seventh imam, Isma'il, as living embodiment of the imam.

The majority of Twelver Shi'a Muslims in the UK regard the Iraq-based scholar Syed Ali Sistani as their spiritual representative.

At present, Karim Aga Khan is the 49th imam in direct lineal descent from Muhammad through Ali and Fatima. See www.akdn.org/imamat/imamat.html.

Key beliefs

- Shi'as believe that the hidden imam will return as the imam mahdi to rule before the Last Day – until then his guidance is through his specially chosen earthly imams. Isma'ilis believe that at the end of each cycle of seven hereditary imams, there is a possibility that the Mahdi will arrive.
- Shi'as do not accept that the Qur'an is eternal, but they believe that there is secret knowledge hidden within it that was told to Ali by Muhammad, and this has been passed down through their imams. Shi'as consider that knowledge is evolving and reason is not therefore contrary to faith.
- Shi'as celebrate additional festivals, such as the birth of Ali and Ashura, or the martyrdom of Husayn on the tenth of Muharram. It is a very emotional festival of weeping and self-mutilation. It is believed that Husayn's death can remove sin.

Sufi Islam

Sufi or 'tasawwuf' Islam developed as a reaction to Islamic legalism. Historically, it is difficult to tell when it emerged, but gradually it came to be accepted by mainstream Islam. Sufism stresses the mystical aspect of religious and Muslim experience: the sense of the inner spiritual journey to union with God, living a God-conscious life, overcoming the lower bodily self and preparing oneself spiritually for the hereafter. The two aims of Sufism are: living an ideal life based on pleasing God, and discovering what form of practice is suited to achieving this.

What is Sufism?

No one quite knows what sufi means. It could mean 'wool', because of the wool clothing the early ascetic Sufis wore, or 'wisdom' from the Greek 'sophia'.

Further reading

Read chapter 13 of *Islam* by Ruqaiyyah Maqsood. Consider why some aspects of Sufism might be shirk.

Sufis believe that the Qur'an provides the basis for the mystical and ascetic life. God is near to answer all calls (2: 186), he is closer to a person than their jugular vein (50: 16), God's face is to be found in all things (2: 115), and, in the famous 'light verse' (24: 35), God is described as the lamp inside a glass that can be experienced in all places and religions. They also cite the example of Muhammad's life – from his initiation experience of God on the Night of Power to

Ascetism refers to a very disciplined religious way of life, focused on spiritual practices rather than everyday living.

Moses' experience of the burning bush is also important for Sufis.

sayings about his life as an ascetic, and great importance is given to the inner meaning of the Night Journey (17: 1).

See pages 55–57 of the *OCR AS Guide*.

Key concepts

- **Dhikr** comes from a verse in the Qur'an (33: 21) meaning to mention God often. Prayers such as the *la ilaha illa'illah* are said many times as a form of mantra.
- **Tawakkul** means to have total trust in God and to shun the world. Later Sufi thinkers, notably al-Ghazali, adapted this idea so as to make Sufism more a part of mainstream Islam. In his famous book *Revivification of the Religious Sciences*, he spoke of the need to make worship more spiritual by looking at the inner dimension of prayer.
- **Fana** is the spiritual experience of 'dying' and 'absorption' into God (based on the Qur'an, 55: 26–27). Having experienced this, the Sufi is then to communicate this experience to his followers in carrying out his Muslim duties.
- **Wahal al-wujud** is the particular doctrine of Muhyaddin Ibn al-Arabi (1165–1240), and refers to the 'unity of all things'. This almost pantheistic teaching considers that there is hardly any distinction between humans and God, and that the purpose of creation is to produce a perfect human who reflects the true glory of God. The prophets were the *waliy*, or friends of God, and were reflections of the perfect man. Ibn al-Arabi was considered to be the 'seal' of the waliy, just as Muhammad was the seal of prophecy.
- **Tariqa** literally means path, but quickly came to refer to the groups of Sufis living with a spiritual master or **shaykh**. Shaykhs claim a spiritual heritage that goes back to Muhammad, Ali, one of the Companions or another great shakyh. A **zawiysas** was originally the house where a Sufi group met with its master, but soon came to refer to different Sufi 'schools' named after a founding shaykh.

Further discussion

What do you think al-Ghazali meant when he said, 'The beginning of guidance is outward piety and the end of guidance is inward piety'?

Family life

Further reading

Read chapter 5 of *Islam: A Very Short Introduction* by Malise Ruthven.

General principles

Men and women

The role of the Muslim man is to protect and provide for the family by earning money and maintaining the morals of the family for the Day of Judgement. This means abstaining from alcohol, gambling, stealing or hoarding, and sexual immorality. He must set an example of manhood to his family. The image that is often used is that he must fortify the family home as its guardian. The Qur'an's view of men and women is 'equal but different'. Men and women are spiritually the same but in the world they are designed to complement each other: hence the contrast between 'Have fear of your Lord, who created you from a single soul' (4: 1) and 'Women shall with justice have rights similar to those exercised against them, although men have a status above women.' (2: 228). The Qur'an and Muhammad enhanced the place of women in society and developed the family as the heart of Muslim society. Khadijah and especially Aisha provide important role models for women today. One of Muhammad's most famous hadith sayings is: 'Paradise lies at the feet of your mother.'

For example, a woman is entitled to inheritance and protection from her husband (33: 35).

Marriage and divorce

Traditionally marriage is for the containment of the sex drive. According to tradition, Shari'ah marriage or **nikah** is a contract sanctioned by God, in which a woman's guardian or **wali** (usually her father) enters the contract on her behalf. She should be able to marry a man of her own choice, but local customs and the strong sense of family unity have developed a wide range of different traditions. A woman should be a virgin at marriage, and is responsible for home and family. She can have a job, provided that it does not harm the family, and in return she can expect as a right the protection of her husband. She retains all her own property on marriage.

Marriage

'Young men, those of you who can support a wife should marry, for it keeps you from looking at women and preserves your chastity' (hadith). For this reason, in Shi'a Islam a man may enter a temporary marriage (muta) from one hour to 99 years.

In the Shi'a view, the woman is 'a full legal entity coequal with her male counterpart': see page 101 of Ruthven's *Islam*.

There is much discussion about polygyny. The Qur'an permits a man to marry up to four wives, providing he treats them all as equals. Traditionalists interpret this as a question of economic/social provision, so that no woman is left without means of survival. Each is to have equal shares of the household income. Modernists on the other hand argue that it means equal psychological care. Nowadays it means that polygyny is effectively redundant.

Polygyny

You will most likely see or hear this issue discussed as polygamy: having more than one spouse. Polygyny refers specifically to having more than one wife (the practice of having more than one husband is called polyandry).

Although Muhammad found divorce distasteful, a husband has the right to **talaq** – repudiation or unilateral declaration of his wife. Divorce occurs after the third time he says 'I divorce you'. According to Shari'ah there has to be a period of waiting (**idda**) after the second declaration to provide time for reconciliation, and to ensure that the woman is not pregnant. The husband usually has custody of boys over seven years old and girls over nine. If a women initiates divorce (**khul**) she forfeits her right to the dowry or (**mahr**).

Divorce

Sexuality

Male/female differences are God-given and fundamental to the understanding and organisation of society. Anything that confuses human sexuality is therefore seen as undermining the divine order. However, the sexual drive should be celebrated and not repressed. Many hadiths record Muhammad's virility, and Paradise itself is described in sexual terms. Al-Ghazali commented that orgasm is a foretaste of the perpetual orgasm of paradise.

'Copulate and procreate, for I shall gain glory from your numbers at the Day of Judgement.' Hadith quoted on page 103 of Ruthven, *Islam: A Very Short Introduction*.

Homosexuality is considered to be a reversal of the natural order and a crime against the rights of women. The crimes of Sodom and Gomorrah (homosexual sex) are condemned in the Qur'an for these reasons: 'You lust after men instead of women. Truly, you are a degenerate people' (7: 81).

Homosexuality

Traditionally, women who are married are restricted to the company of females and a **mahram**: a collective of men who are legally unavailable to her (sons, father, brother, uncle, in-laws and so on). The mahram reinforces the ties of kinship and family – although many Muslim societies have relaxed their views on this subject. Female chastity is a symbol of the purity of the family. Women's special place in the family is **harim**: sacred. She reflects the Qur'anic idea that God is both hidden and revealed. This idea is much discussed and modernists have considered that women can preserve their public role in society without compromising their family duties. However, because women are subject to pollution taboos (birth, menstruation) they cannot have public roles in religious practice.

Female sexuality

Route Q: Developments in Christian Thought with Islam. Read pages 117–125 and 157–158 of the *OCR AS Guide*.

Further reading

Read pages 185–195 of *Discovering Islam* by Akbar Ahmed (Routledge 1988).

It is important not to impose a false consciousness on Muslim women, however. A western interpreter may view rules such as wearing the hijab as oppressive; a Muslim woman may feel grateful for the modesty and freedom from male attention it provides.

Feminism

Globalisation and colonisation have meant that the old family structures and the place of the mahram have come under considerable pressure over the past century. Muslim societies have reacted in several ways. Akbar Ahmed has suggested that 19th-century western colonisation introduced alien values to Muslim societies. As a result, ancient tribal customs have suddenly been rediscovered as a means of reasserting cultural identity in the face of alien cultures. Islamic cultures have often reacted by reducing the rights of women, to differentiate themselves from western values. Feminism is seen to stress the wrong values about the role of women: sexual freedom, lesbianism, shunning of marriage and Marxism, for example.

Muslim feminists

Further reading

Read Leila Ahmed *Women and Gender in Islam: Historical Roots of a Modern Debate* (Yale University Press 1993).

Those who consider themselves Muslim feminists approach these issues in very different ways. Modernist feminists argue that the Qur'an should be read for its spiritual values and that its rulings should be seen in their historical context. For example, when the Qur'an forbids a woman to give a testimony by herself, this is because at that point women were not literate and needed someone to protect them in the law courts. These **reconstructionist** feminists have looked at Muhammad's life in Madinah and considered it far more radical than the conservative Abbasid period that followed. Less radical approaches have looked at the hadiths, especially those concerning Aisha and her political role following the assassination of Uthman in 656 CE.

Test yourself

1. 'The split between Sunni and Shi'a Islam was political, not religious.' Discuss.
2. 'Only the Qur'an contains the revelation of God.' Discuss.
3. 'Shari'ah is only useful today in family law.' Discuss.
4. 'Tawhid undermines human free-will.' Discuss.

Connections

Route F: Philosophy of Religion with Islam

Further reading

Death and Eternal Life by John Hick (Macmillan 1984) is still very useful. See also pages 16–19 of this guide.

Contribution made by Islam to discussions of death and the after-life. Consider the similarities of Akhirah with Christian teaching on resurrection, Hick's modern replica theory and the place of God. Consider problems of language and interpretation of the ineffable. Does reincarnation present a different view of justice and morality that is contrary to the Qur'an?

Further reading

Read pages 37–40 of the *OCR AS Guide* and the chapter on Judaism in this book.

Inspiration and authority of the Qur'an, in comparison with views about the nature of the Bible. Consider the meaning of nazala through the prophets (rasul and nabi), the Qur'an as final and complete revelation and the Qur'an's view of Torah and the Gospels. Look at Orthodox and Progressive Jewish views of the Hebrew Bible as well as fundamentalist, conservative and liberal Christian views, and traditional, Islamist and modernist Muslim commentaries (tafsir) today.

Muslim arguments for the existence of God. Compare the kalam argument with other cosmological arguments, together with knowledge of modern physics. Note also Muslim caution against reducing God to mere 'cause'. Consider the idea of the 'balance' and design arguments. Consider the views of traditionalist and modernist Muslim scholars.

Further reading

Read pages 19–22 of the philosophy of religion chapter in this book, as well as pages 92–95 of *The Miracle of Theism* by J L Mackie (OUP 1982).

The nature of religious experience in Islam. Consider hadith of Muhammad's experience of the 'Night of Power' and his own scepticism. Look at the Sufi emphasis on the mystical experience of God as nur (light) and consider this in the light of the arguments of William James. Consider Muslim criticisms of Sufism and general problems of interpretation.

Read pages 69–70 of the *OCR AS Guide*.

Test yourself

1. Compare Muslim ideas about life after death with the view that when people die they are reincarnated.
2. 'Religious experience is more important than kalam arguments for the existence of God.' Discuss.
3. 'The Qur'an, like the Bible, reflects the times in which it was written.' Discuss.

Route M: Religious Ethics with Islam

Ethics of Islam in relation to issues of war and peace. Compare the concept of the lesser jihad (holy war) with other views such as the Just War and pacifism. Compare and contrast Muslim teaching on the Last Day with Christian eschatology, with reference to different views of pacifism.

Further reading

Read page 153 of the *OCR AS Guide*; pages 46–47 of the religious ethics chapter of this book; chapter 6 of *Issues of Life and Death* by Michael Wilcockson (Hodder 1999); and chapter 6 of *Islam: A Very Short Introduction* by Malise Ruthven.

Ummah and its implications for ethics. Consider Ummah as a source of equality, and contrast it with subjective theories such as egoism and utilitarianism. Compare the concept of Ummah with various forms of prescriptivism (notably Kant's universalism) and with virtue ethics 'communitarianism'.

See page 156 of the *OCR AS Guide*.

Muslim morality as given by Allah in comparison with ethical theories. Consider Kant's categorical imperative in terms of Muslim duties (especially those which are fard); utilitarianism as a means of updating Muslim custom; and moral relativism that allows for ijtihad – individual decision-making. Consider also Shari'ah as the source of virtue and character, and compare this with recent western developments in virtue ethics.

Read pages 75–81 of the *OCR AS Guide*.

Muslim approaches to issues of practical ethics. Consider Shari'ah teaching on God as the sole giver of life and apply it to issues of abortion and euthanasia. Where does ijtihad fit in to this? Consider **environmental** issues in terms of the relationship of God to his creation and the role of humans as khalifa. Consider Shari'ah teaching on the family, sex, marriage and its cohabitation with current Christian and humanist teaching. Look particularly at the role of the woman and developments within feminism.

Further reading

For all these issues, read chapters 15, 18, 19, 23 and 26 of *Islam* by Ruqiayyah Maqsood. See also the religious ethics chapter of this book, and pages 81–85 of the *OCR AS Guide*.

Test yourself

1. 'The aim of war is to establish God's justice.' Discuss.
2. Compare and contrast Muslim teaching on cohabitation with the approach of Utilitarianism.

3. 'Muslim teaching on moral duty is less satisfactory than the Categorical Imperative.' Discuss.

Route Q: Developments in Christian Thought with Islam

> **Further reading**
>
> Read pages 121–122 of the *OCR AS Guide* and chapter 16 of *Muslims* by Andrew Rippin.

Feminism. Consider what is meant by liberation, and the traditionalist views of the roles of men and women, sexuality, marriage, harim and public/private roles. Look also at different types of Christian feminisms and compare to traditional, Islamist and modernist Muslim approaches.

> **Further reading**
>
> Read pages 37–40 of the *OCR AS Guide* and chapter 3 of *Reason and Religious Belief* by Michael Peterson (OUP 2002).

Christian and Muslim views of God's revelation through sacred texts. Compare the traditionalist, Islamist and modernist Muslim interpretations of the Qur'an with fundamentalist, conservative and liberal interpretations of the Bible. Look in particular at fundamentalism in its Muslim and Christian forms.

Read pages 125–131 of the *OCR AS Guide*.

Liberation Theology and the role of Ummah in Islam. Consider the centrality of Moses as law-giver in the Qur'an as the basis of Ummah with the exodus theme and the Church as *iglesia popular* as developed at Medellin in Latin America. Compare Muhammad as statesman with Jesus as liberator.

Read pages 107–114 of the Developments in Christian Thought chapter.

Ways in which Christians and Muslims view the validity of other world religions. Compare Muslim views of Isa with those of Hick. Look at: Qur'an verses which have a favourable view of 'people of the Book' (inclusivist); unbelievers' debates about imam (faith); views on the Last Day (exclusivist/inclusivist); and the modernist argument that all religions require true commitment (islam) to their God (pluralism). Compare the Sufi emphasis on mystical religious experience with Christian pluralist arguments.

Test yourself

1. 'A plural view of religions undermines Islam and Christianity.' Discuss.
2. 'Feminism has always been an aspect of Muslim and Christian teaching.' Discuss.
3. Compare and contrast the ways in which Christian Liberation Theology and Muslim teaching on Ummah have achieved social justice.

Judaism

The significance of the concept of the Land of Israel

Historical context of the Land of Israel as the Promised Land

The notion of **the land** is at the heart of the Abrahamic covenant: God promises to a nomadic people the land that will enable them to become a great nation. The land, therefore, is the one occupied by Abraham, where symbolically he purchased his first plot from Ephron the Hittite, in the Cave of Machpelah (Gen 25: 7–11). The land is also fundamental to Moses' covenant, and the establishment of a civilised and holy people living according to a single law in accordance with God's will.

The land is associated with Israel's obligation to nurture and tend it, because they are a people made in God's image (Gen 1: 26–2: 4a). It is associated with the Law of Jubilee (see Lev 25), the Sabbath, and even harvest laws, which give rights to the poor to gather the leftovers – all of which assumes the understanding that *all* the land and its inhabitants are morally and spiritually related.

Land is also eschatologically linked with the messianic age – as the time when it will be cleansed from all conflict and will enjoy freedom from foreign rule, so that 'each man shall sit under his grape vine or fig tree with no one to disturb him' (Mic 4: 4). In exile, the land and Jerusalem (or Zion) in particular form the basis of hope and are a symbol of God's redemption. The love of Israel (ahavat Yisrael) is part of Jewish consciousness, and became an important part of Zionism and 19th-century settlement in Israel.

Although the destruction of the Temple in 70 CE is usually thought to be a decisive turning point in Jewish history, as far as the land is concerned the moment is marked by the failure of **Bar Kokhba's** revolution to secure Jerusalem back from the Romans around 135 CE. Although a small number of Jews continued to live in the land, as Abba Eban concludes: 'The Jews no longer held any real hope of reclaiming Jerusalem or rebuilding the Temple. There would be no more Jewish rebellions. There would be self-defence against massacres and pogroms, but more than 1,800 years would pass before the Jews would again rule anywhere in Palestine and be masters of Jerusalem.'

The new exile or **galut** has been understood in various ways: as a punishment, as suffering for others or simply as a way in which the **diaspora** has developed a new understanding of itself. The fundamental question is whether a return to the land is appropriate for Judaism in the light of almost 2,000 years' development. Until the late 19th century, there was almost unanimous agreement from Orthodox and Reform Jews alike that there should be no *active* return to the land. In Orthodox Judaism the 'land' symbolises the special Torah-people relationship, which will only become a reality when the diaspora ends and God decides that the galut is over. For Reform Jews and many others, the gradual emancipation of Jews as full citizens in their own countries turned the idea of the land (and Zion in particular) into a spiritual symbol of the world's universal redemption. The rise of Zionism and the establishment of the state of Israel have challenged all these ideas.

Further reading

Read pages 535–541 of *Contemporary Jewish Thought* by A. Cohen and P. Mendes-Flohr (The Free Press 1988). You might also wish to read Martin Buber's classic book *Israel and Palestine: The History of an Idea* (Strauss and Young 1952). A very good introduction to the whole topic is chapter 17 of *Judaism* by C. Pilkington (Hodder 2003).

Route R: Jewish Scriptures and contemporary issues. Consider how the Bible has been used to support and reject Zionism.

Route V: Islam and nature of God. Consider what kind of God is revealed in Jewish history.

See the section on page 163 on messianic hope.

'By the rivers of Babylon, there we sat, sat and wept as we thought of Zion… If I forget you, O Jerusalem, let my right hand wither, let my tongue stick to my palate if I cease to think about you…' (Ps 137: 1, 5–6).

Emperor Hadrian (ruled 117–138 CE) forbade all Jewish practices; the names Judea and Jerusalem were removed from all maps and the area was settled by Gentiles.

Jews have continuously lived in Jerusalem, Safed, Jaffa and Hebron.

Further reading

See page 100 of *Heritage: Civilization and the Jews* by Abba Eban (Summit Books 1984).

'Diaspora' means dispersion and refers to all Jews living outside Israel.

Further discussion

Which is the more appropriate name for the land of Israel: 'The Holy Land' or the 'Promised Land'?

Relationship between the religious idea of the land and the present state of Israel

The establishment of the state of Israel in 1948 was the result of more than 100 years of active development of a variety of religious and secular movements, collectively referred to as Zionism. The fact that there are so many different forms of Zionism helps to explain the political situation in Israel today.

Further reading

Read pages 1069–1076 of *Contemporary Jewish Thought* by A Cohen and P Mendes-Flohr (The Free Press 1988).

Secular Zionism

Autonomy. For the early Zionists, centuries of oppression contrasted with the rise of European wealth and emancipation from class and religion. Enlightenment thinkers such as Kant, Locke and Hume suggested that humans flourish when they can act autonomously and rule themselves. Symbolically for political Zionism, the 'Balfour Declaration' of 1917 recognised the Jewish claim for an autonomous political state.

Lord Balfour's letter expresses the view of the government in favour 'of a national home for the Jewish people', promising to 'use their best endeavours to facilitate the achievement of that object…'.

Anti-Semitism. Despite the gradual emancipation of Jews from ancient restrictive laws, anti-Jewish attitudes still run deep. One example of this was **Captain Dreyfus**, who was accused of selling military secrets to Germany. His trial deeply divided society but it demonstrated to **Theodor Herzl** just how anti-Semitic French society was, despite its egalitarian ideology.

Alfred Dreyfus (1859–1935) came from an assimilated Jewish family.

Theodor Herzl (1860–1904) wrote *The Jewish State* (1896) and is often regarded as the father of modern Zionism. He realised early on that the Zionist project could not happen without the support of religious Jews.

Pogrom and holocaust. The pogroms in Russia and the holocaust demonstrated to Zionists the practical necessity of finding a refuge for Jews with their own homeland. Those who had helped fund the **Yishuv** or community of settlers prior to the foundation of the State of Israel had long seen Palestine as a place of refuge.

The assassination of Tsar Alexander II in 1881 led to a new wave of Jewish massacres (pogroms) under the May Laws of 1882. This resulted in the migration of many Jews to Palestine.

Nationalism. The 19th century witnessed the development of the concept of the nation-state. Language, culture and romantic ideas of identity shifted geographic boundaries throughout Europe.

Ideology. Younger Jewish intellectuals were inspired by the atheistic writings of Marx and Nietzsche. Marxism called them to 'shake off their chains' of slavery – especially the 'opium' of religion as a false consciousness – and viewed history as a series of class struggles. This echoed the Jewish experience, which now called for immediate political action for Jewish emancipation. In Nietzsche's dislike of the inferior 'slave mentality' they saw the Jewish tendency towards introversion, servitude and powerlessness. Nietzsche's call to 'transvaluate' society and develop a new consciousness – again without being slave to God – inspired these strongly non-religious Jews to abandon Torah and Jewish custom in the struggle for freedom.

Socialist Zionists today come into the greatest conflict with religious Jews because for them the state of Israel is an entirely secular state.

Assimilation. Some who rejected the existence of God and the authority of the Torah nevertheless resisted the pressure to abandon their Jewish heritage. In the 19th century, being accepted by society for promotion or place in government often meant converting to Christianity. The 19th century saw a large number of Jews assimilating in order to enjoy emancipation. Some who for cultural reasons felt an affinity for the land of Israel (**Eretz Israel**), and its Jewish history (**Am Israel**) saw a solution to the problem of assimilation through the establishment of a Jewish state.

Asher Ginzberg (1856–1927), known as 'Ahad Ha Am' (One of the People), was the inspiration behind this particular form of Zionism. Read pages 552–556 of *The Jewish Philosophy Reader* by D Frank, O Leaman and C Manekin (Routledge 2000) for an extract of one of his writings.

The Messianic Age. Some religious Jews reject the notion of a state of Israel on the eschatological grounds that the messiah has not arrived, that it is wrong for humans to bring about the state which is God's and that a secular state is incompatible with religious Judaism. The Orthodox anti-Zionist position is sceptical of the state of Israel. Although the ultra-orthodox who live in Israel today have secured a significant place in the Knesset and control laws on marriage and divorce, Sabbath and food, they do so for pragmatic or practical reasons. A solution to the problem of secularism was notably developed by **R Abraham Kook** (1864–1935). Kook's argument was that secularism is part of the evolutionary process of historic change, and acts as a means of cleansing Judaism of many introverted and backward practices. The state of Israel is part of this process towards the messianic age and religious renewal.

Religious Zionism

Further reading

For an interesting essay on religious Zionism and the problems posed by traditional halakhah, read David Harman's 'The Challenge of Modern Israel' (1987) in *The Jewish Philosophy Reader* (Routledge 2000).

The ultra-Orthodox Neturei Karta, sees the holocaust as a punishment for secularism and Zionism. Look at www.nkusa.org.

Boundaries of the Land. One political-messianic Zionist position is taken by the **Gush Emunim** (founded in 1967) who consider that all land won in the 1967 and 1973 wars forms part of the ancient lands of Israel. They resist any movement to return the land to the Arabs. Many believe the only legitimate use of force is for peace not land.

Aliyah as personal religious and moral fulfilment. Another major change has been the attitude of Reform Judaism to Zionism. The Pittsburgh Platform (1885) rejected Zionism on the grounds that the covenant was aimed at the universal brotherhood of mankind. The Colombus Platform (1937) accepted the refuge argument (although the refuge did not necessarily have to be Israel), but the San Francisco 1976 perspective presented a view reminiscent of Ahad ha Am – that aliyah was part of every Jew's love of Israel: 'The State of Israel and the Diaspora, in fruitful dialogue, can show how a people transcends nationalism even as it affirms it, thereby setting an example for humanity.' By 1997, at the Miami Platform, aliyah was endorsed to a much greater extent, as a way in which Jewish people could take responsibility for the running of society in a Torah-centred way, and so give the individual 'full potential of their individual and communal strivings'.

Aliyah literally means 'ascent' (as in ascending mount Zion) and has come to mean immigration to Israel.

Further discussion

Consider to what degree living in the secular state of Israel today can actually reduce the fear of assimilation, and be a way of being more religiously Jewish.

Route R: Jewish Scriptures and authority. Read pages 62–65. Consider how the Bible has been interpreted by orthodox and non-orthodox Jews to support and reject messianic hope.

Messianic hope

Messianic hope is an element of Jewish eschatology and part of three connected ideas: the messiah, the Kingdom of God and the Coming Age (the *olam ha ba*). There is no clear doctrine about any of these three ideas; indeed, many writers stress that Judaism is very much a 'this worldly' religion, and that discussion of the messiah as a redeemer is unbiblical and unJewish. This reaction may be in part a means of distancing Jewish ideas of the messiah from Christianity and the notion that the Torah is fundamental to Judaism. Even so, there is a long prophetic tradition that God's chosen one would be instrumental in the establishment of God's kingdom, when Israel would live in peace and harmony with her neighbours. The idea of the messiah is preserved in many liturgies and prayers such as the **Amida** and **Mourner's Kaddish**.

Further reading

The three ideas are clearly set out and discussed in chapter 9 of *Judaism* by Nicholas de Lange (OUP 2003).

The Mourner's Kaddish begins, 'May he establish his kingdom during your life and during your days, and during the life of all the house of Israel, evenly, speedily and at a near time, and say ye, Amen.' (Hertz *Authorized Daily Prayer Book* page 213). The Amida is perhaps the oldest Jewish prayer. The fifteenth benediction states, 'Speedily cause the offspring of David, thy servant, to flourish, and lift up his glory by thy divine help because we wait for thy salvation all the day.' (Hertz *Authorized Daily Prayer Book* page 147).

The word messiah comes from the Hebrew **mashiah** meaning 'to anoint'. In the Bible, kings, high priests and judges were all anointed with oil to signify their role and special relationship to

God. The actual term is rarely used in biblical texts; here the idea of a future redeemer is much more general and usually associated with a descendent of King David. The key passage is from **2 Samuel 7** where God says, 'I will raise up your offspring after you, one of your own issue, and I will establish his royal throne for ever' (2 Sam 7: 12–13). In most of the later discussion of the messiah's role by the rabbis and others, he is not a redeemer in himself but rather the one who ushers in the Kingdom of God or the **Messianic Age**; it is only God who can be Israel's redeemer.

The Kingdom of God is widely used by the rabbis to distinguish it from other kingdoms ruled by humans. In the Messianic Age, as many rabbis have said, 'The only difference between this world and the days of the Messiah is the subjection of Israel to the nations of the world' (BT *Sanhedrin* 91b).

Isaiah and Malachi

Further reading

Make sure you have looked up the biblical references given here. Quotations are given from *Tenakh* (Jewish Publication Society 1985).

Isaiah 1–39 is often thought to have been written pre-exile in the 8th century BCE (during the Assyrian invasion of the northern kingdom), Isaiah 40–55 during the end of the exile and Isaiah 55–66 during the restoration. However, there are several major themes that appear continually throughout the book, which suggest that there is a view of Judaism particular to Isaiah.

Isaiah

Further reading

Detailed discussion of Isaiah 40–42 and 53 can be found in the Jewish Scriptures chapter, pages 53–55.

A land and people restored. Isaiah 35 is an important chapter that describes a time when all physical imperfections will be removed from the people: 'Then shall the eyes of the blind be opened, and the ears of the deaf shall be unstopped, then shall the lame leap like deer and the tongue of the dumb shall shout aloud' (35: 5–6). This need not be taken absolutely literally and can relate to Isaiah's frequent claim that the people are morally and spiritually blind and deaf (6: 10). But in addition, the restored people will have a land of their own, free from travellers and wild animals (35: 8–9). The redeemed will live in Zion (Jerusalem) in everlasting joy and gladness (35: 10). Some aspects of Isaiah suggest that foreigners (non-Jews) who respect God will be included in this messianic age and will worship in the restored Temple. So the transformed world is one in which 'all flesh shall come to worship Me' (66: 23).

'As for foreigners who attach themselves to the Lord, to minister to Him and to love the name of the Lord, to be His servants – all who keep the Sabbath and do not profane it, and who hold fast to My covenant – I will bring them to My sacred mount...for My House shall be called a house of prayer for all peoples.' (Is 56: 6–7).

Messiah. There is no messiah as such in Isaiah. In Isaiah 40–55, reference is made to a 'servant' who is instrumental in the establishment of a restored Israel – his identity raises some interesting implications for later messianic thinking. The servant might be the people or a righteous group collectively, or an individual such as a man of outstanding moral integrity, or possibly a foreigner. But Isaiah describes how a young girl's son will be a sign to the faithful remnant (7: 3) that God's promises will be given to the descendants of David's dynasty. The symbolic name of the child (7: 14) is 'Immanuel' (meaning 'God is with us') and he represents a time when the people will be living in splendour 'feeding on curds and honey'. Isaiah 11: 1–11 has also been interpreted messianically to refer to an ancestor of David (11: 1) of great wisdom and devotion, who will bring justice and peace in a world where 'the wolf shall dwell with the lamb' (11: 6).

Malachi

There is a major divergence between Hebrew Bible and English Bible chapter divisions. 3: 19–24 in the Hebrew corresponds to the English 4: 1–6. References here are to the Hebrew Bible.

The book of Malachi was probably written in the Second Temple period, possibly during the time of Ezra and Nehemiah, c. 480 BCE, though there is no consensus. The book comprises a number of dialogues in which accusations are made about God's relationship with his people and the people's relationship with God:

- God has not loved his people and acted for them (1: 2–5).

- ✦ The priests have failed to carry out their duties in the Temple (1: 6–2: 10).
- ✦ The people have failed to worship the one God by worshipping a foreign goddess and men have divorced their wives too easily (2: 10–16).
- ✦ God has failed to judge evildoers (2: 17).

'You have wearied the Lord with your talk. But you ask, "By what have we wearied Him?" By saying, "All who do evil are good in the sight of the Lord, and in them He delights" or else, "Where is the God of justice?"' (Mal 2: 17).

In response to the question in 2: 17 Malachi gives two answers:

- ✦ God will send his messenger, who will prepare the people and purify Temple worship before the Day of the Lord. This will be a time of purging and judgement. As an imminent worldly event, the people are challenged to keep to God's laws and put God to the test (3: 10) so that he will bless them.
- ✦ Those who have remained righteous will be rewarded. They will have their names written in the book of life (3: 16; Dan 12: 1) and take comfort that the wicked will be destroyed at judgement day.

The identity of the messenger is confusing. Here it appears to be the angel who carried out God's will at the Passover (Exodus 14: 19), but in 3: 23 he is associated with Elijah, see 2 Kings 2: 11.

'For lo! That day is at hand, burning like an oven. All the arrogant and all the doers of evil shall be straw and the day that is coming – said the Lord of Hosts – shall burn them to ashes' (Mal 3: 19).

Importance of messianic hope

Many Jewish writers are at pains to explain that messianic hope is a subsidiary element to the main principles of Judaism. Green and Silverstein make a strong case for what they call Judaism's **levitical religion**, that is Judaism at first represented by the priests, the Temple and the regular round of sacrifices. After 70 CE, the levitical religion was replaced with piety, good works and the study of the Torah. Both are means of maintaining the good order of society and the creation. This, they argue, is the Jewish normative position, which of itself has no need for a 'redeemer, saviour or messiah'. Nevertheless, the biblical vision as we have seen in Isaiah and Micah, and in particular the experience of the exile – when kingship ceased and the role of the Temple became less central – provided a strand of eschatological thinking that the rabbis integrated.

Further discussion

Discuss what Jacob Neusner meant when he said: 'The messiah theme fits into primary categories but is itself divisible among them.' See page 248 of *The Blackwell Companion to Judaism* by J Neusner and A Avery-Peck (Blackwell 2003).

Further reading

The Blackwell Companion to Judaism (Blackwell 2003), page 251.

The Mishnah has frequent references to the Kingdom of God and the 'Days of the Messiah'. But the Mishnah is more interested in everyday life than the future. The messiah is one who heralds the messianic age; he does not cause it – only God can act to do this.

The rabbis of the Talmud developed this further and established a principle that determined all later messianic thinking. This might be called the principle of **quietism,** that the Kingdom of God must not be forced by human agency, because even the messiah is subject to the divine will. The coming of the messiah and the messianic age would not affect worship or the study of the Torah; the major difference is that Israel would be able to worship freely.

R Helbo says: '...He imposed an oath on Israel not to rebel against the kingdom and not to force the end, not to reveal its mysteries to the nations of the world and not to go up from exile by force.' (Song of Songs Rabbah 2: 7)

In medieval times, Maimonides (1135–1204) recorded how varied Jewish thought was about the messiah and the Coming Age. His own naturalist view (which he acknowledged was not mainstream) was to treat most of these ideas as symbols rather than historical events. But he did think that the messiah would be a descendent of King Solomon who would gather in the exiles and establish Jewish sovereignty of Israel. The messiah is mortal, and after his death his descendents would rule for a thousand years over a perfect society, which would live by the Torah in order to establish the Coming Age.

However, from the time when Bar Kokhba (132 CE) was proclaimed messiah there have been many so-called messiahs. **Sabbeteanists** considered that Shabbetai Zevi (1626–1676) was the messiah in May 1665. Zevi belonged to the mystical Jewish **Lurianic Kabbalah** movement, which claimed that God had lost sparks of his divinity in the evil material world. The Jewish task was to restore these sparks by carrying out the halakhah. By 1665, Zevi's community considered the task almost complete and believed that he, as messiah, would be able to announce the final moment. His followers regarded even his conversion to Islam as his means of rescuing more trapped sparks of divinity. There have been subsequent Sabbatean groups. Most Jews regarded the movement as failing on two counts: its **antinomianism** as a means of bringing Israel closer to redemption; and its emphasis on human means of redemption rather than God. Despite these criticisms, various forms of modern messianic movements have developed Sabbatean thinking.

Interpretations of messianic hope today

> **Further reading**
> Read pages 260–266 of *The Blackwell Companion to Judaism* (Blackwell 2003).

Two significant factors in Judaism over the past 150 years have been the development of Zionism and the State of Israel, and the effects of the enlightenment (haskalah). Some orthodox Jewish thinkers acknowledge that events in the last two centuries have been significant enough to radically adapt some of the rabbinic messianic principles.

Orthodox

In the 19th century, two rabbis questioned the teaching that the Jews should remain a people in exile until such time as God should choose otherwise. R Judah Alkalai (1798–1878) and R Zvi Hirsch Kalischer (1795–1874) founded the Harbingers of Zionism which advocated a **gradualist** settlement in Israel. Their justification distinguished two kinds of messianic theology: process and goal. In the first stage, the Messiah ben Joseph would arrive after Israel had prepared herself politically; only then could Messiah ben David arrive and mark the moment of God's redemption. Orthodox critics rejected the idea that occupying the land could in anyway be considered redemptive.

R Abraham Isaac Kook (1865–1935) and his son **R Zvi Yehudah Kook** (1891–1981) argued that the world was entering a new phase. They maintained that the dawn of the messianic age had been heralded by pogroms and holocaust, establishing the end of the exilic phase of Jewish history and the return to the Eretz Israel. The return was an act of repentance and redemption. The influence of messianic Kabbalism justified the role of human agency to take collective responsibility for the establishment of a new society.

This form of religious Zionism is characterised as 'messianism without a messiah'.

The most recent messianic development has not involved Zionism but the deep-seated prophetic notion of a new moral age. In what has been called **messianism of prosperity**, the ultra-orthodox Lubavitch Hasid, Rebbe Menachem Mendel Schneerson declared that in the light of the holocaust (which marked the 'birth pangs' of the messianic age) and the end of the USSR, the Noachide covenant was now being established worldwide and the time of redemption was dawning. In 1991 he spoke to his community of the coming of the messiah. Following his death in 1994, some of his followers consider that he was the messiah.

> **Further reading**
> See pages 90–91 of the *OCR AS Guide* for the universal elements of the Noachide covenant.

'The belief that the Messiah may die without accomplishing his mission and return to earth at a later time is a dramatic departure from tradition.' Nicholas de Lange, *Judaism* (OUP 2003) page 130.

Progressive Jews have questioned the focus and supernatural beliefs of traditional Judaism, especially the idea of a specific messianic figure, the Coming Age and the immortality of the soul. Many consider that the development of the messiah has occurred only during times of stress, when hope in a heroic figure overcoming the enemy has diverted Judaism away from its this-worldly view of religion and morality. This is reinforced by the Enlightenment's dislike of the more speculative aspects of religion. However, this hasn't meant the abandonment of all messianic hope, rather the abolition of the concept of a specific figure bringing in a new age at a specific time.

Progressive

In other words, progressives share the prophetic universalism of many of the Hebrew prophets.

The **Pittsburgh Platform** (1885) stated that the messianic hope should only be considered in universal terms because 'we consider ourselves no longer a nation but a religious community'. Therefore, the rule of the messiah, the return to Israel, and the Temple and its sacrifices have ceased to have any meaning.

Further study

Consider the following quotation and discuss to what degree traditional Orthodoxy and Progressive Judaism actually differ on their view of messianic hope. 'Abraham was called not in order to be "saved" let alone bring salvation, but to be a model and paradigm of the righteous and blessed life, to be a paradigm of blessing (and not a source of blessing)...' R J Zwi Werblowsky in *Contemporary Jewish Thought*, page 599.

20th-century holocaust and post-holocaust theology

In Jewish history three major communal disasters have had a fundamental effect on Judaism: Nebuchadnezzar's destruction of the Temple and defeat of Judea in 587 BCE, the fall of Jerusalem to the Romans in 70 CE, and the extermination of six million Jews by the Nazis. It is the scale and brutality of the holocaust or **shoah** which makes this last event in Jewish history different.

Further reading

Approaches to Auschwitz by Richard Rubenstein and John Roth (Westminster John Knox Press 2003) is a very good comprehensive guide to the history, literature and theology of the holocaust. See also chapter 8 of *Judaism* by Brian Close (Hodder and Stoughton 1991).

Effects on world Jewry

Education

Rabbi Albert Friedlander has said that no Jew can discuss the holocaust without confronting the issue of survival. What purpose does the memory of the holocaust serve? Those who survived have had to reconcile their lives with those who died. One response is to use the holocaust as a means of educating the world.

Geographical

The holocaust changed the Jewish map of the world – in Europe, 70 per cent of Jewry died. For example, of the 3.3 million Jews (10.5 per cent of all Jews) who lived in Poland, 2.6 million died. Of the 140,000 Lithuanian Jews (7.6 per cent), 104,000 died.

Further reading

Martin Gilbert *Atlas of Jewish History* (William Morrow, 1993).

Psychological

In the 1970s Reeve Brenner polled 1000 Israeli survivors to discover the effect of the holocaust on their religious thinking. More than 700 replied. 69 per cent believed in God before the holocaust; 47 per cent stated the holocaust had no effect on their faith. Of the 53 per cent whose faith was changed, three quarters lost their faith, while for the remainder their faith was strengthened. The believers were asked if the existence of Israel was worth the holocaust, and all said 'no'.

'It's really a wonder that I haven't dropped all my ideals because they are so absurd and impossible to carry out. Yet, I keep them, because I spite of everything I still believe people are really good at heart...I can feel the sufferings of millions and yet, if I look into the heavens, I think that it will all come right, and that this cruelty too will end, and that peace and tranquillity will return again.' *The Diary of Anne Frank*, 15 July 1944 (Pan Books 1954) pages 218–219.

The holocaust has been a major factor in the creation of the State of Israel. It has served to save those in the Diaspora from persecution; for example, those who survived the holocaust itself (30,000 Poles immigrated to Israel) and the dramatic air-rescue of the Ethiopian Jews in 'Operation Solomon' in 1991.

Literary

Literary responses to the holocaust can express in human terms the seemingly inexpressible, without having to be philosophically and theologically systematic. Rubenstein and Roth outline seven types of literary response: **lamentation** (Yitzhak Katzenelson, *Song of the*

Further reading

Approaches to Auschwitz chapter 9.

Murdered Jewish People), **resistance** (Andre Schwarz-Bart, *The Last of the Just*), **endurance** (Ka-tzetnik, *Star Eternal*), **survival** (Primo Levi, *If This is a Man*), **honesty** (Tadeusz Borowski, *This Way for the Gas, Ladies and Gentlemen*), **choice-making** (William Styron, *Sophie's Choice*) and **protest** (Elie Wiesel, *Night*).

Orthodox and Progressive responses to the holocaust

> **Further reading**
>
> For a comprehensive set of extracts from many Jewish and Christian writers, read *Holocaust Theology: A Reader* ed. Dan Cohn-Sherbok (New York University Press 2002).

For almost 20 years, almost nothing theological was said about the religious meaning of the holocaust. Perhaps the profound effect it had was too complex to be articulated. As Jonathan Sacks has said, it was 'a mystery wrapped in silence'. Post-holocaust theology is contextual and perhaps only able to be done by Jews. Some consider that, as important as it is, holocaust theology is limited in its aims – it is not directly concerned with Jewish practice or ethics, but the nature of God's relationship with his people. Holocaust theology is not just interested in **theodicy** but also questions of covenant, Torah and election of Israel.

Rubenstein: the death of God

> **Further reading**
>
> See pages 308–316 of *Approaches to Auschwitz*.

After 20 years of silence, Richard Rubenstein's radical book *After Auschwitz* (1966) appeared in the USA and caused a storm of protest, followed by a series of theological responses to the holocaust that continue to this day. Rubenstein's theology is very much influenced by his assimilated, philosophical and North-American cultural background to the problem of God's action in the world.

- **Death of God**. Rubenstein argues that the holocaust does not disprove the existence of God, but that the experience of the concentration camps finally killed the traditional view of God acting in history to save his people.
- **God as Holy Nothingness**. The holocaust was *not* God's punishment. Hitler was not God's agent in the same way as Nebuchadnezzar was God's agent in destroying the Temple in 587 BCE, because God is 'Holy Nothingness'. The holocaust forces us to rethink the nature of God in terms of his utterly incomprehensible existence. Mystically God just *is* – he is not a thing or person. When God is thought of in this way, it is impossible to think of God as someone who has deliberately caused suffering. 'Nothingness' describes God existentially, as a non-personal ground of being.
- **Jewish tradition**. Rubenstein was impressed that what gave the people courage and hope was the enactment of ancient traditions, prayers and rituals, sometimes in the face of terrifying brutality. Being Jewish, living in a community and following tradition is the existential means of giving and creating meaning. The creation of the State of Israel is one example of the way in which the tenaciousness of Jewish tradition against disaster can create good out of evil.

Berkovits: the hidden God

> **Further reading**
>
> *Faith After the Holocaust* (New York Ktav 1973). See pages 233–236 of *Judaism* by C Pilkington (Hodder).

Eliezer Berkovits' argument is often regarded as the most Jewish response to the holocaust. Unlike Rubenstein, his arguments depend far more on the Bible and Jewish history; he doesn't regard the holocaust as a unique event in Jewish history.

- **Protest**. Like Job, the prophets and so many others, Berkovits begins by asking why God appeared not to be helping his faithful, the elect, during their time of suffering – 'My God, my God, why have you abandoned me?' (Psalm 22: 1).

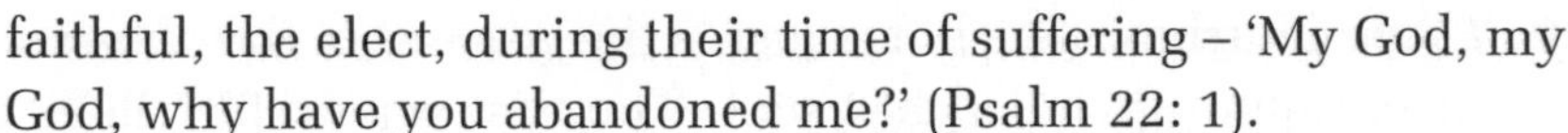

Route R: Jewish Scriptures with Judaism. Look at Job's protest at his innocent suffering and the answer given (see the Jewish Scriptures chapter). If Job does not die, can the book be used in holocaust theology?

- **Hiddenness of God** (*Hester Panim*). In biblical terms, God hides himself so that his people have the freedom to develop their own morality. In philosophical terms, this is the 'free-will defence'. It might appear that God is absent – 'Why do you hide Your face ignoring our affliction and distress?' (Ps 44: 24) – but God is there in their affliction as the object of faith.

'You are indeed a God who concealed Himself, O God of Israel, who brings victory!' Isaiah 45: 15.

- **Suffering for the world**. Using Isaiah's Suffering Servant, Berkovits argues that the innocent suffering of the Jewish people was for the sins of the world and to fulfil the rabbinic notion of **Kiddush ha Shem** – to sanctify God's name through martyrdom. The numerous examples of pious Jews dying in the death camps is the great witness for God's presence in suffering.

Further reading

See Isaiah 52: 13–53: 12 and the Jewish Scriptures chapter in this guide.

- ***Akedah* and faith**. *Akedah* or the 'binding of Isaac' (Gen 22), when Abraham was commanded by God to sacrifice his son, symbolises the ultimate mystery of the holocaust. It is a test of faith, although to what end remains a mystery.

Remember also the theme of Job that his suffering is also a test (Job 2: 10).

Fackenheim: mending the world

Emil Fackenheim (1916–2003) was born in Halle, Germany. While studying for the Reform rabbinate in 1938, he was arrested by the Gestapo and briefly held in the Sachsenhausen concentration camp. In 1940, he succeeded in leaving Germany and emigrated to Canada.

Further reading

Rubenstein and Roth *Approaches to Auschwitz* pages 316–329.

- **614th commandment**. To the Torah's 613 mitzvot or commandments, Fackenheim adds one more: to survive. 'It is our duty to live, and not give Hitler posthumous victory by ending Jewish life.' This includes remembering those who perished in the holocaust and not falling into despair, cynicism or escape into otherworldliness. In the past, idolatry was the great sin; for the Jew today 'it is to respond to Hitler by doing his work'.
- **Commanding Voice**. The Voice at Auschwitz remembers what has happened and reminds the world so that it never happens again. The uniqueness of the holocaust gives the Jews a special place in the world. But, as the book of Job concludes, there can be rational reasons for understanding the holocaust – intelligibility must be a human response through faith and action.
- **Mending the world**. Fackenheim's theology can be summarised by the rabbinic term *Tikkun olam* – the command to mend the world – that is, to break down differences between people, to protest against injustice and to establish God's rule on earth.

Maybaum: God's punishment

As a European Reform rabbi, the theology of Ignaz Maybaum (1897–1976) shares the Reform view of Israel's position as a moral 'light to the world', so the holocaust is a means of cleansing Judaism of its collective sins.

Further reading

See pages 303–308 of *Approaches to Auschwitz* by Rubenstein and Roth.

- **Purification and the Day of the Lord**. Many of the prophets of ancient Israel viewed the sins of the people and their consequent punishment by God as a prelude to the re-establishment of the covenant. Like many others, Maybaum considered that Judaism (especially from eastern Europe) had become too introvert and had failed to modernise. Hitler was God's instrument of purification just as Jeremiah saw Nebuchadnezzar (Jer 21: 7).

The Day of the Lord in Amos, Isaiah and Micah is God's judgement on good and bad alike. See pages 61–62 on Amos.

- ✦ **Three Churban**. The holocaust is the greatest of the *churban* or catastrophes that God has sent. The first was in 587 BCE, the second in 70 CE and the third 1933–1945. Each time the Jews have reformed themselves. Maybaum says: 'These catastrophes are a 'small moment', a 'little wrath' measured against the eternal love which God showers on his people.'

Cohn-Sherbok: justice

> **Further reading**
> See *Holocaust Theology* by Dan Cohn-Sherbok (Marshall Morgan and Scott 1989).

Rabbi Cohn-Sherbok takes the controversial position that without a belief in the after-life the holocaust remains a theological and social perplexity. In the past – from the time of the Maccabees – a belief in the after-life helped sustain Jews through atrocities, and it was evident that the Jews assumed the reality of the after-life to help them through their suffering and death. However, most writers have avoided this traditional position.

- ✦ **Kiddush ha Shem**. Cohn recounts how an old man in a concentration camp was singing *zimrot* (psalms) very loudly at Sukkot. When warned of the danger this was putting him in he said: 'What can they do to me? They can take my body but not my soul. Over the soul they have no authority. Here they are powerful but in the Other World they are powerless.' Without a belief in the after-life, it is impossible to believe in the goodness of God.
- ✦ **Death as a sacrifice of faith**. Those who died believed in the absolute judgement of God to reward their faith. They saw their lives as 'an interlude between two eternal states of darkness, they saw their suffering and death as a prelude to a more glorious future'.
- ✦ **Justice and hope**. The reward to the faithful in the Age to Come illustrates the goodness and love of God. 'Only in this way will the Jewish people who have experienced the Valley of the Shadow of Death be able to say, in the ancient words of the Psalmist: "I shall fear no evil, for thou are with me."'

Quotations from *Holocaust Theology*.

Jewish traditions in the United Kingdom

Perhaps the major difference between orthodox Judaism and the non-orthodox traditions is the authority given to the Torah, either as God's direct **revelation** to Moses (orthodoxy) or as God's inspired word as interpreted by humans (non-orthodoxy). But the factors that determine the authority of revelation and therefore distinguish Jewish traditions are much more complex. Consideration should also be given to:

- ✦ The place of the Talmud, halakhah, messiah, land of Israel, use of Hebrew, role of women, sacrifice and the Temple, authority of the mitzvot.
- ✦ The historical background out of which orthodoxy and non-orthodoxy have developed. This is especially important when comparing European Judaism with Judaism in the United States.

> **Further reading**
> Read chapters 4 and 5 of *Judaism* by C Pilkington, and chapter 13 of *The Jews* by Alan Unterman (Sussex Academic Press 1996).

> **Route G: Philosophy of religion and authority of scripture.** Look at different Jewish views of the revelation. **Route V: Islam and divisions.** Consider the circumstances that have led to different Jewish and Muslim divisions.

> **Further study**
> Consider how Jonathan Sacks, the Chief Rabbi, deals with orthodoxy and globalisation in *The Dignity of Difference* (Continuum 2002).

Orthodoxy

Until the French Revolution (1789), the term 'orthodoxy' did not exist. Jews called themselves **Haredim** ('men of awe') or **Yereim** ('God-fearers'). Since the development of non-orthodox Judaism, orthodoxy has become a term to refer to what others would prefer to call 'religious' (*datiyim* in modern Israel) or 'observant' Judaism. Until the 19th century, most Jews regarded themselves as being members of the *galut* – a people in exile – and defined themselves through their adherence to the Torah and halakhah. But as societies have given Jews greater rights, the *Orah Hayyim* have become more important than *Hoshen Mishpat*. In the USA, orthodox Jews are a minority (nine per cent), while in the UK, 50 per cent belong to the United Synagogue (which appoints the Chief Rabbi) and another 25 per cent are affiliated to the Union of Orthodox Congregations. Orthodoxy is also significant in Israel – although it does not represent the majority.

Orah Hayyim are discussions about rituals and customs. *Hoshen Mishpat* are discussions about civil war.

With the orthodox view that the Torah was 'from heaven' (Aboth 1: 1 refers to both Written and Oral Torah), questions of when and where it was written are of little concern, but there have always been orthodox scholars: interpreters such as Gaon and Rashi. Abraham Ibn Ezra was the first to suggest that the Book of Isaiah may have had more than one author.

Revelation

Further reading

Read pages 159–162 of the *OCR AS Guide*.

See page 53.

The observance of halakhah is generally what has distinguished orthodox Judaism from non-orthodoxy. The traditional view is that halakhah seeks to express the eternal truths of Written and Oral Torah regardless of history. But recent changes, especially in the formation of the state of Israel, have questioned many well-established halakhic laws. This can be most clearly seen in the split between the Gush Emunim (pro-Zionist) and Neturei Karta (anti-Zionist) orthodox groups in Israel today, and the teaching of the sages about aliyah. Likewise, the influential teaching of R Kook illustrates that halakhah can be seen to evolve.

Halakhah

Further study

Are the Writings or Ketuvim as binding as Torah?

R Kook sanctioned the formation of the State of Israel in terms of a developing view of history in the establishment of the messianic age.

Orthodoxy has always resisted the formation of a creed and senior clerics have preferred to develop rulings according to the degree of respect and learning given to a particular rabbi. Yet within what is sometimes referred to as **ultra-orthodoxy**, which comprises various Hasidic traditions, the degree of authority of the rebbe to decide on matters of practice is contrary to orthodox practice. This debate about right-practice or orthopraxis is one that presently occupies orthodoxy, especially in Israel. For example: should Jews be obedient to the laws of a secular state? Should women be obliged to carry out military service? Should women be allowed to read in the synagogue now that the medieval halakhah against women studying the Torah has been abolished? Should the land be left uncultivated every sabbatical year?

Orthopraxis

The rebbe is the 'righteous man' (zaddik) whose authority comes through mystical tradition from the founder of Hasidism, Israel Baal Shem Tov (1700–1760) in the 18th century.

Further discussion

Consider what it means to be an 'observant Jew'. Is keeping a kosher kitchen or separate seating in the synagogue for men and women necessarily an indication of orthodoxy?

Neo-orthodoxy

Neo-orthodoxy was developed by the German rabbi **Samson Raphael Hirsch** (1808–1888) in response to the liberal development of Reform Judaism and the very traditional *hadarim* or orthodox religion schools. He rejected the historical approach to the Torah and halakhah of the Reformists, and argued that Judaism has an eternal symbolic structure which enables it to be applied to any time and culture. His famous catchphrase was a quotation from the Mishnah: 'Torah is good together with *derekh eretz*' (Aboth 2: 2). His interpretation of *derekh eretz* was to engage with 'worldly occupation'. In practice, this meant rejecting the Talmudic method of *pilpul* – minute study of Talmud and hair-splitting debate – and instead attempting to apply the halakhah in a way that took into account current cultural thought and experience. The aim was to produce the 'Israelite Man': the ideal human being who embodies both reason and spiritual values.

Reform

Further reading

Jonathan Romain *Faith and Practice: A Guide to Reform Judaism Today* (Reform Synagogues of Great Britain 1991).

Reform Judaism developed towards the end of the 18th century in Germany, influenced by the European enlightenment. The enlightenment stressed human reason over emotion and non-rational claims of traditional religion. Science, politics, law, even religion were judged and developed by human rationality. The reform movement emerged as Jewish thinkers responded to the challenges of these ideas and the increasing numbers of those who were abandoning their traditional Judaism and assimilating either to Christianity or secularity (agnosticism or atheism).

Cohens are those families whose ancestors were priests in the Temple.

Israel Jacobson (1768–1828) is often considered to be the father of reform. He taught that Torah is the word of God as interpreted by humans and that every generation tests these ideas. The aim of rabbinic Judaism, Jacobson argued, was not to ensure that Judaism remained up-to-date – that was the aim of Reform Judaism. For example, the halakhah which forbade cohens from marrying divorced women based on the teaching of the Torah (Lev 21: 7) was redundant – without the Temple, the division of Jews into priests, Levites and Israelites is no longer applicable, and Jews should not impose a hierarchy on one another. The debate as to which mitzvot are binding and which are not continues.

The other influential factor in reform was the desire to make **worship** more dignified and spiritual. Many Jews were impressed by the emphasis in Christian worship on personal prayer. The reformers developed the use of the edifying sermon, the use of the local language rather than Hebrew and a sense of decorum (shorter services, which, by beginning and ending at a certain time, would ensure better concentration). Some have introduced **confirmation** in addition to bar/bat mitzvah as being more personal.

However, inspired by a new land unrestrained by tradition, the German Reform Jews who settled in the USA were more radical. The Reform movement has challenged many important orthodox ideas. At the first meeting of Reform Synagogues in the USA, the **Pittsburgh Platform** (1885) set out a radical agenda: the Jews are not a holy *nation* but a community; the only moral laws which should be followed are those which 'sanctify our lives'; there is no personal messiah and there should be no state of Israel. More recent developments have been less radical and have re-introduced the use of Hebrew and traditional forms of liturgy.

Reform Judaism in Britain has been less ideologically driven than in Germany and the USA. It is less radical than these reform traditions and is much closer to American Conservative Judaism.

The emphasis on the autonomy of the individual against tradition is also a characteristic of Reform Judaism in Britain and its origins were prompted initially by debates over style and content of worship.

Origins of reform in Britain

www.wls.org.uk

In 1840, members of the Bevis Marks synagogue in the East End of London left to form the West London Synagogue of British Jews. The congregation of mainly Sephardi Jews took the opportunity to revise their prayer book (1841–1842), although the main debate was over the authority of halakhah.

This continues to be a major area of controversy.

One of the most controversial areas is the extent to which women can participate in synagogue worship and leadership. As Pilkington illustrates, the distinction is not a sharp one. In Reform traditions, women may read from the sefer Torah, lead worship and become rabbis. But women have their own special forms of worship in orthodoxy – the issue is the degree of public inclusion dictated by the mitzvah of **minyan**. Some argue that the if halakhah exempts women from some forms of prayer or the minyan there is no reason why they shouldn't waive the exemption or even take on mitzvah.

Place of women and worship

Further reading

Judaism pages 71–77.

A minyan is defined as the minimum number of people necessary for saying certain prayers. Usually this is ten men.

For example, some women in Reform have taken on the mitzvot of wearing taillith and tephillin traditionally applicable only to men.

Liberal

In the UK, Liberal synagogues represent the more radical end of **Progressive** synagogues. Liberal Judaism was developed as an offshoot of Reform Judaism in 1902 by Claude Montefiore and Lily Montagu, and is closer to the more freely thinking elements of American Reform synagogues. Like Reform in the USA, it has shifted its views on Zionism but it regards traditional teaching on the messianic age to be symbolic – or, at worst, false wish-fulfilment. It treats halakhah merely as examples of past interpretation and radically considers that Jewishness passes down either the male or female line.

Progressive is the collective term sometimes used for Reform and Liberal synagogues in the UK.

Further study

Use this quotation to decide what liberals consider to be important about Judaism. 'The Jewish Religious Union was founded in order to win back for Judaism those who were drifting away from it, to awaken in them a new understanding of their heritage, a new respect for it, a new commitment to it. That remains our aim.' John Hooker and Bernard Rayner, *Judaism for Today* page 5.

Conservative

Conservative Judaism represents slightly different attitudes and practices in the USA than the UK. However, Conservatives aim to balance the tradition of orthodoxy and the liberalism of modernity less radically than the Reform tradition has often done.

Traditional Conservatism began in 1886 in the USA. It retained Hebrew in worship and regarded the halakhah as part of Jewish tradition. The 1946 prayer book omitted all references to the restoration of the Temple and negative statements about women.

Conservatism is the largest Jewish group in USA.

Reconstructionist Conservatism was developed by Mordecai Kaplan, who was the first to introduce (1922) the ceremony of bat mitzvah for girls. Reconstructionism regards halakhah as *minhag* (custom) and considers individual religious experience to be important.

For example, the 1994 prayer book addresses God as the 'Compassionate One'.

Masorti (tradition) is the name of Conservative Judaism in the UK (and Israel). **Louis Jacobs** brought Masorti to the UK after his expulsion from the Jews' College in London, caused by his book *We have Reason to Believe* (1957). The major difference can be seen in the application of halakhah. Masorti rabbis take into account modern views of science, philosophy and politics when making their judgements. They accept that, as society changes, so must Jewish responses to it. For example, Masorti states that it is only tradition that has forbidden women to read the Sefer Torah. Masorti synagogues differ as to whether they permit this to happen or not. As Louis Jacobs has said, just because the rabbi says the chicken is kosher, doesn't mean you have to eat it.

We have Reason to Believe considers the Torah to be divinely inspired but composed by humans.

Further study

A good summary of Masorti can be found at www.masorti.org.uk

Test yourself

1. 'The establishment of the Land of Israel is not part of religious Judaism.' Discuss.
2. 'The Messianic Age does not need a Messiah to establish it.' Discuss.

3. 'No Jew can believe in a loving God after the holocaust.' Discuss.

4. 'Conservative Judaism fails to take halakhah seriously enough.' Discuss.

Connections

Philosophy of Religion with Judaism (Route G)

Post-Holocaust theology. Consider the problem of evil and suffering, especially in relation to the problem of theodicy. Look at arguments for the death of God, hidden God, the 614th Commandment, divine punishment and the World to Come. Compare to Augustine and Irenaeus, and consider how these Christian views differ with their view of the Fall.

> **Further reading**
> Read pages 71–72 of the *OCR AS Guide*.

Authority of scripture. Consider debates about whether scripture should be read in Hebrew; whether this is for cultural reasons or because of its divine origins. Consider the relationship of Torah and halakhah, and Progressive/Conservative views (e.g. halakhah as custom, not Oral Torah).

Revelation. Consider the relationship between revelation that is 'propositional' (God-given instruction) and religious experience that is 'existential' (a human sense of the Divine expressed in human terms). Compare orthodox and Progressive views of Torah as propositional/non-propositional or existential.

> **Further reading**
> Read pages 69–70 of the *OCR AS Guide*. For examples from the Jewish Scriptures read pages 98–106 in *The Original Story: God, Israel and the World* by John Barton and Julia Brown (DLT 2004).

Religious experience. Consider Jewish contributions to understanding how humanity can have a relationship with God through worship in the synagogue – the covenant as people; carrying out the mitzvot (from mezuzah to kashrut, to personal prayer and use of tephillin). Consider Jewish ambivalence about the miraculous, visions and conversion (except in the cases of the biblical prophets). Look at exceptions in Hasidism and some modern messianic movements.

Test yourself

1. 'In Judaism God reveals himself primarily through history.' Discuss.

2. To what extent does the holocaust illustrate what happens when people do not worship God?

3. 'Authentic Jewish religious experience occurs in the synagogue, not to individuals.' Discuss.

Religious Ethics with Judaism (Route N)

Read the chapter on religious ethics in this guide.

Free will and determinism. Consider Jewish responses to hard and soft determinism. Compare different attitudes to messianic hope: when establishing the Messianic Age, will God or humans bring the present age to close? Look at Talmudic teaching on quietism and present attitudes to Zionism. Consider moral responsibility in the debates about reward in the after-life/olam ha ba.

> **Further reading**
> Read pages 75–77 and 159–162 of the *OCR AS Guide*.

Jewish ethics. Consider the Categorical Imperative and the place of individual autonomy and responsibility. Does Kant place reason before Torah? Consider different types of mitzvot – those that are universal (Noachide code) and those that are specifically Jewish.

Consider the relationship of Utilitarianism and kavannah (right intention) with preference utilitarianism, against obedience to the Torah. To what degree is Oral Torah/halakhah situational (bear in mind attitudes to the binding nature of halakhah)? Consider moral relativism and the relationship of Judaism to prevailing cultures – the influence of feminism, dietary customs, philosophical ideologies, and debates between orthodoxy and Progressive Judaism about the extent to which Judaism should assimilate non-Jewish ideas.

Further reading

Read pages 77–81 of the *OCR AS Guide* and note the different types of utilitarianism.

Further reading

Read pages 21 and 79–80 of the *OCR AS Guide*.

Jewish approaches to practical ethics issues. Consider Jewish principles of **life and death**: to choose life (Deuteronomy 30: 19) because it is God-given. The Mishnah states that killing one individual is like destroying the world (Sandedrin 4: 5) but consider how the exceptions (to prevent murder, incest and idolatry) might be applied to euthanasia, abortion and so on. Consider how the range of opinion about the afterlife affects care for the dying. Consider attitudes to **war** and Zionist action, peace and justice. Consider different attitudes to **sex and relationships**, such as the Torah's view of sex as primarily for procreation (Lev 18–20) versus sex for love and pleasure (*Shir HaShirim*/Song of Songs). Consider the condemnation of adultery and bestiality with present Jewish debates about homosexuality, cohabitation, sex before marriage and feminist arguments. Consider the **environment** and the Jewish notion of *tikkun olam* (repairing the world), and the biblical eschatological visions of a land and people restored.

Further reading

Read the chapter on Religious Ethics and *Renewing the Vision: Rabbis Speak Out on Modern Jewish Issues* ed. Jonathan Romain (SCM Press 1996) pages 64–73, 98–105, 192–202.

Ethical monotheism and conscience. Consider to what extent conscience is the 'voice of God' speaking to people, or reason based on given moral principles (although the Bible and rabbinic literature make no reference to conscience as such). Consider the tension between revealed law (Torah) and reason as a God-given human quality.

Further reading

Read page 17 of the *OCR AS Guide*, the chapter on religious ethics in this guide and pages 87–89 of *Contemporary Jewish Thought* by Cohen et al.

Test yourself

1. Compare and contrast the Utilitarian approach to environmental issues with a Jewish approach.
2. 'Judaism teaches that life should be preserved at all costs.' Discuss.
3. 'Judaism rejects moral relativism.' Discuss.

Islam with Judaism (Route V)

Nature of God/Allah. Consider Muslim and Jewish eschatology, i.e. God as Judge and holder of destiny – but note the Jewish reluctance to speculate on the Coming Age. Consider God as Creator, his immanent role in history, problems of free-will and recognising God's will. Compare the role of the prophets, the various views on the mahdi and the messiah as God's agents.

Revelation of God/Allah through sacred texts. Consider the traditional Muslim and orthodox Jewish view that the Qur'an and Torah are the revealed word of God given to Muhammad and Moses. Consider the Muslim view that the Jewish version of the Torah has become corrupted. To what extent might Progressive Jews agree? Consider modernist Muslim interpretations of the Qur'an in its historical setting and Islamist revisionist

Further reading

Read pages 58–60 of the *OCR AS Guide*.

interpretation with Progressive, Conservative and Neo-orthodox responses to the enlightenment. Consider also the relationship of Talmud and hadith in terms of developing revelation.

The Qur'an sometimes refers to the Talmud.

Further reading

See page 155 of the *OCR AS Guide*.

Attitudes to war. Compare Jewish and Muslim views on holy war. Can using war to expand territories be justified? Consider the religious Zionist position in Israel today. Compare the greater Jihad as personal struggle to righteousness with the Jewish pursuit of holiness. Compare attitudes to martyrdom.

Divisions within Judaism and Islam. If Islam has fewer divisions than Judaism, is this due to the notion of Ummah? Look at the impact of history (colonisation, persecutions) on development of Islam/Judaism and resistance to secular/non-Muslim/non-Jewish as causes for reactionary (Islamist/Ultra-orthodox) traditions. Consider effects of science and philosophy on modernising movements. Compare Hasidism and Sufism.

Further reading

Read pages 155–156 of the *OCR AS Guide*.

Worship. Consider how different forms of worship illustrate the relationship between humanity and God or Allah. Compare Jumu'ah (Friday) prayers with the Shabbat, with family worship at home and community worship at the mosque/synagogue. Consider the role of women in worship and the extent to which they are allowed to be religious leaders (especially in Progressive Judaism).

Test yourself

1. 'Worship in the home is equally important for Jews and Muslims.' Discuss.
2. 'The Muslim view of God stresses His transcendence more than the Judaism.' Discuss.
3. To what extent do Judaism and Islam both hold same the view of war?